Lecture Notes in Computer Science 4764

Commenced Publication in 1973
Founding and Former Series Editors:
Gerhard Goos, Juris Hartmanis, and Jan van Leeuwen

Editorial Board

Pekka Abrahamsson   Nathan Baddoo
Tiziana Margaria   Richard Messnarz (Eds.)

Software Process Improvement

14th European Conference, EuroSPI 2007
Potsdam, Germany, September 26-28, 2007
Proceedings

 Springer

Volume Editors

Pekka Abrahamsson
VTT Technical Research Centre of Finland
E-mail: Pekka.Abrahamsson@vtt.fi

Nathan Baddoo
University of Hertfordshire, UK
E-mail: N.Baddoo@herts.ac.uk

Tiziana Margaria
University of Potsdam, Germany
E-mail: margaria@cs.uni-potsdam.de

Richard Messnarz
ISCN, Austria
E-mail: rmess@iscn.com

Library of Congress Control Number: Applied for

CR Subject Classification (1998): D.2, K.6, K.4.2

LNCS Sublibrary: SL 2 – Programming and Software Engineering

ISSN   0302-9743
ISBN-10   3-540-74765-6 Springer Berlin Heidelberg New York
ISBN-13   978-3-540-74765-9 Springer Berlin Heidelberg New York

Springer is a part of Springer Science+Business Media

springer.com

© Springer-Verlag Berlin Heidelberg 2007

Typesetting: Camera-ready by author, data conversion by Scientific Publishing Services, Chennai, India
SPIN: 12167821   06/3180   5 4 3 2 1 0

Preface

This textbook is intended for use by SPI (software process improvement) managers and researchers, quality managers, and experienced project and research managers. The papers constitute the research proceedings of the 14th EuroSPI (European Software Process Improvement, www.eurospi.net) conference in Potsdam, September 26-28, 2007, Germany. Conferences in this series have been held since 1994 in Dublin, 1995 in Vienna (Austria), 1997 in Budapest (Hungary), 1998 in Gothenburg (Sweden), 1999 in Pori (Finland), 2000 in Copenhagen (Denmark), 2001 in Limerick (Ireland), 2002 in Nuremberg (Germany), 2003 in Graz (Austria), 2004 in Trondheim (Norway), 2005 in Budapest (Hungary), and 2006 in Joensuu (Finland). EuroSPI established an experience library (library.eurospi.net) which will be continuously extended over the next few years and will be made available to all attendees. EuroSPI also established an umbrella initiative for establishing a European Qualification Network in which different SPINs and national initiatives join mutually beneficial collaborations (EQN - EU Leonardo a Vinci network project).

With a general assembly during October 15–16, 2007 through EuroSPI partners and networks, in collaboration with the European Union (supported by the EU Leonardo da Vinci Programme), a European certification association has been created for the IT and services sector to offer SPI knowledge and certificates to industry, establishing close knowledge transfer links between research and industry. The biggest value of EuroSPI lies in its function as a European knowledge and experience exchange mechanism for SPI know-how between research institutions and industry.

September 2007   Richard Messnarz

Organization

Organization Committee

EuroSPI 2007 was organized by the EuroSPI partnership (www.eurospi.net), internationally coordinated by ISCN, and locally supported by the University of Potsdam.

Program Committee

Conference Chair	Richard Messnarz (ISCN, IRL)
Scientific Program Chair	Pekka Abrahamsson (University of Oulu, Finland)
Scientific Program Chair	Nathan Baddoo (University of Hertfordshire, UK)
Scientific Program Chair	Tiziana Margaria (University of Potsdam, Germany)
Industrial Program Chair	Jorn Johansen (DELTA, Denmark)
Industrial Program Chair	Mads Christiansen (DELTA, Denmark)
Industrial Program Chair	Nils Brede Moe (SINTEF, Norway)
Industrial Program Chair	Risto Nevalainen (STTF, Finland)
Tutorial Chair	Richard Messnarz (ISCN, Ireland)
Organizing Chair	Stephan Goericke (ISQI, Germany)
Organizing Chair	Adrienne Clarke (ISCN, Ireland)

Reviewers

Abrahamsson Pekka, VTT Electronics, Finland
Ambriola Vincenzo, Universita di Pisa, Italy
Aurum Aybke, University of New South Wales, Australia
Baddoo Nathan, University of Hertfordshire, UK
Biffl Stefan, Technische Universität Wien, Austria
Biro Miklos, Corvinus University of Budapest, Hungary
Ciolkowski Marcus, TU Kaiserslautern, Germany
Dalcher Darren, School of Computing Science, UK
Daughtrey Taz H., James Madison University, USA
Desouza Kevin C., University of Illinois at Chicago, USA
Dingsoyr Torgeir, SINTEF IKT, Norway
Duncan Howard, Dublin City University, Ireland
Dyba Tore, SINTEF Telecom and Informatics, Norway
Gorschek Tony, Blekinge Institute of Technology, Sweden

Table of Contents

Introduction

Enforcement, Alignment, Tailoring

Focus on SME Issues

Improvement Analysis and Empirical Studies

New Avenues of SPI

SPI Methodologies

Testing and Reliability

Software Process Improvement
– EuroSPI 2007 Conference

Pekka Abrahamsson[1], Nathan Baddoo[2], Margaria Tiziana[3],
and Richard Messnarz[4]

[1] VTT Technical Resarch Centre of Finland, P.O. Box 1100, FIN-90571, Oulu, Finland
[2] University of Hertfordshire, Hatfield, Hertfordshire AL10 9AB, UK
[3] University of Potsdam, August Bebel Straße 89, 14482 Potsdam, Germany
[4] EuroSPI, c/o ISCN LTD, Bray, Co. Wicklow, Ireland
http://www.eurospi.net

Abstract. This book constitutes the refereed research proceeding of the 14th
European Software Process Improvement Conference, EuroSPI 2007, held in
Potsdam, Germany in September 2007. The 18 revised full papers presented
were carefully reviewed and selected from 60 submissions. The papers are
organized in topical sections on agile methods, software process improvement
studies, improvement methods, engineering and development, and quality and
knowledge concepts.

1 EuroSPI Overview

EuroSPI is a partnership of large Scandinavian research companies and experience
networks (SINTEF, DELTA,STTF), the ASQF as a large German quality association,
the American Society for Quality, and ISCN as the co-coordinating partner. EuroSPI
collabrates with a large number of SPINs (Software Process Improvement Network)
in Europe.

EuroSPI conferences present and discuss results from software process
improvement (SPI) projects in industry and research, focusing on the benefits gained
and the criteria for success. Leading European universities, research centers, and
industry are contributing to and participating in this event. This year's event is the
14th of a series of conferences to which international researchers contribute their
lessons learned and share their knowledge as they work towards the next higher level
of software management professionalism.

The greatest value of EuroSPI lies in its function as a European knowledge and
experience exchange mechanism for Software Process Improvement and Innovation of
successful software product and service development. EuroSPI aims at forming an
exciting forum where researchers, industrial managers and professionals meet to exchange
experiences and ideas and fertilize the grounds for new developments and improvements.

1.1 Board Members

EuroSPI Board Members represent centres or networks of SPI excellence having large
experience with SPI. The board members are collaborating with different European
SPINS (Software Process Improvement Networks).

P. Abrahamsson et al. (Eds.): EuroSPI 2007, LNCS 4764, pp. 1–6, 2007.
© Springer-Verlag Berlin Heidelberg 2007

The following six organisations have been members of the conference board in the last 8 years:

ASQ, http://www.asq.org
ASQF, http://www.asqf.de
DELTA, http://www.delta.dk
ISCN, http://www.iscn.com
SINTEF, http://www.sintef.no
STTF, http://www.sttf.fi

1.2 EuroSPI Scientific Programme Committee

EuroSPI established an international committee of selected well known experts in SPI who are willing to be mentioned in the program and to review a set of papers each year. The list below represents the research program committee members. EuroSPI also has a separate industrial program committee responsible for the industry/experience contributions.

ABRAHAMSSON Pekka, VTT Electronics, FINLAND
AMBRIOLA Vincenzo, Universita di Pisa, ITALY
AURUM Aybke, University of New South Wales, AUSTRALIA
BADDOO Nathan, University of Hertfordshire, UK
BIFFL Stefan, Technische Universitt Wien, AUSTRIA
BIRO Miklos, Corvinus University of Budapest, Hungary
CIOLKOWSKI Marcus, TU Kaiserslautern, GERMANY
DALCHER Darren, School of Computing Science, UK
DAUGHTREY Taz H., James Madison University, USA
DESOUZA Kevin C., University of Illinois at Chicago, USA
DINGSOYR Torgeir, SINTEF IKT, NORWAY
DUNCAN Howard, Dublin City University, IRELAND
DYBA Tore, SINTEF Telecom and Informatics, NORWAY
GORSCHEK Tony, Blekinge Institute of Technology, SWEDEN
GRESSE VON WANGENHEIM Christiane, Universidade do Vale do Itajai, BRAZIL
LANDES Dieter, Fachhochschule Coburg, GERMANY
MCQUAID Patricia, California Polytechnic State University, USA
MÜLLER Matthias, EnBW AG, Germany
MÜNCH Juergen, Fraunhofer IESE, GERMANY
OIVO Markku, University of Oulu, FINLAND
PRIES-HEJE Jan, IT University of Copenhagen, DENMARK
RICHARDSON Ita, University of Limerick, IRELAND
RUHE Guenther, University of Calgary, CANADA

1.3 EuroSPI Scientific Chairs

For EuroSPI 2007 the conference board decided to appoint three research programme committee chairs, Dr. Pekka Abrahamsson, Dr. Nathan Baddoo and Dr. Tiziana Margaria, who all have an outstanding SPI experience record.

All four chairs, the general and the research chairs, have a quite complementary and interesting profile. Dr Messnarz works in close collaboration with Austrian research institutions (universities of applied sciences) and large German automotive companies. Dr. Pekka Abrahamsson is a research professor at VTT (a leading Finnish research centre) with an outstanding SPI experience record in SMEs and large companies in the telecom field. Dr. Nathan Baddoo is a professor at the University of Hertfordshire, UK, and he has published scientific articles about the human factors in SPI and has performed studiers at major European organisations applying motivation techniques in SPI. And finally, Dr. Tiziana Margaria, is a professor at the University of Potsdam and she is a program chair and co-chair in various international conferences concerning electronics and software design. The experience portfolio of the chairs covers different market segments, different sizes of organisations, and different SPI approaches.

This strengthens then fundamental principal of EuroSPI to cover a variety of different markets, experiences, and approaches.

Dr Richard Messnarz
General Chair of EuroSPI
ISCN, Ireland and Austria
rmess@iscn.com

Dr. Pekka Abrahamsson
EuroSPI Scientific Programme Committee Chair
VTT Technical Research Centre of Finland
Pekka.Abrahamsson@vtt.fi

Dr. Nathan Baddoo
EuroSPI Scientific Programme Committee Chair
University of Hertfordshire, UK
N.Baddoo@herts.ac.uk

Dr. Tiziana Margaria
EuroSPI Scientific Programme Committee Chair
University of Potsdam, Germany
margaria@cs.uni-potsdam.de

2 How to Read the Proceedings

Since its beginning in 1994 in Dublin, the EuroSPI initiative outlines that there is not a single silver bullet to solve SPI issues but you need to understand a combination of different SPI methods and approaches to achieve concrete benefits. Therefore each proceeding covers a variety of different topics and at the conference we discuss potential synergies and combined use of such methods and approaches. This proceeding contains selected research papers for 6 topics each having three research papers:

>Section I: Enforcement, alignment, tailoring
>Section II: Focus on SME issues
>Section III: Improvement analysis and empirical studies
>Section IV: New avenues on software process improvement
>Section V: Software process improvement methodologies
>Section VI: Testing and reliability.

Each of the section will be briefly outlined in the following.

2.1 Research Contents

Section I presents three studies addressing three different use cases of process models and standards in a software organization. Hanssen et al. perform a systematic literature review to find out what is the current state-of-the-art research in introducing and tailoring Rational Unified Process (RUP) in different industrial contexts. They conclude that most of the studies are anecdotal and they actually address the effects of RUP rather than the tailoring aspect. Soto and Münch address the alignment of process standards evolving in parallel to derived process models. They use an actual industrial example to illustrate whether a strongly tailored model can still be aligned with its parent standard and to assess the potential cost of such an alignment. The paper by Biro and Molnár attempts to discover the multifaceted synergies discovered between the ISO/IEC 15408 (Common Criteria) IT Security Evaluation standard, software quality evaluation standards and the Capability Maturity Model Integration (CMMI). They demonstrate the use of their findings by real world case studies.

It is well acknowledged that majority of the software companies globally are quite small in their size and volume. Papers in section II focus on issues dealing with processes of an SME organization. Garcia et al. help SME companies to discover which of their project management practices are executed even if not document. Based on the CMMI standard and a questionnaire study, they also point out issues where these companies should focus their improvements. Chen and Staples argue that it is critical to understand the business and practice needs of SMEs in order to increase the relevance and benefits of software process improvement for SMEs. When studying SMEs they place their analytical focus on practice outcomes. They find that SMEs perceive most value for working on project-related outcomes, and for planning and doing work on product-related outcomes. As an empirical conclusion, Chen and Staples present a framework for categorization of project-related practices for further study about CMMI and other SPI approaches. Savolainen et al. present a practical approach to software process improvement in small organizations. Their approach is validated by a case study in a small software company. Their approach helped the

---

CMMI is registered in the U.S. Patent & Trademark Office by Carnegie Mellon University.

company independently implement quite significant improvements for identified problems.

The papers in section III present empirical studies on improving software processes. Cerpa et al. argue that SPI models are difficult to understand because they lack visual representations relating concepts to text. They propose a Systems Modular Analysis (SMA) as a graphical modelling approach to facilitate understanding of SPI models. Based on a real world experiment, authors conclude that SMA significantly improves understanding of the properties and structure of CMM-SW Level 2. Pries-Heje and Krohn find find it problematic that software process improvement work is not organized systematically. They summarize experiences from seven years of improvement work at a company. They show empirically that different types of improvement work requires different ways of organizing. As a pragmatically valid conclusion, Pries-Heje and Krohn propose five ways of organizing for five types of improvement work. Ziemer and Canova Calori have earlier developed a decision modeling approach for analyzing requirements configuration trade-offs in time-constrained web application development. Their method aims at bringing stakeholders together to share knowledge and to decide on a configuration for the next release that satisfies all stakeholders. In this paper they report results from an industrial experiment where the method has been tried out with positive results.

The field of software process improvement quickly evolves and develops. Session IV presents some new approaches to SPI. Rejas-Muslera et al. have noticed that current software process improvement models do not properly include processes for legal audits and more concretely legal risks management for each phase of the software development lifecycle. Authors argue that this bears a significant risk since the potential cost of an inadequate management of legal aspects can even contribute to the failure of the project. Authors propose a process for managing legal risks by a sequence of steps to be taken in each life-cycle phase. López-Cortijo et al. address an important problem in the SPI field, namely, how to convince senior management to sponor SPI initiatives. Authors introduce a concept SPI value management, which enables benchmarking with successful histories by means of case studies. This is supported by a technique to formalize the information enclosed in an SPI case study providing an easy access to the relevant information of an SPI initiative. Dingsøyr et al. approach software process improvement from the knowledge management perspective. In their exploratory study, they try to improve organizational learning by systematically reviewing the results of a series of project postmortem reviews.

The papers in section V present new approaches and methodologies to better implement SPI in organizations. The paper from Levent Yilmaz illustrates, for instance, that there is a need for a software process simulation framework that represents not only technical activities, policies, and procedures, but also the resources, preferences, and human factors, together with functional and social organization and strategic management, all in unified and coherent terms. M. Zhang et.al. describe in their paper how complexity metrics are used in open source development projects to analyze specific situations, such as the relationship of complexity and the number of faults in the components. The analysis based on the CVS version control system of Eclipse JDT open source project and compared three different complexity metrics to perform such an analysis. M. Montoni et.al. analyzed critical success factors in SPI projects. The paper lists 25 major success criteria and statistically analyzed their importance in SPI projects. The result of the study shows that certain success criteria are related to each other which needs to be considered in the implementation of SPI programs.

The papers in section VI present new approaches and methods for testing and reaching a high reliability of systems. Lars-Ola Damm et.al illustrate in their paper experiences with using TDD (Test Driven Development) approaches in agile development and how this positively impacted the quality of the systems and software development based on fault statistics. Lech Madeyski et.al. additionally describe how the TDD approach helps to increase the productivity in the development. And finally the paper from Jon Arvid Børretzen et.al. describes how the analysis of faults (root causes and their common cause) resulted in process improvement decisions and by comparing previous and actual data the success of improvement actions is evaluated.

2.2 Recommended Further Reading

In [1] we integrated the proceedings of 3 EuroSPI conferences into one book which was edited by 30 experts in Europe. In [2] you find the EuroSPI research proceeding published by Springer and based on EuroSPI 2004. In [3] you find the EuroSPI research proceeding published by Springer and based on EuroSPI 2005. In [4] you find the most recent EuroSPI research proceeding published by Springer and based on EuroSPI 2006.

References

1. Messnarz, R., Tully, C. (eds.): Better Software Practice for Business Benefit - Principles and Experience. pages 409, IEEE Computer Society Press, Los Alamitos (September 1999)
2. Dingsøyr, T. (ed.): Software Process Improvement. LNCS, vol. 3281, p. 207. Springer, Heidelberg (2004)
3. Richardson, I., Abrahamsson, P., Messnarz, R. (eds.): Software Process Improvement. LNCS, vol. 3792, p. 213. Springer, Heidelberg (2005)
4. Richardson, I., Runeson, P., Messnarz, R. (eds.): Software Process Improvement. LNCS, vol. 4257, pp. 11–13. Springer, Heidelberg (2006)

Tailoring and Introduction of the Rational Unified Process

Geir Kjetil Hanssen[1,2], Finn Olav Bjørnson[2], and Hans Westerheim[1]

[1] SINTEF ICT, NO7465 Trondheim, Norway
[2] NTNU/IDI, NO7491 Trondheim, Norway
ghanssen@sintef.no, bjornson@idi.ntnu.no,
hans.westerheim@sintef.no

Abstract. RUP is a comprehensive software development process framework that has gained a lot of interest by the industry. One major challenge of taking RUP into use is to tailor it to specific needs and then to introduce it into a development organization. This study presents a review and a systematic assembly of existing studies on the tailoring and introduction of RUP. From a systematic search for study reports on this topic we found that most research is anecdotal and focus on the effects of RUP itself. Only a few number of studies address tailoring and introduction. We have found that tailoring RUP is a considerable challenge by itself and that it must be closely related to existing best practices. We see a tendency of turning from large complete process frameworks towards smaller and more light-weight processes which may impose a smoother transition from process model to process in use.

Keywords: software development process, method tailoring, method adoption, rational unified process.

1 Introduction

As software development is a highly complex process; methodology support is a prerequisite for the completion of a successful software development project. There exist a wide variety of software development methodologies, spanning from heavy and bureaucratic processes to light-weight and dynamic processes, lately agile processes have gained a lot of interest both by the industry and academia. A more mature direction within software development methodologies is the Unified Process[1] (UP) and its commercial variant Rational Unified Process (RUP). There exist no exact figures on how many organizations that have tried and use (R)UP – in any variant; however an overview of experience reports from software engineering conferences, books and magazine publications indicate a considerable interest in UP and RUP. RUP is an extensive framework that is a collection of best practices described as a structured collection of process components; activities (what to do and how to do it), roles (by whom) and artifacts (what are the input and/or result of the activities). RUP contains detailed descriptions of these components and how they relate to each other. To establish structure, these components are organized in two dimensions; first by phases from inception to elaboration and then by a set of disciplines adhering to common SE activities. In addition, RUP is based on a few

P. Abrahamsson et al. (Eds.): EuroSPI 2007, LNCS 4764, pp. 7–18, 2007.

basic values; it is architecture centric, it is use-case driven and it is an iterative and incremental process. Having this completeness and complexity it is not intended to be a silver bullet process for all development project situations – RUP is a framework that must be tailored to the situation of use. It is an absolute necessity to do so to get the intentional value from using RUP. Despite this indisputable interest, the total amount of empirical studies on the *adoption* and *introduction* of RUP is surprisingly low. A search for empirical studies identified only five studies that to some extent explain tailoring and introduction of RUP. We separate clearly between simple lessons-learned reports that don't present information on context and study method and those that present these details as well as findings, analysis and conclusions. This leads to the aim of this paper: What do the software industry and the research community know about the limitations, benefits, prerequisites and costs of tailoring and introducing RUP? Thus, cost and benefit of RUP in *use* is outside the scope of this paper. As RUP covers more or less all aspects of SE it may seem easy to take it into use. However there are many challenges in doing so successfully. How do you know which parts to keep, exclude or alter? Who should get involved in the process? How much time does it take? How is the result to be taken into use? How do you know that the result was good? To be able to answer such questions and to pinpoint further research needs, at least in part, we have done a literature review of all existing relevant studies on tailoring and introducing RUP - holding a minimum of methodological quality. In addition, we extend this compiled overview with three case studies of the introduction and use of RUP that the authors have done over the past few years [2-5] thus bringing together all available empirical experience on the topic. This paper first describes our research method, both for the literature review and for our own case studies. Then, results are presented giving an overview of identified experience reports. A discussion summarizes findings from the literature review and own experiences giving a conclusion addressing the research aim of this paper.

2 Background: Method Tailoring

There exists a set of guidelines for tailoring and adoption of RUP; one book that specifically targets the issue [6] and one book that covers the issue to some detail [7]. Additionally there exists a guideline documented through a website [8]. In addition there are some guidance in the RUP documentation itself [4] or RUP-related books, however these guidelines tends to be superficial. Despite the existence of these guidelines the authors have not been able to find any experience reports evaluating their outcome and suitability. On the other hand, there exist a set of experience reports addressing tailoring and adoption of RUP done in other ways. These experience reports are summarized and analyzed later in this paper. The term methodology is defined as "A body of methods, rules, and postulates employed by a discipline: a particular procedure or set of procedures" by the Merriam-Webster dictionary [9]. Basically, a methodology describes how someone, e.g. an organization performs a task, e.g. software development. In our context we talk about methodologies for running projects with a defined customer having more or less defined goals initially.

The process of adapting RUP can possibly take many forms. IBM Rational, the provider of RUP has defined the Process Engineering Process (PEP) [8]. This is a comprehensive adaptation process requiring a fairly big amount of resources (people and time). This may very well be appropriate for larger companies, but for the small ones this process may be too expensive. Adaptation of a framework, such as RUP, can take one of (at least) three approaches. The first is to do it in one step, for each project, thus representing a heavy job in each case. This can be justified for large projects. This approach may be called situational method engineering, as defined by ter Hoefstede and Verhoef in [10]. The second approach is to do an up-front adaptation producing a subset of the framework, still being a framework, but now tuned to the organizations general characteristics (technology, customers, domain, traditions etc.). This is the intentional process of PEP and may be called method engineering, as defined by Brinkkemper in [11]. The thirds approach is to first identify and describe a set of recurring project types. Having knowledge of characteristics and differences of these types, an adaptation is done for each type. No matter which approach being used; in the last step, a final adaptation is done to each case (project). Adapting RUP in practice means to decide on which process elements to keep, remove, alter, add or merge. These decisions can be based on assumptions, experience, goals and visions. It is the quality of this underlying knowledge and experience that determines how good these decisions are. Having decided the content and principles of a process it must be made available to the users – the project team(s). Traditionally process descriptions have taken the form of voluminous printed descriptions. Today the most common form is through web-based process guides, RUP Online is such an example. In the case of RUP, IBM Rational provide a set of software tools to assist the reengineering of the process elements of RUP to build a coherent web based presentation of the result. Edwards et al. [12] emphasize the importance of actively involving stakeholders in the process of tailoring situational specific methods. This will both ensure that necessary detailed information becomes available and affects the tailoring process and that the resulting process actually is taken into use due to ownership and relevance. Various acceptance models such as TAM, TAM2, PCI and others [13] may help to explain and underline the importance of involving stakeholders that, after the tailoring, are going to use or be affected by the resulting process. For example, stakeholder participation may affect the *Usefulness*-construct (the extent to which the person thinks using the system will enhance his or her job performance) and the *Ease-of-use*-construct (the extent to which the person perceives using the system will be free of effort).

3 Method

In this chapter we first describe the study methods used in our own three studies – each description is based on four parts: 1) a brief overview of the study context, 2) study aim, 3) data collection procedures and 4) method for data analysis and finally, in the last part of the chapter we present the method used to perform the literature review.

Case study A: *Context:* Company A is a Norwegian software consultancy company with 50 employees mainly developing software systems with heavy back-end logic and often with a web front-end, typically portals. However, they also develop lighter solutions with most emphasis on the front-end. All development is done in the form of projects. The authors have followed A for a period of five years - having a varying focus over these years; First we studied how A initially used RUP, out-of-the-box, with no restrictions or guidelines. The study is reported in [3]. Secondly, we carried out an action research project to follow A in an attempt to tailor RUP to a predefined project type. The study is reported in [2]. Thirdly, and finally, we have carried out a case study of a pilot project at A using a heavily downscaled variant of RUP documented in the form of an internal Wiki-web. The results from this study are still not published, however reported in this article.

Study aim: For the three studies, the study aims were respectively; *to present an industry case to provide lessons learned and answers with respect to process uptake and effect.* The second study aimed *to provide others considering remodeling and adapting a process framework in general, and RUP particularly, an insight in how this has been done in a small software company.* The third study aimed *to study the use and effects of an extensively downscaled variant of RUP documented in the form of a Wiki-web.*

Data collection: For the first study we first interviewed four project managers (claiming to be using RUP in four projects) to make a usage map per project to see what parts of RUP actually was being used. Then, we arranged semi structured interviews with five employees with varying roles to document main experiences and find potential explanations for use/no-use of RUP. For the second study we took an action research approach [14] following A in the whole process of tailoring RUP, as a group-process, to a defined project-type. In the third study we have interviewed the project manager and analyzed internal mid term- and end- PMA-evaluations [15] of the pilot project being studied.

Analysis: As all three studies have been descriptive with no hypothesis to validate we have done a qualitative analysis. For the first study, interviews were documented on-the-fly in a usage-map (excel spreadsheet) showing which RUP process components had been used or not with potential explanations from the interviewees. Further on, the interviews were transcribed and analyzed using the constant comparison technique [16]. In the second study which was organized according to the principles of action research our report [2] contains a discussion that extracts and summarizes key learning's. In the third study we also used the constant comparison technique to extract key learning's from the transcribed interview and the internal project evaluations.

Case study B: *Context:* Company B is the software development department (300 persons) within a large Norwegian company with a total of 2000 employees. B is focused at both software development and consulting services within the domain of banking and transportation services. The authors have followed B over period of two years, entering the scene about a year after the company's RUP specialization had been taken into use by projects. This study is reported in[4].

Study aim: The aim of the study was *to investigate the level of use of a large-scale RUP specialization, explaining positive and negative experiences using the tailored process and reasons for use/no-use.*

Data collection: In this case study we used three main sources of information; 1) a main contact person which was the leader of the tailoring of RUP prior to our study, 2) the process advisory board responsible of the tailoring and the introduction of the new process in the organization and 3) project managers and software developers. Our main method of data collection was workshops and semi structured interviews with these roles. We had three workshops with the project advisory board; information was recorded on-the-fly using mind-maps. We did two rounds of interviews, the first – interviewing representatives from eight projects face-to-face, mainly project managers. The second round of interviews was carried out one year later with the same eight interviewees, this time over telephone. All 16 interviews were recorded and transcribed for later analysis. The aim of the interviews was to document experiences from the introduction of the tailored RUP, find effects – both positive and negative, and to investigate the level of use and correspondingly explanations.

Analysis: All transcribed interviews was analyzed using the constant comparison technique, the first eight interviews were coded and analyzed using the NVivo™-tool, the last eight were coded manually by two researchers in pair using a whiteboard. Lessons learned and experiences were counted across the interviews to find key learning's of most significance.

Case study C: *Context:* Company C was a company specializing in the development of web applications with a high emphasis on the user experience of the web sites. The company had software developers and psychologists employed. The latter ones worked as producers, specifying the look and feel of the web sites, as well as the logical aspects of the use of the web pages. The company did develop both ecommerce applications and more entertainment types of sites. This study is reported in [5] and [17].

Study aim: The aim of the study was to investigate how RUP could support the specifications and development of non-functional parts of a web site. The company had its own tailored RUP, where the original disciplines and the structure of RUP were not changed. The tailoring was a new user experience discipline, with dedicated activities to be performed by new roles.

Data collection: In this case study the main data source was the conducted Postmortem [15] analyses. Data from six different projects is included in the case study. The tailoring of RUP was already in place when the researchers started to cooperate with the company.

Analysis: The data in the PMA reports was analyzed using constant comparison.

Literature review method: A systematic review is a strategy for gathering and systematizing results from several independent studies sharing more or less the same thematic focus. The intention is to establish a compiled overview of all relevant experiences and to identify gaps in existing knowledge, thus implicating the directions for further research. In this case we did a simplified review inspired by the guidelines described by Kitchenham [18], hence we call it a literature review. Systematic reviews have traditionally been used to systematize quantitative research, typically as a means of doing statistical meta-analysis. However, most software engineering method-focused experience reports so far are qualitative single-case studies. We therefore needed to adopt practices to be able to systematize qualitative data. This resulted in a review-protocol that we used to 1) define a common research question, 2) search for relevant literature, 3) select studies to include in an analysis and 4) systematize findings and lessons learned.

Step 1 - A common research question: We defined the following question for the review: *What are the challenges, prerequisites and success criteria's for tailoring and introducing RUP?*

Step 2 - Finding relevant literature: The following SE index databases; ISI Web of science, Compendex and ACM Digital Library were searched using the phrase *unified process AND software.*

Step 3 – Select studies to keep: All three authors participated in the evaluation of the search results using the following routine:

Deselect on title: a coarse deselection of studies was done based on title, removing studies with an obvious wrong focus. The exclusions and inclusions were based on a few simple selection criteria's: The study aim or topic had to be within the frames of *tailoring/adopting/specializing/introducing the Unified Process or Rational Unified Process* This resulted in 100 unique studies.

Deselect on title and abstract: The second selection criterion was: the study must present empirical data beyond anecdotal evidence. This left 36 studies.

Deselect on full text: Studies was excluded if they had insufficient quality with respect to 1) a well defined and limited study aim, 2) an adequate description of the study method, 3) a sufficient description of the study context, 4) a presentation of the study results, 5) a thorough analysis of the results and 6) giving conclusions or answers with respect to the defined study aim. This left 5 studies.

Final, group based selection: Each resulting study was reviewed by each of the three authors discussing the six quality criterions defined above. This final step left 2 studies. The complete list of idendified reports are not presentet here due to space limitations but can be obtained from the authors on request.

Step 4 - Systematize findings and lessons learned: The main learnings or conclusions from the resulting studies were identified and expressed as claims. A claim can be seen as a hypothesis supported by at least one study.

4 Results

The results are here presented in a common form; each study is briefly summarized and discussed. The main findings or conclusions relevant to tailoring and introduction of RUP is expressed as claims (separate pieces of knowledge that are supported by an empirical study).

Case study A: The first part of the study, addressing RUP-use out-of-the-box concludes that a direct use of a framework, such as RUP, with no assistance, tailoring or guidelines results in low use. Introducing RUP is an investment beyond the license fee. In this case the outcome could have been better if the introduction of RUP was carefully managed and not left as an autonomous effort in each project. The second part of the study concludes that a success factor in tailoring RUP to a defined project type is to have focus on the features of the defined process and that a tailoring workshop should consist of persons with proper experience from case projects of the defined type. In the third study we saw that the main objection with the use of the small footprint process guide was lack of content, the project manager typically had a demand for more and better check lists. However, the content was still under development. The project manager commented that it has to be a balance between content size and the lightness as one of the main positive experiences was the simplicity of the guide – it was easy to find relevant guidance. As the process guide is a Wiki-web the project manager clearly saw a need of defining an editor role as editing is free to all and may compromise the content. The content which basically is a collection of activity descriptions organized over the four RUP phases seemed appropriate for the case project, only four new activity descriptions was suggested. Beyond task guidance the project manager strongly demanded practical process support tools such as estimation models, project follow-up support, a testing framework etc. When asked to comment the difference between this light process guide and the complete RUP the project manager emphasized the ease of use and clear relevance of the new guide as opposed to RUP's well of information that may be hard to find one's way through. However, interestingly, a definite premise of using such a minimum version of RUP is that the user must have an good understanding of the principles of RUP.

Claim A.1: RUP, out-of-the-box is over-comprehensive and will provide more confusion than guidance and consequently low uptake and use.

Claim A.2: Tailoring RUP efficiently must be based on best practice from the native organization and relevant project cases.

Claim A.3: RUP may be downscaled extensively to increase relevance and ease of use, however, a successful use requires a good knowledge of RUP principles.

Case study B: The findings resemble with known models of technology acceptance[13]; little knowledge of RUP and thereby low motivation results in low or no use. On the other hand, knowledge and motivation for RUP results in medium/extensive use. In relation, education seems to be an important factor, not only prior to the process but also continuously trough the use. Further on, we found that management support seemed to be an important factor with respect to uptake and to continuously improve the process during use; this also resembles with other similar studies[19].

Claim B.1: Low knowledge of RUP creates low motivation and further low uptake and use.

Claim B.2: Management support is a success factor in tailoring and using RUP efficiently.

Case study C: The main result, when it comes to introduction of RUP, is that formalization of roles makes them more visible and understandable to others in a project. In this case, new roles related to graphical design were added to the RUP process resulting in a higher acceptance from more technical roles which consequently increased the uptake and use of RUP in the project.

Claim C.1: Explicit definition of roles makes them visible to other project members and thus positively affects the use of the process.

Our search for empirically justified claims on RUP tailoring and adaptation resulted in only two study reports; a clear signal that more research is needed in this area. In this chapter we summarize the claims these papers add to the research community. To assess the validity of these claims, we also include a short summary of the setting and research method described in each of the papers. The papers we identified were by Folkestad et.al. [20] and Bygstad [21].

Folkestad et.al. [20]:

Context: The specific case being studied was a project to transfer an existing system from mainframe architecture to a client-server based architecture. The company saw the project as an opportunity to rebuild and enhance the competence of their staff and was willing to spend resources on this. They chose to use a version of Unified Process as their software development approach. The size of the project was about 30 man-years and lasted three years.

Study aim: The study aims are clearly stated as 1) Identify the effects of changing to a new process. 2) Identify the causes for these changes. 3) Identify what properties of the new work process that was instrumental in the change.

Data collection: The data was gathered after the project had been running for one year. The main sources were seven semi-structured depth interviews with members of the software developer group. In addition some data was gathered through informal discussions and from the business' documents regarding the development process and the project.

Analysis: The data was analyzed qualitatively using a method called Activity Theory, which can be considered "a framework for the understanding of human activity".

Limitations: Openly discussed in the paper. Since it is a single case study, it is not easy to generalize the results. Factors like openness, flat hierarchy, and confident staff may be the cause behind the results, just as much as UP itself.

Findings: We have extracted the following findings based on this paper:

Claim R.1: The iterative approach of Unified Process will ensure large effects in terms of learning.
Claim R.2: Unified Process will improve on communication and work distribution in a company.
Claim R.3: Unified Process helps constrain activities and leads to developers being more focused on their tasks, and hence it has a positive influence on productivity and quality.
Claim R.4: As a project develops, elements of Unified Process will become internalized and become tools for the developers. Or in other words, the developers will focus less and less on UP in itself, but focus more on following the practices that they decide to adopt.

Bygstad : [21]

Context: A RUP development project at Scandinavian Airline System (SAS), carried out by the Scandinavian IT Group (SIG) (owned by SAS). The goal of the project was to establish a web based marketing channel, enable easy publishing and integrating it with the existing booking systems. SAS had chosen RUP as their standard software methodology two years prior to this project. RUP was tailored to the project, and was linked to established practices in SIG.

Study aim: The research questions are 1) how can the project manager control the integration challenge? And 2) what support is there in the software engineering frameworks, like RUP?

Data collection: The case was followed for 18 months. Interviews were conducted over three intervals, project meetings were observed and project documentation analyzed.

Analysis: All data was coded with in-vivo codes, using only domain (project) terms. Then each iteration of the project was analyzed qualitatively using constant comparison methods.

Limitations: There is no discussion concerning external validity, but since it is a single case study, the results may not be easy to generalize. The internal validity is discussed in the paper with emphasis on how they addressed the principles of dialogical reasoning, multiple interpretations and member verification in their analysis.

Findings: Claim R.5: RUP provides good support for internal technical integration and poor support for external technical integration.

Claim R.6: RUP provides weak support for internal stakeholder integration throughout a project.
Claim R.7: RUP provides strong support for external stakeholder integration in the early phases, but weak support in the later phases.
Claim R.8: RUP gives strong declarational support to step-wise external integration, but too little practical support.
Claim R.11: Using RUP as a basis, linking it to existing best practices results in a process that is actually used.

5 Discussion

The search for relevant empirical studies, with sufficient quality, on tailoring and introduction of RUP resulted in only two study reports. In addition to our three own studies this forms a very small experience base and it has shown to be hard to see trends across these studies.

From the studies we see that RUP initially is too complex to be used without any tailoring which in practice means that the project manager must make more or less ad-hoc decisions. This becomes an error prone process if the knowledge of the content of RUP is low and thus makes it hard to decide upon which elements to keep, alter or avoid [3]. The RUP-online documentation is a comprehensive collection of process elements and their relations containing about 3700 web pages – which makes it necessary to have a detailed knowledge about the content to be able to select a consistent subset suitable for a given context of use. In the first attempt to deselect RUP elements in case study A we saw that insufficient knowledge of such details quickly became a problem. In case study B a dedicated team needed to get assistance from a trained RUP mentor to be able to accomplish a successful tailoring. In the second attempt in case study A, a bottom-up approach was used – building a small process guide based on existing best practices using RUP merely as inspiration rather than a commodity. This approach made it at least possible to accomplish the task and resulted in a complete process guide that was taken into use by project teams. In this case, almost all users of this heavily downscaled RUP-process had very high knowledge of RUP through training. This made it possible to use simplistic guidelines as the users knew the details or at least where to find them when needed. The resulting process guide itself in case A was a simple overview of the most important high-level tasks to perform in a development project – no templates or process maps were included. So, the resulting process and its web-based representation can be characterized as minimalistic, thus rising the question of what RUP is; how much do you have to keep unaltered to still call it RUP and when is it merely inspired by RUP that by it self is a collection of already existing best practices and guidelines? As a contrast to case A where the basic knowledge of RUP was high we saw in case B that the intended users had little knowledge which clearly affected their motivation for use which consequently also resulted in low uptake of the new process - even though it in this case was tailored to their project characteristics by a dedicated tailoring team. Other studies also support this in the case of acceptance and uptake of electronic process guides [19]. It is reasonable to believe that low knowledge negatively affects these motivational factors. Further on, in case B, we found that management support was a success factor – one project in this case study was found to actually use RUP and report a certain level of success of doing so. In this case the management had been clear in their expectations that the project should use RUP and supported this. In other projects in the same case study, management was more absent which made the project members use their own varying best practices in an uncoordinated way, thus hampering the goal of establishing a corporate unified development process. Another potential success factor for uptake was found in case study C. As RUP clearly defines roles it became evident how each role was needed and how they related to each other through joint activities and shared artefacts. This increased the acceptance of existing roles that was not documented to be a part of the total development process. We have not followed our own cases to assess the use of RUP over time, however Folkestad et al. found that developers, over time, will focus less and less on the process in itself, but focus more on following the practices that they decide to adopt [20]. Thus, the value of introducing RUP may have important effects when it comes to learning a new shared process.

An interesting note in the context of RUP and the challenge of making it fit to local needs and context is the recent spirited development of agile processes [22]. Ivar Jacobson, one of the original contributors to RUP has recently initiated a total remake of RUP, resulting in something called the Essential Unified Process (EssUP). This is intended to be a great improvement of RUP and Jacobson says in a whitepaper [23]: *"The Unified Process became too heavy, the process improvement programs required too much boring work..."*. This is interesting since RUP for years has been marketed as a framework that could help most software organizations in professionalizing software development effectively. EssUP can simply be described as a combination of RUP – which may be seen as a heavy type of process – and agile software development principles [24]. Our findings, both from our own studies and others support this view that RUP is too heavy and that it may require too much tedious and difficult work to make it fit. The question is; will a join of RUP and agile be a better approach? Others as well has addressed the challenge of making RUP simpler and agile which, in sum, can be seen as a shared opinion that RUP has its limitations despite its comprehensiveness. This adds to our findings summarized in this paper.

RUP has since its creation gone through several transformations, all leading towards a more light-weight approach of designing and developing software. This has resulted in various variants and spin-offs of the process, followed by numerous books and even more presentations, speeches, courses and consultant services. It is hard to predict where this will end; however, based on our findings we see a clear need of simplifying RUP to ensure uptake and efficient use. The development turns clearly towards the agile side of the spectrum – perhaps in search for a balance between discipline and agility [25].

6 Conclusions

Based on our own, and a few other empirical studies on tailoring and introduction of RUP into development organizations we found that there exist few or none (reported) direct success stories. All experiences pull in the same direction; RUP is, out of the box, too complex, however, tailoring it to specific needs is also too complex. Looking at the evolution of RUP itself over the past years and the cases we summarize here we see a clear need for, and movement towards, a more agile process that can bee tailored with less effort.

Acknowledgment

The authors would like to thank the participants from the case companies. We would also like to thank the SPIKE and EVISOFT projects, funded by the Research Council of Norway under grant 156701/220 and 174390/I40.

References

1. Jacobson, I., Booch, G., Rumbaugh, J.: The Unified Software Development Process. In: Booch, G., Jacobson, I., Rumbaugh, J. (eds.) Object Technology Series, p. 463. Addison Wesley Longman Inc., Reading, Massachusetts (1999)
2. Hanssen, G.K., Westerheim, H., Bjørnson, F.O.: Tailoring RUP to a defined project type: A case study. In: Bomarius, F., Komi-Sirviö, S. (eds.) PROFES 2005. LNCS, vol. 3547, Springer, Heidelberg (2005)
3. Hanssen, G.K., Westerheim, H., Bjørnson, F.O.: Using Rational Unified Process in an SME - A Case Study. In: Richardson, I., Abrahamsson, P., Messnarz, R. (eds.) Software Process Improvement. LNCS, vol. 3792, Springer, Heidelberg (2005)
4. Westerheim, H., Hanssen, G.K.: The Introduction and Use of a Tailored Unified Process - A Case Study. In: Euromicro 2005, Porto, Portugal (2005)

5. Westerheim, H., Hanssen, G.K.: Extending the Rational Unified Process with a User Experience Discipline: a Case Study. In: Richardson, I., Runeson, P., Messnarz, R. (eds.) Software Process Improvement. LNCS, vol. 4257, Springer, Heidelberg (2006)
6. Bergström, S., Råberg, L.: Adopting the Rational Unified Process, pp. 165–182. Addison-Wesley, Reading (2004)
7. Kroll, P., Kruchten, P.: The Rational Unified Process Made Easy - A Practitionare's Guide to the RUP, ed. O.T. Series. Addison Wesley, Reading (2003)
8. Rational PEP. Available from: http://www-1.ibm.com/ support/ docview.wss?uid= swg 21158199
9. Merriam-Webster dictionary
10. ter Hofstede, A.H.M., Verhoef, T.F.: On the feasibility of situational method engineering. Information Systems Journal 22(6), 401–422 (1997)
11. Brinkkemper, S.: Method engineering: Engineering of information systems development methods and tools. Information and Software Technology 38(4), 275–280 (1996)
12. Edwards, H.M., Barrie Thompson, J., Hardy, C.J.: Developing situationally specific methods through stakeholder collaboration. In: COMPSAC. Computer Software and Applications Conference (1998)
13. Riemenschneider, C.K., Hardgrave, B.C., Davis, F.D.: Explaining Software Developer Acceptance of methodologies: a Comparison of Five Theoretical Models. IEEE Transactions on Software Engineering 28(12), 1135 (10) (2002)
14. Avison, D., et al.: Action Research. Communications of the ACM 42(1), 94 (4) (1999)
15. Birk, A., Dingsøyr, T., Stålhane, T.: Postmortem: Never Leave a Project without It. IEEE Software 19(3), 43–45 (2002)
16. Seaman, C.B.: Qualitative methods in empirical studies in software engineering. IEEE Transactions on Software Engineering 25(4), 557–572 (1999)
17. Westerheim, H., Dingsøyr, T., Hanssen, G.K.: Studying the User Experience Discipline extension of the Rational Unified Process and its effects on Usability - The design of a case study. In: Bunse, C., Jedlitschka, A. (eds.) Empirical Studies in Software Engineering: Proceedings from the first international workshop, December 2002, pp. 69–74. Fraunhofer IRB Verlag, Rovaniemi, Finland (2002)
18. Kitchenham, B.: Procedures for Performing Systematic Reviews. Keele University and Empirical Software Engineering National ICT Australia Ltd. p. 33 (2004)
19. Dybå, T., Moe, N.B., Mikkelsen, E.M.: An Empirical Investigation on Factors Affecting Software Developer Acceptance and Utilization of Electronic Process Guides. In: METRICS 2004, Chicago, USA (2004)
20. Folkestad, H., Pilskog, E., Tessem, B.: Effects of Software Process in Organization Development - A Case Study. In: Melnik, G., Holz, H. (eds.) LSO 2004. LNCS, vol. 3096, Springer, Heidelberg (2004)
21. Bygstad, B.: Controlling Iterative Software Development Projects: The Challenge of Stakeholder and Technical Integration. In: Hawaii International Conference on System Sciences, Hawaii, USA (2004)
22. Cockburn, A.: Agile Software Development. In: Cockburn, A.H.J. (ed.) The Agile Software Development Series, Addison-Wesley, Reading (2002)
23. Jacobson, I., Ng, P.W., Spence, I.: The Essential Unified Process - a Fresh New Start (2006)
24. Agile Manifesto, http://www.agilemanifesto.org/
25. Boehm, B., Turner, R.: Balancing Agility and Discipline - A Guide for the Perplexed, p. 266. Addison-Wesley, Reading (2004)

Maintaining a Large Process Model Aligned with a Process Standard: An Industrial Example

Martín Soto and Jürgen Münch

Fraunhofer Institute for Experimental Software Engineering,
Fraunhofer-Platz 1, 67663 Kaiserslautern, Germany
{soto,muench}@iese.fraunhofer.de

Abstract. An essential characteristic of mature software and system development organizations is the definition and use of explicit process models. For a
number of reasons, it can be valuable to produce new process models by tailoring existing process standards (such as the V-Modell XT). Both process models
and standards evolve over time in order to integrate improvements or adapt the
process models to context changes. An important challenge for a process engineering team is to keep tailored process models aligned over time with the standards originally used to produce them. This article presents an approach that
supports the alignment of process standards evolving in parallel to derived
process models, using an actual industrial example to illustrate the problems
and potential solutions. We present and discuss the results of a quantitative
analysis done to determine whether a strongly tailored model can still be
aligned with its parent standard and to assess the potential cost of such an
alignment. We close the paper with conclusions and outlook.

Keywords: process modeling, process model change, process model evolution,
model comparison, process standard alignment.

1 Introduction

Documenting its software development processes is a step that every software organization striving to achieve a high level of process maturity must take sooner or later.
One problem that many organizations face when first attempting to perform this cru-
cial task is the lack of appropriate expertise: Documenting a complete set of organiza-
tion-wide development processes is potentially a very large undertaking, and doing it
successfully requires highly specialized knowledge that organizations often lack. For
these reasons, customizing an existing standard process model can be an excellent
option for many organizations, as opposed to documenting their processes "from
scratch". A standard process model (e.g., the German V-Modell XT [1]) offers them a
solid framework, which can greatly help to guarantee that the resulting process documentation is complete and detailed enough, and that it is structured in such a way that
it is useful to process engineers and process performers alike.

Since tailoring is central to process standard adoption, standard models should ide-
ally offer a mechanism for making adaptations in a systematic way, and for keeping
those adaptations separated from, but properly linked to, the original standard. Unfortunately, most existing models have not yet reached the point where they can support

P. Abrahamsson et al. (Eds.): EuroSPI 2007, LNCS 4764, pp. 19–30, 2007.
© Springer-Verlag Berlin Heidelberg 2007

this type of advanced tailoring out-of-the-box. Therefore, most customization is performed in practice by directly modifying a copy of the original model until it reflects the practices of a given organization. This way, organizations can quickly get up to speed with their own process definition, requiring only access to a standard process model and its corresponding editing tools (which are often distributed together with the model, or are freely available.)

Although very useful in practice, this type of *ad hoc* process model tailoring also introduces some problems, the largest of which is probably long-term maintenance. As soon as tailoring starts, the organization-specific model and the standard model take different paths, and after some time, they will probably diverge significantly. At some point, every organization relying on a customized process model will be confronted with the problem of deciding if it should try to keep it *aligned* with the standard, or if it should rather maintain it as a completely separate entity.

This decision is not easy at all. On the one hand, maintaining the customized model separately implies that, potentially, many corrections and improvements done at the standard level will not be adopted, and also involves the risk that the practices documented for the organization deviate unnecessarily from mainstream accepted practices. On the other hand, keeping the model aligned with the standard implies integrating changes from the standard into the local documentation at regular intervals, a task that, to our knowledge, is not well supported by existing tools and that can be very expensive and unreliable if performed manually.

We believe that this and other similar problems related to process model maintenance can be greatly mitigated by properly managing the evolution of process models. We have devised our *DeltaProcess* [2, 3] approach for process model difference analysis with this goal in mind. The approach makes it possible to efficiently and reliably identify changes in newer versions of a process model with respect to its older versions. It also makes it possible to perform analyses that classify changes in a model (e.g., a process standard) according to their relevance to another model (e.g, a customized model). We expect that by making use of this information, process engineers will be able to save significant effort and produce much more reliable results when trying to align complex process models.

We are currently conducting a study intended to investigate the above hypothesis. In the study, we are trying to help a company to align a process model, customized over a period of about one and a half years, with its corresponding process standard. The rest of this paper uses this case study as an example to illustrate the problems involved in keeping complex process models aligned. The paper is organized as follows: Section 0 describes the process alignment problem and the challenges it presents to process engineers. Section 0 presents a brief description of our *DeltaProcess* approach. Section 0 describes an analysis we performed as part of our ongoing case study to determine the viability of aligning two large process models. Section 0 closes the paper with conclusions and future work.

2   Aligning a Customized Process Model with a Standard

In this section, we provide a more detailed description of the problem that occupies us in our case study, namely, aligning a large industrial-grade, customized process model with the standard from which it was originally derived. In order to provide the reader with a complete view of the problem, we describe the process model standard (the German V-Modell XT), the company performing the customization, and the extent and characteristics of their customized model. The section concludes with a discussion of related work, and of why existing approaches are not completely adequate to solve the problem we are dealing with.

2.1 The German V-Modell XT

The V-Modell XT [1] is a prescriptive process model intended originally for use in German public institutions, but finding increasing acceptance in the German private sector. Its predecessor, the so-called V-Modell 97, was developed in the 1990s and released originally only in the form of a text document. The V-Modell XT is the result of a recent effort by a publicly-financed consortium of private companies, and government and research institutions to "modernize" the original V-Modell. This effort included converting the original document-based process description into an actual process model with formalized entities and relationships, creating a set of tools to manage instances of the model in this new representation, and improving and extending the actual model contents.

As of this writing, three major versions of the V-Modell XT have been released, namely 1.0 (finished in January 2005 with a minor update in March 2005), 1.1 (finished in July 2005) and 1.2 (finished in January 2006 but released in May 2006.) Further active development by a team of experts from the development consortium is still ongoing. All V-Modell XT releases are freely available and can be downloaded at no cost from the Internet (see [1].)

For editing purposes, instances of the V-Modell are stored as XML files that can be processed using a set of specialized tools (also freely available as an Internet download). The model is structured as a hierarchy of process entities, each having a number of attributes. Entities can be connected to other entities through a variety of relations. Version 1.2 of the V-Modell XT is comprised of about 2100 process entities with over 5000 attributes, and connected by some 4100 entity relations. The paper documentation generated automatically from this model is 620 pages long. Also, the current model schema contains 38 classes and 43 different types of relations. Most of these numbers are only approximate, but should be able to give the reader a general idea of the size and complexity involved.

2.2 A Customized Version of the V-Modell XT

We are performing our case study in the context of a medium-sized (about 1200 employees), privately-held company that is an early adopter of the V-Modell XT. Although information technology is not its main business, this company has a software development division with about 70 employees, which is mainly dedicated to the development and maintenance of the company's own information systems. The idea of introducing the V-Modell XT arose in 2005 as part of a software process improvement effort. Since it was judged that the V-Modell XT in its standard form was not adequate for internal use, the company's software process group started a customization effort at the end of 2005, whose first results were seen a year later with the introduction of the model as official guidance for new development projects. The tailored model is based on version 1.1 of the V-Modell, which was the current version at the time the customization effort was started.

The tailored model differs significantly from the standard V-Modell XT. During customization, more than half of the original entities were erased because they were considered irrelevant for the company. The resulting trimmed model was afterwards extended with a number of new entities. Many of the entities preserved from the original model were also adapted, by changing names and descriptions as necessary to fit the local processes and terminology. Despite the extensive changes, the final model still uses the original V-Modell XT metamodel without modification.

As mentioned above, Version 1.2 of the V-Modell XT was released in May 2006, when the company's process customization effort was already quite advanced. As of this writing (March 2007), no attempt has been made to integrate any of the additions and corrections present in version 1.2 into the company's customized model, although members of the software process group have expressed their interest in doing this at least to some extent. This is currently not a high priority because the customization process was finished only recently, but it is acknowledged that there may be corrections and additions in the new V-Modell XT version that could benefit the tailored model.

Due to the size and complexity of the models involved, it is very difficult to manually determine the actual extension of the changes performed on each one of them, and this, in turn, makes it difficult to estimate the effort involved in aligning the tailored model with the standard. As discussed in the following section, determining the extent of the changes and analyzing them to find those that are suitable for incorporation into the tailored model and those that may lead to conflicts has been, until recently, a mainly manual, and thus potentially expensive and unreliable, process.

2.3 Difference Identification in the V-Modell

Comparing source code versions and analyzing the resulting differences is a task software developers perform on a daily basis for a variety of purposes, including sharing of changes, review and analysis of changes done by others, and space-efficient storage of multiple versions of a program. Such comparisons can be performed using widely available software, such as the well-known diff utility present in most UNIX-like operating systems, and other similar programs. Diff relies on interpreting files as being composed of text lines (sequences of characters separated by the newline character) and then finding *longest common subsequences* (LCS) of lines by using an efficient algorithm (see [4] for an example). Lines not belonging to a common subsequence are considered to be differences among the compared files.

In most practical cases, entities in a process model are connected in an arbitrary graph structure (the V-Modell XT is a good example of this). Since LCS algorithms can only operate on sequential structures, it is thus impossible to apply them directly to most process models. Nonetheless, the idea of using diff or a similar LCS-based program on process models is still appealing. The reason is that many useful tools, including most source code versioning systems, rely on an LCS algorithm implementation as their only comparison mechanism, and it would be valuable if these tools would work on process models, as opposed to working only on program source code.

For the the team working on the V-Modell XT, for example, it was necessary to introduce a code versioning system to support collaborative work, since members of the team work separately and in parallel on different aspects of the model's contents. In order to do that, each team member changes a separate copy of the model, and later uses the versioning system to *merge* the changes into the main development branch. The merge operation, however, is based on finding a minimal set of changes using diff, and, thus, requires diff to produce somewhat usable results when applied to the V-Modell XML representation. The V-Modell solution to this problem is to format XML files in a special way, carefully controlling the order of elements in the file, and ingenuously introducing line breaks and comment lines into the XML representation. When working with XML files formatted this way, diff is able to recognize simple changes, like added or deleted entities or changed attributes, as separated groups of inserted, deleted, or changed lines.

Although this approach has effectively enabled the use of collaborative versioning tools for the model's development and maintenance, it is not free of problems. First of all, change integration works mostly correctly when integrating *non-conflicting* sets of changes, i.e., sets of changes that affect completely separate areas of the model. If, on the other hand, the change sets happen to touch the same area of the model (e.g., by altering the same attribute in different ways), a conflict is detected and marked. Solving the conflict requires a human being to look into the XML file where the changes have been merged and correct the conflicting lines manually using a text editor. This is a cumbersome process that requires detailed knowledge of the XML representation.

3 The *DeltaProcess* Approach

Considering the problems discussed in the previous section, we developed the *DeltaProcess* approach with the following goals in mind:

- Operate on models based on a variety of schemata. New schemata can be supported with relatively little effort.
- Be flexible about the changes that are recognized and how they are displayed.
- Allow for easily specifying change types that are specific to a particular schema or even to a particular application.
- Be tolerant to schema evolution by allowing the comparison of model instances that correspond to different versions of a schema (this sort of comparison requires additional effort, though.)

We claim that our approach is suitable for *difference analysis* as opposed to just difference identification (i.e., simple comparison). First of all, instead of defining a set of interesting change types in advance, we make it possible for the user to specify the types of changes that interest him in a schema-specific way. Additionally, since we use queries to find changes, it is possible for a user to restrict results to relevant areas of a model, according to a variety of criteria. Finally, postprocessing allows for applying specialized comparison and visualization algorithms to the resulting data, making it possible to display changes at a level of abstraction that is adequate for a specific task.

In this section, we provide a brief description of the *DeltaProcess* approach and its implementation *Evolyzer*. Readers interested in the inner workings of the approach are invited to read [2] and [3].

3.1 Description of the Approach

In order to compare models, the *DeltaProcess* approach goes through the following steps:

1. Convert the compared models to a normalized triple-based notation.
2. Perform an identity-based comparison of the resulting models, to produce a so-called *comparison model*.
3. Find relevant changes by using queries to search for patterns in the comparison model.
4. Postprocess the resulting change data, in order to refine the results or produce task-specific visualizations.

We explain these steps in some more detail in the following paragraphs.

The first step normalizes the compared models by expressing them as sets of so-called *statements*. Statements make simple assertions about the model entities (e.g., *e1 has type Activity* or *e1 has name "Design"*), or define relations among entities (e.g., *e1 produces product p1*). Although we could have defined our own notation for the statements, we decided to use the standard RDF notation [5] for this purpose. Beside the standardization benefits, RDF has the formal properties required by our approach.

In general, using a normalized triple notation has a number of advantages with respect to other generic notations like XML:

- It is generally inexpensive and straightforward to convert models to the notation. Since the set of possible assertions is not limited and can be defined separately for every model, models in arbitrary notations can be converted to RDF without losing information.
- Models do not lose their "personality" when moved to the notation. Once converted, model elements are often still easy for human beings to recognize.
- The results of a basic, unique-identifier based comparison can be expressed in the same notation. That is, comparisons are models, too. Additionally, elements remain easy for human beings to identify even inside the comparison.
- Thanks to normalization, a single, simple pattern notation can be used to describe a large number of interesting changes.

In step 2, two or more normalized models (in our case study, we perform many analyses using a three-way comparison) are put together into a single so-called *comparison model*. In this new model, statements are marked to indicate which of the original models they come from. One central aspect of the comparison model is that it is also a valid RDF model. The theoretical device that makes this possible is called *RDF reification,* and is defined formally in the RDF specification [5]. The main purpose of RDF reification is to allow for statements to speak about other statements. This way, it is possible to add assertions about the model statements, telling which one of the original models they belong to.

Changes appear in the comparison model as combinations of related statements that fulfill certain restrictions. For example, the change *a1's name was changed from "Design" to "System Design"* appears in the comparison model as the statement *a1 has name "Design"* marked as belonging only to the older version of the model, and the statement *a1 has name "System Design"* marked as belonging only to the newer version of the model. Since the number of statements in a comparison model is at least as large as the number of statements in the smallest of the compared models (the three-way comparison model used for the case study contains almost 18,000 statements), automated support is necessary to identify such change patterns reliably. For this reason, in step 3, a pattern-based query language is used to formally express interesting change types as queries. By executing the queries, corresponding changes are identified in the comparison model. There is already a standardized notation (SPARQL, see [6]) to express patterns in RDF models. With minimal adaptations, this notation makes it possible to specify interesting types of changes in a generic way. Our *Evolyzer* system (see Section 0) provides an efficient implementation of SPARQL that is adequate for this purpose.

The final step involves postprocessing of the change data obtained in step 3 in order to prepare the results for final display. One important purpose of this step is to allow for applying specialized comparison algorithms to particular model elements. For example, changed text descriptions in the V-Modell can be compared using a word-level, LCS-based algorithm to determine which words were changed. We also use this step to generate a variety of textual and graphical representations of change data.

One important limitation of the *DeltaProcess* approach is the fact that it requires that entities have unique identifiers that are consistent in all of the compared model instances. Otherwise, it would be impossible to reliably compare the resulting statements. Although this limitation may appear at first sight to be very onerous, our experience shows that, in practice, most modeling notations actually contain the identifiers, and most modeling tools do a good job of keeping them among versions. The V-Modell is not an exception, since its entities are always given a universal, unique, aleatory identifier at creation time.

3.2 Implementation

Our current implementation, *Evolyzer,* (see Fig. 1) was especially designed to work on large software process models, such as the V-Modell and its variants. Nevertheless, since the comparison kernel implements a significant portion of the RDF and SPARQL specifications (with the remaining parts also planned), support for other types of models can be added with relatively small effort.

The current implementation is written completely in the Python programming language, and uses the MySQL database management system to store models. Until now, we have mainly tested it with various process models, including many versions of the V-Modell (both standard releases and customized versions.) Converted to RDF, the latest released version of the V-Modell (1.2) contains over 13.000 statements, which describe over 2000 different entities. A large majority of the interesting comparison queries on models of this size (e.g., those used for producing the results presented in Section 0) run in less than 5 seconds on a modern PC.

3.3 Related Approaches

A number of other approaches are concerned with identifying differences in models of some type. [7] and [8] deal with the comparison of UML models representing diverse aspects of software systems. These works are generally oriented towards supporting software development in the context of the Model Driven Architecture. Although the basic comparison algorithms they present could also be applied to this case, the approaches do not seem to support the level of difference analysis we require.

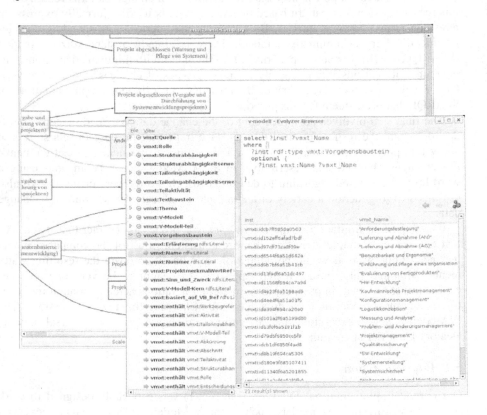

Fig. 1. The *Evolyzer* tool working on the V-Modell XT

[9] presents an extensive survey of approaches for software merging, many of which involve a comparison of program versions. Some of the algorithms used for advanced software merging may be applied to the problem of guaranteeing consistent results after a model merge operation, but this is a problem we are not yet trying to solve.

[10] provides an ontology and a set of basic formal definitions related to the comparison of RDF graphs. [11] and [12] describe two systems currently under development that allow for efficiently storing a potentially large number of variants of an RDF model by using a compact representation of the differences between them. These

works concentrate on space-efficient storage and transmission of difference sets, but do not go into depth regarding how to use them to support higher-level comparison tasks.

Finally, an extensive base of theoretical work is available from generic graph comparison research (see [13]), an area that is basically concerned with finding isomorphisms (or correspondences that approach isomorphisms according to some metric) between arbitrary graphs whose nodes and edges cannot be directly matched by name. This problem is analogous in many ways to the problem that interests us, but applies to a separate range of practical situations. In our case, we analyze the differences (and, of course, the similarities) between graphs whose nodes can be reliably matched in a computationally inexpensive way (i.e., unique identifiers.)

4 An Alignment Viability Analysis

As part of our ongoing case study, we performed an analysis aimed at determining the viability of aligning the company's customized process model with the V-Modell, by incorporating a subset of the changes that occurred in the V-Modell between versions 1.1 and 1.2. In order to perform this assessment, we decided to count the number of entities, entity attribute values, and relations affected by certain types of changes. The purpose of these measurements was to obtain a general impression of the number of separate changes that need to be considered by the process engineers while doing the alignment work.

In order to obtain the values, we defined a change pattern query for every change type, and used the *Evolyzer* tool to execute it and count the results. Although we are only presenting consolidated numbers, the individual changes are available from the tool and could be used by a process engineer as input for the actual alignment task. Regarding effort invested into the analysis, it was performed by one engineer in a single day, with the models having been imported previously into the tool's database.

The table below summarizes our results. The first column numbers the rows for reference, and the second column contains a description of the analyzed change type. The columns labeled "Entities", "Attributes", and "Relations" contain the respective counts of affected model elements. When a change type does not affect a particular type of model element, the corresponding cell remains empty.

Rows 1 to 3 present the total entity counts involved. It is clear that the tailoring process deleted a significant portion of the original. Another important observation is that 64% or about two thirds of the entities in the tailored model are still shared with the V-Modell. This portion seems large enough to justify attempting an alignment.

Rows 4 to 6 count the number of changed entities (defined as entities with changed attributes). Lines 5 and 6, in particular, count entities changed by the V-Modell that are still present in the tailored model. The count in 5 (96) corresponds to entities without conflicts, whereas the count in 6 (180) corresponds to entities with conflicts. The sum (276) is the total number of changed entities to consider. Notice that this number is about one half of the total of entities changed by the V-Modell (536). The difference (260) is the number of changed entities that do not have to be considered because they were deleted from the tailored model.

#	Change Type	Entities	Attributes	Relations
1	Total entities in the V-Modell (1.2)	2107		
2	Total entities in the tailored model	1231		
3	Entities present in both models (common entities)	789		
4	Changed entities in the V-Modell	536	670	
5	Common entities changed only by the V-Modell	96	99	
6	Common entities containing conflicting attributes	180	210	
7	New entities in the V-Modell	286		
8	New entities in the V-Modell that are contained in preexisting entities	150		
9	New entities in the V-Modell that are contained in entities still present in the tailored model	109		
10	Entities deleted from the V-Modell that are still present in the tailored model	0		
11	New entities in the V-Modell that reference preexisting entities	170		393
12	New entities in the V-Modell that reference entities that are still present in the tailored model.	100		189
13	Preexisting entities in the V-Modell that reference new entities	81		109
14	Entities still present in the tailored model that reference new entities in the V-Modell.	26		41
15	New relations between preexisting entities in the V-Modell			67
16	New relations in the V-Modell between entities that are also present in the tailored model			7
17	Deleted relations (between preexisting entities) in the V-Modell			127
18	Relations deleted in the V-Modell between entities still present in the tailored model			1
19	Entities in the V-Modell moved to another position in the structure.	86		
20	Entities still present in both the V-Modell and the tailored model, which were moved by the V-Modell but not by the tailored model	14		
21	Entities moved to conflicting positions in the structure by the V-Modell and the tailored model	0		

Rows 7-18 try to quantify the size of totally new additions present in the V-Modell. 7 and 8, respectively, count all new entities (286) and new entities contained in preexisting entities. The latter is probably the most relevant count, because the remaining entities are subentities of other new entities, and will probably be considered together with their parents. The subsequent rows try to determine whether it is possible to filter some of these new entities by analyzing their relations to preexisting entities. The resulting values suggest that this is possible, and that a significant number (40 to 50%) can probably be discarded because they have no connections to any of the entities in the tailored model. Line 10, in particular, contains good news: no entity deleted by the V-Modell is still being maintained by the tailored model.

The last three rows (19-21) are an attempt to measure a particular type of structural change, namely, movement of entities in the containment hierarchy. From 86 total changes in the V-Modell, only 14 affect the tailored model, and there are no conflicting changes.

Without historical effort data, it is difficult to produce an exact estimation of the effort involved in performing a model alignment. However, a few conclusions can be extracted from this data. First, integrating the changes done to existing entities (lines 1-3) is probably possible with relatively little effort. Informal observation of the versioning changelogs tells us that many of the changes are small grammar and spelling corrections, but to confirm this, we would need to exactly measure the extent of the changes done to text attributes.

Second, although integrating the new V-Modell elements is likely to take more work, it is also probably viable in a few days time, because the number of entities to consider is relatively small (around 100). Finally, the analysis shows that in this case, the total number of model elements to consider for alignment can be reduced to about half by filtering those elements that were already deleted from the tailored model or that are not connected to elements in the tailored model. This fact alone represents a significant effort saving, which is not achievable with any other method we are aware of.

5 Conclusions and Future Work

Organizations trying to document their software processes for the first time may greatly benefit from adopting an existing process standard and customizing it. However, since both process standards and the models derived from them evolve over time, sooner or later they diverge to a point where their lack of alignment becomes problematic. Realigning large process models, however, is a complex problem. Manual alignment is tedious and unreliable, and automated tool support for this task has been insufficient.

Our *DeltaProcess* approach and its *Evolyzer* implementation are a first step to remedy this situation. They provide a framework for identifying changes in process models and for analyzing these changes in order to support particular tasks. The implementation works efficiently on models of the size of the German V-Modell XT.

As the analysis presented in Section 0 shows, our approach can be used effectively to identify relevant changes and filter irrelevant changes when trying to align large process models that were changed independently from each other for an extended period of time. We have not yet started doing the actual alignment as part of our current case study, but expect to be able to attempt it in the following months. A complete experience report will be produced from that effort.

We are also working on extending our tools, which currently concentrate on change analysis, to also support altering the analyzed models. This way, we expect to make it easier for process engineers to work on complex model alignment tasks, by being able to move seamlessly from the change data to the actual model contents.

Acknowledgments. This work was supported in part by the German Federal Ministry of Education and Research (V-Bench Project, No.01I SE 11 A).

References

1. V-Modell XT (last checked 2006-03-31), available from http://www.v-modell.iabg.de/
2. Soto, M., Münch, J.: Process Model Difference Analysis for Supporting Process Evolution. In: Richardson, I., Runeson, P., Messnarz, R. (eds.) Software Process Improvement. LNCS, vol. 4257, Springer, Heidelberg (2006)
3. Soto, M., Münch, J.: The DeltaProcess Approach for Analyzing Process Differences and Evolution. Internal report No. 164.06/E, Fraunhofer Institute for Experimental Software Engineering (IESE) Kaiserslautern, Germany (2006)
4. Black, P.E. (ed.): Algorithms and Theory of Computation Handbook, Longest Common Subsequence. From Dictionary of Algorithms and Data Structures. NIST. CRC Press LLC (1999)
5. Manola, F., Miller, E.R. (eds.): Primer. W3C Recommendation (2004) (last checked 2006-03-22), available from http://www.w3.org/TR/rdf-primer/
6. Prud'hommeaux, E., Seaborne, A. (eds.): SPARQL Query Language for RDF. W3C Working Draft (2006) (last checked 2006-10-22), available from http:// www.w3. org/ TR/ rdf-sparql-query/
7. Alanen, M., Porres, I.: Difference and Union of Models. In: Stevens, P., Whittle, J., Booch, G. (eds.) «UML» 2003 - The Unified Modeling Language. Modeling Languages and Applications. LNCS, vol. 2863, pp. 2–17. Springer, Heidelberg (2003)
8. Lin, Y., Zhang, J., Gray, J.: Model Comparison: A Key Challenge for Transformation Testing and Version Control in Model Driven Software Development. In: OOPSLA Workshop on Best Practices for Model-Driven Software Development, Vancouver (2004)
9. Mens, T.: A State-of-the-Art Survey on Software Merging. IEEE Transactions on Software Engineering 28(5) (2002)
10. Berners-Lee, T., Connolly, D.: Delta: An Ontology for the Distribution of Differences Between RDF Graphs. MIT Computer Science and Artificial Intelligence Laboratory (CSAIL) (last checked 2006-03-30), online publication http:// www.w3.org/ DesignIssues/Diff
11. Völkel, M., Enguix, C.F., Ryszard-Kruk, S., Zhdanova, A.V., Stevens, R., Sure, Y.: SemVersion - Versioning RDF and Ontologies. Technical Report, University of Karlsruhe (2005)
12. Kiryakov, A., Ognyanov, D.: Tracking Changes in RDF(S) Repositories. In: KTSW 2002. Proceedings of the Workshop on Knowledge Transformation for the Semantic Web, Lyon, France (2002)
13. Kobler, J., Schöning, U., Toran, J.: The Graph Isomorphism Problem: Its Structural Complexity. Birkhäuser (1993)

Synergies Between the Common Criteria and Process Improvement

Miklós Biró and Bálint Molnár

Corvinus University of Budapest
{miklos.biro,balint.molnar}@informatika.uni-corvinus.hu

Abstract. This paper summarizes multifaceted synergies discovered between the ISO/IEC 15408 (Common Criteria) IT Security Evaluation standard, software product quality evaluation standards and the Capability Maturity Model Integration (CMMI). In addition to serving research motivated interest, the usefulness of the synergies is demonstrated through case studies related to significant systems development projects.

Keywords: Security, Quality, Assessment, Evaluation, Capability, Maturity, Classification, Categorization.

1 Introduction

Security is naturally present in all systems of software product quality criteria, and plays a significant role in the approporiate implementation of many software and systems engineering process areas. The development of the Information Society made this criterion of even higher significance, which resulted in the distinguished attention of international standardization bodies for example, resulting in the ISO/IEC 15408 (Common Criteria) standard.

Certification needs and the constraints of the standardization process led to the flexibility in both the product standards (ISO/IEC 9126, ISO/IEC 14598) and the process methodologies (CMMI , ISO/IEC 15504) which allows for evaluation modules based on a more elaborated background (ISO/IEC 15408, ISO/IEC 12207) as well as other modules based on simpler measurements.

Even if some of the underlying standards evolved independently of each-other, the discovery of synergies between their structure can contribute to the establishment of a cost and resource effective multiple certification process [Taylor, Alves-Foss, Rinker, 2002].

The combination of software process and product quality standards has already been studied in [Boegh, Régo, 2000]. In this paper we examine the synergies between the ISO/IEC 15408 (Common Criteria) standard and software quality and process capability evaluation methodologies. In addition to serving research motivated interest, the usefulness of the synergies is also demonstrated through case studies related to significant systems development projects.

® CMMI is registered in the U.S. Patent & Trademark Office by Carnegie Mellon University.

P. Abrahamsson et al. (Eds.): EuroSPI 2007, LNCS 4764, pp. 31–45, 2007.
© Springer-Verlag Berlin Heidelberg 2007

2 The Common Criteria

The history of the ISO/IEC 15408 (Common Criteria~CC) standard goes back to the 80's with the following non-exhaustive list of milestones:

- 1980- **TCSEC:** Trusted Computer System Evaluation Criteria (USA)
- 1991   **ITSEC:** Information Technology Security Evaluation Criteria v 1.2 (France, Germany, the Netherlands, U.K.)
- 1993 **CTCPEC:** Canadian Trusted Computer Product Evaluation Criteria v 3.0
- 1993 **FC:** Federal Criteria for Information Technology Security v 1.0 (USA)
- ➔ **CC Editorial Board**
- 1996 **CC v 1.0 ➔ ISO Committee Draft (CD)**
- 1998 **CC v 2.0 ➔ ISO Committee Draft (CD)**
- 1999 **CC v 2.1 = ISO/IEC 15408**

CC v 2.1 consists of the following parts:
   Part 1: Introduction and general model
   Part 2: Security functional requirements
   Part 3: Security assurance requirements

It is a common perception that understanding the Common Criteria (CC) evaluation process **requires painstakingly inspecting multiple documents and cross referencing innumerable concepts and definitions** [Prieto-Díaz, 2002]. The first challenge is the digestion of the abbreviations of which here is a brief extract for our immediate purposes:

- **TOE:** Target of Evaluation — An IT product or system and its associated administrator and user guidance documentation that is the subject of an evaluation.
- **TSP:** TOE Security Policy — A set of rules that regulate how assets are managed, protected and distributed within a TOE.
- **TSF:** TOE Security Functions — A set consisting of all hardware, software, and firmware of the TOE that must be relied upon for the correct enforcement of the TSP.
- **PP:** Protection Profile — An implementation-independent set of security requirements for a category of TOEs that meet specific consumer needs.
- **ST:** Security Target — A set of security requirements and specifications to be used as the basis for evaluation of an identified TOE.
- **EAL:** Evaluation Assurance Level — A package consisting of assurance components from Part 3 that represents a point on the CC predefined assurance scale.

Figure 1 and Figure 2 give an overview of the CC evaluation context and process.
   Here is an illustrative list of the classes of security functional requirements discussed in Part 2 of the CC introducing more abbreviations:

- **FAU** Security audit
- **FCO** Communication
- **FCS** Cryptographic support
- **FDP** User data protection
- **FIA** Identification and authentication
- **FMT** Security management
- **FPR** Privacy

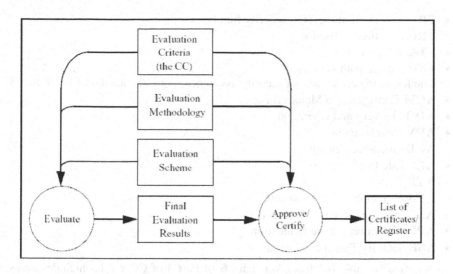

Fig. 1. Evaluation context (Source: Common Criteria for Information Technology Security Evaluation Introduction and general model, August 1999 Version 2.1)

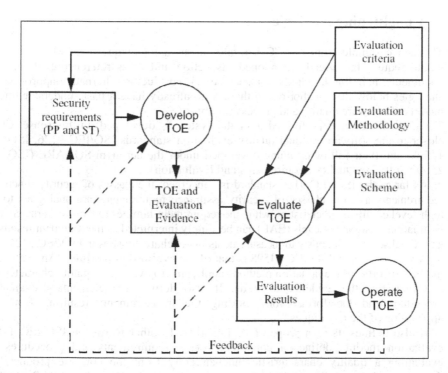

Fig. 2. TOE evaluation process (Source: Common Criteria for Information Technology Security Evaluation Introduction and general model, August 1999 Version 2.1)

- **FPT** Protection of the TOE security functions
- **FRU** Resource utilisation
- **FTA** TOE access
- **FTP** Trusted path / channels
  The following are classes of security assurance requirements discussed in Part 3:
- **ACM** Configuration Management
- **ADO** Delivery and Operation
- **ADV** Development
- **AGD** Guidance Documents
- **ALC** Life Cycle Support
- **ATE** Tests
- **AVA** Vulnerability Assessment
- **AMA** Maintenance of Assurance
- **APE** Protection Profile Evaluation
- **ASE** Security Target Evaluation

And finally, table B.1 from Appendix B of Part 3 of CC v 2.1 which describes the relationship between the evaluation assurance levels and the assurance classes, families and components (Table 2).

3 Enlightening Analogies

The above sample from the CC naturally raises a lot of questions whose answers would require the already mentioned inspection and cross referencing of multiple documents including hundreds of pages. As an introductory alternative approach, the analogies below offer a shortcut to those who already have a basic understanding of models of software quality and process capability.

CC certification is performed after the system is developed. In this sense, CC is closer to the software product quality evaluation standards ISO/IEC 9126, ISO/IEC 14598, and their follow-up being developed under the acronym SQUARE (ISO/IEC 25000 Software Quality Requirements and Evaluation).

As far as the ISO/IEC 9126 standard is concerned, the classes of security functional requirements and the classes of security assurance requirements are analogous to the high-level quality characteristics, while the requirement families to the subcharacteristics. Evaluation Assurance Levels (EAL) can be simply interpreted as measurement results on an ordinal scale analogously to measurements of subcharacteristics in ISO/IEC 9126.

A key concept of ISO/IEC 14598 is that of the **evaluation module**. "An evaluation module specifies the evaluation methods applicable to evaluate a quality characteristic and identifies the evidence it needs. It also defines the elementary evaluation procedure and the format for reporting the measurements resulting from the application of the techniques."

It also defines its own scope of applicability. In other words, an ISO/IEC 14598 evaluation module defines a consistent set of requirements and procedures for evaluating a quality characteristic independently from the concrete product, but depending on its application environment. If we consider the concept of **Protection Profile** (PP) as an implementation-independent set of security requirements for a category of TOEs that meet specific consumer needs, as introduced above, we can immediately see the analogy with the ISO/IEC 14598 evaluation module.

Even-though CC certification is performed after the system is developed, its structure shows a striking analogy with the system of continuous and staged representation structures of the Capability Maturity Model Integration (CMMI). In order to highlighting the analogy, let us consider Figure 3.5: Target Profiles and Equivalent Staging in the CMMI for Development, Version 1.2 showing the process area capability level (CL) target profiles of the Continuous Representation making an organization's maturity level equivalent to a maturity level (ML) defined in the Staged Representation (Table 3).

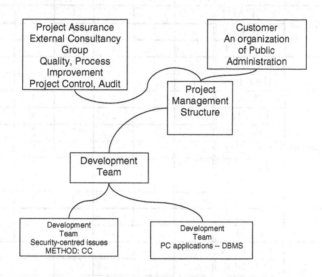

Fig. 3. Project structure

Let us equivalently transform this table so that the last columns contain maturity levels instead of capability levels, and the cells underneath contain the capability level of the given process area necessary for achieving the given maturity level (Table 5).

The analogy between Table 2 and Table 5 is immediately apparent if we consider the following analogies of the concepts of the Common Criteria and of CMMI (Table 1):

Table 1. Analogies of the concepts of the Common Criteria and of CMMI

Common Criteria	CMMI
Assurance Family	Process Area
Evaluation Assurance Level (EAL)	Maturity Level
Assurance value	Capability Level
Classification of Security Requirements	Categorization of Process Areas

This analogy not only helps those already familiar with CMMI to better understand the Common Criteria, but provides a new perspective on CMMI itself as well.

Table 2. Relationships in CC between the evaluation assurance levels and the assurance classes, families and components

Assurance Class	Assurance Family	Assurance Components by Evaluation Assurance Level						
		EAL1	EAL2	EAL3	EAL4	EAL5	EAL6	EAL7
Configuration management	ACM_AUT				1	1	2	2
	ACM_CAP	1	2	3	4	4	5	5
	ACM_SCP			1	2	3	3	3
Delivery and operation	ADO_DEL		1	1	2	2	2	3
	ADO_IGS	1	1	1	1	1	1	1
Development	ADV_FSP	1	1	1	2	3	3	4
	ADV_HLD		1	2	2	3	4	5
	ADV_IMP				1	2	3	3
	ADV_INT				1	2	3	
	ADV_LLD				1	1	2	2
	ADV_RCR	1	1	1	1	2	2	3
	ADV_SPM				1	3	3	3
Guidance documents	AGD_ADM	1	1	1	1	1	1	1
	AGD_USR	1	1	1	1	1	1	1
Life cycle support	ALC_DVS			1	1	1	2	2
	ALC_FLR							
	ALC_LCD				1	2	2	3
	ALC_TAT				1	2	3	3
Tests	ATE_COV		1	2	2	2	3	3
	ATE_DPT			1	1	2	2	3
	ATE_FUN		1	1	1	1	2	2
	ATE_IND	1	2	2	2	2	2	3
Vulnerability assessment	AVA_CCA					1	2	2
	AVA_MSU			1	2	2	3	3
	AVA_SOF		1	1	1	1	1	1
	AVA_VLA		1	1	2	3	4	4

4   CC in Software Development as Process Improvement Tool

The case study context:

Companies specialized in certifying and devising products using the CC take it for granted to make use of the Common Criteria not only as a tool for certification of software and hardware products but as a product development method as well. In this interpretation, the prescribed security and quality inspection steps in CC can be

Table 3. Target Profiles and Equivalent Staging in CMMI®

Name	Abbr	ML	CL1	CL2	CL3	CL4	CL5
Requirements Management	REQM	2	Target Profile 2				
Measurement and Analysis	MA	2					
Project Monitoring and Control	PMC	2					
Project Planning	PP	2					
Process and Product Quality Assurance	PPQA	2					
Supplier Agreement Management	SAM	2					
Configuration Management	CM	2					
Decision Analysis and Resolution	DAR	3	Target Profile 3				
Product Integration	PI	3					
Requirements Development	RD	3					
Technical Solution	TS	3					
Validation	VAL	3					
Verification	VER	3					
Organizational Process Definition	OPD	3					
Organizational Process Focus	OPF	3					
Integrated Project Management (IPPD)	IPM	3					
Risk Management	RSKM	3					
Organizational Training	OT	3					
Integrated Teaming	IT	3					
Organizational Environment for Integration	OEI	3					
Organizational Process Performance	OPP	4	Target Profile 4				
Quantitative Project Management	QPM	4					
Organizational Innovation and Deployment	OID	5	Target Profile 5				
Causal Analysis and Resolution	CAR	5					

considered as quality control of product development. The software development life cycle in this perspective can be deduced from the CC overall approach, then the methods and tools that should be applied can be implicitly inferred from the best practice of software engineering and software development. The consequence of these facts is that the quality control focusing on security issues takes place in due course. Quality inspection concentrates primarily on the security functional requirements, the representation techniques. The diagrammatic description for depicting the functional behaviour of the system is not pre-defined. The result of this fact is that the employed system development procedures are heterogeneous, i.e. they differ not only at the various companies using CC as system development method and system development life cycle approach, but they vary from project to project within the same system development company.

Table 4. ISO/IEC 9126 quality characteristics

Criterion	CHARACTERISTIC	Criterion	CHARACTERISTIC
Quality in Use	Effectiveness	Usability	Understandability
	Productivity		Learnability
	Safety		Operability
	Satisfaction		Attractiveness
Functionality	Suitability		Compliance
	Accuracy	Efficiency	Time behavior
	Interoperability		Resource utilization
	Security		Compliance
	Compliance	Maintainability	Analyzability
Reliability	Maturity (hardware/software/data)		Changeability
	Fault tolerance		Stability
	Recoverability (data, process, technology)		Testability
	Compliance		Compliance
		Portability	Adaptability
			Instability
			Co-existence
			Replace-ability
			Compliance

Generally, this seems not to be a serious problem as the system functional and security requirements are conceptualized in a "plain text" format either in a traditional way or a more modern "use case" format in the style of the Unified Process model (UP). There is no known example for creating a strong coupling between the CC "system development" process steps and — in the case of business or mission critical software development — a structured system development methodology as e.g. SSADM (Structured System Analysis and Development Method) or UML / UP (Unified Modelling language, Unified Process) object oriented methodology. The checking of the syntactic and semantic properties of descriptions and systems can be effortlessly carried over to the checking of the conformance of function calls and parameter passing to security standards. This kind of checking, naturally, includes the

Table 5. Capability levels necessary for achieving the given maturity levels in CMMI®

Name	Abbr	ML 1	ML 2	ML 3	ML 4	ML 5
Requirements Management	REQM	2	-	2	3	3	3
Measurement and Analysis	MA	2	-	2	3	3	3
Project Monitoring and Control	PMC	2	-	2	3	3	3
Project Planning	PP	2	-	2	3	3	3
Process and Product Quality Assurance	PPQA	2	-	2	3	3	3
Supplier Agreement Management	SAM	2	-	2	3	3	3
Configuration Management	CM	2	-	2	3	3	3
Decision Analysis and Resolution	DAR	3	-	-	3	3	3
Product Integration	PI	3	-	-	3	3	3
Requirements Development	RD	3	-	-	3	3	3
Technical Solution	TS	3	-	-	3	3	3
Validation	VAL	3	-	-	3	3	3
Verification	VER	3	-	-	3	3	3
Organizational Process Definition	OPD	3	-	-	3	3	3
Organizational Process Focus	OPF	3	-	-	3	3	3
Integrated Project Management (IPPD)	IPM	3	-	-	3	3	3
Risk Management	RSKM	3	-	-	3	3	3
Organizational Training	OT	3	-	-	3	3	3
Integrated Teaming	IT	3	-	-	3	3	3
Organizational Environment for Integration	OEI	3	-	-	3	3	3
Organizational Process Performance	OPP	4	-	-	-	3	3
Quantitative Project Management	QPM	4	-	-	-	3	3
Organizational Innovation and Deployment	OID	5	-	-	-	-	3
Causal Analysis and Resolution	CAR	5	-	-	-	-	3

pre- and post-conditions of security function calls but there is little or no emphasis on the other more business like pre- and post conditions. This approach is very effective and efficient from the security viewpoint but provides little or no hint for the other important quality aspects, as stipulated in ISO/IEC 9126.

At first glimpse, there is an imminent conflict between the security-oriented method and the system development process, and which means in fact process improvement opportunities for both approaches.

In practice, at a certain software development exercise — that could be considered as a case study example in this connection —, where the aim was to develop an information system with high security requirement, an *ad hoc* compromise had to be worked out. The ISO/IEC 9126 (Table 4) quality aspects are implicitly built-in the practice of the traditional structured system development methodologies through the functional and non-functional requirements and their step-by-step modeling and implementation.

Since the CC does not put emphasis on quality characteristics other than security and partly safety, the solution was to build up quality criteria checklist based on the ISO/IEC 9126 characteristics and painstakingly include them into the user side quality control and quality assurance exercise.

In order to achieve improvement of software development processes based on principles grounded in CC, the "Target of Evaluation (TOE)", "TOE Security Functions", "Evaluation Assurance Level" subject areas had to be complemented with the quality criteria. These subject areas can be represented as tangible assets in the form of documentation, and can be coupled to groups of quality criteria and system development artifacts (see Table 6).

Table 6. Coupling of groups of quality criteria to system development artifacts

Common Criteria Concept	System Development Concept		Quality Criterion
	Structured Approach	UML / UP	
TOE: Target of Evaluation	Business Context Modelling Requirements Definitions Data Modelling	Business Modelling Artifacts Requirements Artifacts	Functionality
TSF: TOE Security Functions	Function Modelling Behaviour and Process Modelling	Analysis and Design Artifacts	Functionality Reliability
EAL: Evaluation Assurance Level	User Centred Design Database and Physical Process Design	Implementation Artifacts Deployment Artifacts	Quality in Use Usability Maintainability Portability

The subject of the development project was to devise and implement a secure PC-based — moreover laptop-based — distributed system, where a central server with a central database would communicate to effectively mobile, laptop-based clients. The communication media would be commercial radio communication network (GSM) which is able to provide radio coverage even in very distant rural areas.

The developer consortium consisted of a professional company specialized in developing, manufacturing and operating security products, moreover it had major expertise in applying CC both for product audit and product development. The other member was an SME (Small and Medium sized Enterprise) specialized in PC software development. The Customer was a public agency with the assistance of a consultancy group specialized in informatics issues for government.

Having experienced the problems in spite of the promises and official statements of the consortium, the consultancy body started to elaborate quality control steps. For each stage and each product of the development process, a set of criteria was defined based on ISO 9126. As a result, the quality control and the criteria implicitly directed the development process. The development team was replaced with a more experienced staff in information systems development, and more receptive to the end-users' requirements partly embodied into the quality criteria to be checked at the quality review.

Process improvement has been achieved within the CC methodology without profoundly modifying it by extending the set of criteria for quality review. There were no new diagram techniques and analysis tools introduced. However, the rigorous functional analysis of the security issues built-in CC proved sufficient with the quality extension to supply information system for the satisfaction of end-users.

In this way, the CC security-centred engineering approach and system development quality assurance could be combined to benefit the end-users and their requirements. The results were satisfying but need further research and experimental case studies to provide a sound basis for a systematic engineering method for the combination of two differing world-views instead of a rather *ad hoc* approach.

5 Software Quality Standards in Iterative, Object-Oriented Development

The Unified Modelling Language (UML) and the Unified Process Model have gained popularity among companies involved in systems or software development. However, the buyers of systems and the end-users are not satisfied with the systems shipped to them at all. What are the reasons why the promised quality attributes do not fulfill the expectations of the end-users?

The case study context:
In a system development case, where a public administration institution has outsour-ced its system and software development activities to reduce the costs that have burdened its budget, the vendor had to create a customized method. In order to avoid quality accountability, the detailed method description did not contain quality criteria associated to every single technique and method, in spite of the fact that the method customization was based on a well-known system method and the vendor's proprietary methodology. The ideology behind this decision is articulated in [Ulferts2005] paper: the claim is that the Software Quality Assurance is a built in feature of UP, but the experiences show that this statement might be valid at large

professional organization specialised in UP / UML like system development but not at smaller ones where for reasons of cost-effectiveness, it is the quality assurance that is dropped firstly. The sad and costly consequences of the above mentioned situation is that the end-users' organization who had outsourced the system development should provide a friendly environment for quality assurance and process improvement opportunity for both for the vendor and the customer organization. The critical issue is that the quality criteria for each method, tool, technique and procedure applied in UP / UML development environment are not public, even if they are existent they are included into the proprietary documentation of the proprietary method owned by some system development company. The solution for the customer organization is to assemble quality criteria associated to the artifacts and methods contained in the customized methodology or set of methods. As the company undertaking software development was neither willing nor capable to compile a set of quality criteria for each specific document and artifact of the development processes. The process improvement has been realized by setting up an independent quality assurance team that was totally separate form the developer's organization and practically from the customer. Measuring the quality of products, the ISO/IEC 9126 quality metrics helped to demonstrate the discrepancies between the reviewed products of developers and some widely published results appropriate for international benchmarking. The tangible result for the customer organization is that quality becomes a measurable attribute of the artifacts of system development. The right hand-side columns of Table 2 represent the solution and mappings between the significant end-users' quality criteria incorporated in the ISO 9126 and some essential set of artifacts produced by UP / UML methodology. The use of CC has emerged as a must regarding the privacy of data manipulated by the organization. The CC provides a framework to evaluate the security requirements of products.

5.1   Application of UP / UML

The developer companies released a set of guides and handbooks following the basic principles of UP / UML that contained a customized version of the "disciplines" and documentation standards.

5.1.1   The Business Modelling Discipline

This modelling tool set and method is the imminent conflicting point between the developer companies and public administration organizations. The public administration's basic governing principles come from the legal environment, primarily laws, decrees, ordinances (government's, ministries'), other statutory instruments and then subordinate legislation. Understanding and correctly interpreting the conceptual framework encoded into the textual rules and the every day practice is hard task and the dense texture of the rules are hardly penetrable for people or companies who are not participating day-to-day in the work. The system and software development methodologies as UP / UML provide the detailed steps, techniques, diagram techniques, documentation standards both in format and in content as a feasible and viable tools to control the analysis process and to reflect and describe as close as possible the business processes in terms of users. The "Use Case" diagram and textual description is an apt tool for description the real processes in a correct form in the case of following the rigorous rules of methodology, i.e. depicting the processes using the standard documentation format that expects the description of the pre- and post-conditions, the main-stream scenario, the alternative ones including the "error-prone" branches. The developer company specified the use of the "Business Use-Case modeling" method as it was abovementioned, however never used this way. This fact caused twofold problems, on one side incorrect use of the method both formally and semantically, on the other side the business and system analyst did not understand the business processes correctly. The quality assurance team raised several objections, but the developer team was not competent to fulfil the expectations.

5.1.2 The Requirements Discipline

Regarding the complexity of public administration and the ignorance of developer company, the developers were not able to compile a consistent set of requirements. The customer collected and edited a requirements catalogue, nevertheless the developer company and its analyst were not able to correctly interpret the requirements. The "Use-Case modelling" method was not used correctly within the modelling exercise as well having the same defects as before.

5.1.3 The Analysis and Design Discipline

The customized methodology contained some significant methods and their documentation as Data Model, Design Model. The developer team formally created the documents but keeping a low-profile on the content, i.e. leaving out the detailed data elements analysis, detailed description of relationship among entity classes as degree and relationship realizing data element. The customer's Quality Assurance team had played and important role checking the artifacts and using measurement system for the quality of products, namely the ISO 9126 quality metrics, general criteria for application systems and especially UP conform development. The quality assurance team experiences point at the opportunities of software process development in future. Despite the statement that UP immanently contains the quality control and assurance, there were several problems during the software development that could be handled only by the customer side quality assurance.

5.1.4 The Test Discipline

The testing method, partly conforming to RUP partly not, were extensively used as the defects and errors had been produced the previous stages manifested the testing phase. Enormous number of errors and insufficiencies in requirements specification came to surface. The assessment and evaluation of errors showed the holes in the project management and control on the side of developers. There were no categories for various error types, there were no distinction between errors detected in the alpha and in the beta test for number crunching statistics to see the quality characteristics of the software.

5.1.5 The Deployment Discipline

In spite of the customized method handbooks, the deployment related activities were done in an *ad hoc* manner and not according to the prescription of RUP. However, this caused minor problems because the customer had had a good practice for several years.

5.1.6 The Configuration and Change Management Discipline

A specific handbook among the customized ones treated the change management; specialized software modules had been acquired to support the related activities. However, because of the lack of capability and willingness on the side of developers, the change management was total failure causing several problems on the customer side and during the acceptance phase. The UP and supporting software modules demand theoretical and practical pre-requisites, specialized knowledge and skill. Without the necessary training and commitment on the developer side, the UP method in itself cannot guarantee any success.

There were no Configuration Management Plan, Configuration Audit. The handling of "Change Request" was neither systematic nor keeping track.

5.1.7 Project Management Discipline

The developer side hardly used the project management methods proposed by them. There were no Quality Assurance Plan, Problem Resolution Plan, Risk management Plan, Product Acceptance Plan, Iteration Plan including Iteration Assessment. On customer side, having lack of knowledge of UP like project management, they made up for PRINCE II project management method having wide international acceptance. By this way, the customer side were able to keep in check their own side the developer teams project management was rather chaotic.

5.1.8 Process Improvement and UML / UP

The UML / UP is a theoretically sound system and software development method that have proved its usefulness in practice and in several software projects. In spite of this, the use of method is not straightforward for a given organization as the method provides a wide-range of tools and techniques that should be selected in an appropriate manner in each single iterative phase. This adaptation work is a huge task and leads to failures if the quality side is not taken into consideration, e.g. through the application of the readily available process improvement approaches.

6 Conclusion

The analogies discovered between the complex standards and methodologies described in the paper help those familiar with one of the systems of concepts better understanding the other system of concepts on the one hand, contribute to the potential establishment of a cost and resource effective multiple certification process on the other hand.

Process improvement can be manifested by a mapping approach that meticulously couples the significant quality criteria and the artifacts produced by either the CC method or UP / UML. To be successful, an organizational guarantee is required; a quality assurance team has to be present in the customer organization which ensures that the quality really becomes an integral part of the processes of systems development for the satisfaction of the requirements of end-users. We can conclude that the following thesis has been established: process improvement reflecting higher CMMI levels leads to potentially higher security levels in the CC sense. The two case studies suggest that this statement is correct. However, in order to empirically validating this hypothesis, we need a measurement framework including the CMMI and the CC criteria which should be cross-referenced. The elaboration of such a framework and the performance of such an experiment will be the subject of further research.

Nonetheless, we can deduce that process improvement can help both types of software development approaches investigated in the case studies, whether security-centred or user requirement-oriented.

References

1. Biró, M., Tully, C.: The Software Process in the Context of Business Goals and Performance. In: Messnarz, R., Tully, C. (eds.) Better Software Practice for Business Benefit, IEEE Computer Society Press, Washington, Brussels, Tokyo (1999)
2. Biró, M., Messnarz, R.: Key Success Factors for Business Based Improvement. Software Quality Professional (ASQ, American Society for Quality) 2(2), 20–31 (2000) (July 11, 2007), http://www.asq.org/pub/sqp/past/vol2_issue2/biro.html
3. Biró, M.: Common Criteria for IT Security Evaluation - SPI Analogies. In: Messnarz, R. (ed.) Proceedings of the EuroSPI 2003 Conference, pp. IV.13–IV.21. Verlag der Technischen Universität Graz (2003), ISBN 3-901351-84-1
4. Boegh, J., Rêgo, C.M.: Combining software process and product quality standards. In: The 2nd World Conference on Software Quality, Japan (September 2000)
5. Prieto-Díaz, R.: Understanding the Common Criteria Evaluation Process. Commonwealth Information Center Technical Report CISC-TR-2002-003 (September 2002)
6. Taylor, C., Alves-Foss, J., Rinker, B.: Merging Safety and Assurance: The Process of Dual Certification for Software. In: Proc. Software Technology Conference (March 2002)
7. CCTA (Central Computer and Telecommunication Agency): SSADM Version 4+, Version 4.3. London, HMSO, The Stationery Office (1996)
8. Larman, C.: Applying UML and Patterns, 3rd edn. Prentice Hall, Englewood Cliffs (2002)
9. Muller, P.-A.: Instant UML. Wrox Press Ltd., Birmingham, UK (1997)
10. Ulferts, Karen: Why isn't there a RUP workflow for software quality assurance? (July 11, 2007), http://www-128.ibm.com/developerworks/rational/library/jun05/ulferts/index.html#notes
11. Common Criteria for Information Technology Security Evaluation Introduction and general model: Version 2.1, CCIMB-99-031, ISO/IEC 15408:1999 (August 1999)

Determining Practice Achievement in Project Management Using a Two-Phase Questionnaire on Small and Medium Enterprises

Garcia Ivan., Calvo-Manzano Jose A., Cuevas Gonzalo, and San Feliu Tomas

Languages and Informatics Systems and Software Engineering Department
Faculty of Computer Science, Polytechnic University of Madrid, Spain
ivan@mixteco.utm.mx, jacalvo@fi.upm.es, gcuevas@fi.upm.es,
tsanfe@fi.upm.es

Abstract. This paper aims to obtain a baseline snapshot of Project Management processes using a two-phase questionnaire to identify both performed and non-performed practices. The proposed questionnaire is based on the Level 2 process areas of the Capability Maturity Model Integration for Development v1.2. It is expected that the application of the questionnaire to the processes will help small and medium software enterprises to identify those practices which are performed but not documented, which practices need more attention, and which are not implemented due to bad management or unawareness.

Keywords: Software process improvement, appraisals, questionnaire, project management processes.

1 Introduction

This research advocates the idea that although project management processes are not carried out in many organizations there are isolated members or groups that perform their own project management practices. These practices, however, are usually not documented and consequently are not spread across the organization. Recent years have witnessed an increasing demand for software to solve more and more complex tasks, and with greater added value [27]. Under these circumstances, the following question can be raised: Is the software industry prepared to deliver the software that is needed according to client demands in the coming years? According to the Prosoft Foundation (Program for Develop the Software Process) [28] and researchers such as Oktaba [25], Brodman [4], and Carreira [8] the answer is unfortunately no. The software development process is far from being a mature process.

At the moment, there is a consensus in the software industry sector that such a complex product as software must be developed with the help of engineering and management processes and metrics that enable us to effectively predict the risk levels of software products (primordially, in terms of costs, schedules, and defects) [14]. The fact of the matter, however, is that IT projects usually fail partially or sometimes

P. Abrahamsson et al. (Eds.): EuroSPI 2007, LNCS 4764, pp. 46–58, 2007.

completely [15]. The "software crisis" of 1969 has lasted up to now, with the same old causes of project failure [20] [31]:

- 30% of software projects are cancelled,
- 50% of software projects are abandoned or their costs are excessive,
- Often, 60% of software projects fail due their poor quality , and
- Software delivery is delayed in 9 out of 10 projects.

The lack of management is confirmed in [30] [11]. Throughout the world, a million projects are implemented every year. Cairó [7] indicated that a third of these projects exceed 125% in time and cost. But why is there so much failure? The same study indicates that although there are many reasons, one of the most important is *project management*. Jones [19] has identified three principal causes of failure and delays in software projects: inaccurate estimates, poor communication of project status, and lack of historical information. These are key issues in the areas of *project planning and project monitoring and control*. Furthermore, the Standish Group maintains that software does not cover all the requirements for which they were created, it must be modified frequently and is difficult to maintain. Jones also holds that these causes can be eliminated through an adequate project management process.

A recent Department of Defense (DoD) report on this problem states that: *"After two decades of unfulfilled promises about productivity and quality gains from applying new software methodologies and technologies, industry and government organizations are realizing that their fundamental problem is the inability to manage the software process, the low quality in the risk management area specially"* [3]. Hence, having taken into account old and new causes of project failure, we reached the conclusion that the causes are still the same.

The objective of this paper is to provide a more accurate picture of the Project Management Practices (PMP) of an organization by administering a questionnaire. PMP has been selected because they are considered the cornerstone of the software lifecycle. There is evidence that suggests that deficient PMP may be one of the principal causes of many problems related to later stages in the software development process. The questionnaire proposed in this paper is used as an initial data collection instrument for the appraisal of PMP. The questionnaire was chosen because it provides a quick fix for a research methodology and because the researcher can determine the questions to be asked and the range of answers that can be given. This makes it more precise and easy to analyze from the researcher's point of view [13]. Besides, it has been argued that the application of questionnaires consumes less time, effort and financial resources than other methods of data collection such as interviews and document reviews [2]. Moreover, it offers less accurate results and could be misunderstood. The questionnaire is based on the Capability Maturity Model Integration for Development (CMMI-DEV) [29]. The CMMI option was selected because it is probably one of the best known software process improvement models [1] and because its representation offers flexibility when applying a process improvement program.

2 Motivations

From the beginning of the 90's, industry and researchers interested in Software Engineering have been expressing special interest in Software Process Improvement (SPI)

[26] (see Figure 1). An indicator of this interest is the increasing number of international initiatives related to SPI, such as CMMI-DEV [29], ISO/IEC 15504:2004 [17], SPICE [18], and ISO/IEC 12207:2004 [16].

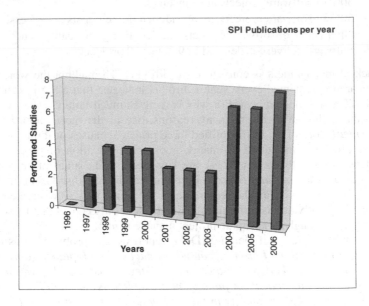

Fig. 1. SPI Publication's tendency per year

In addition, many methods for evaluating improvements in organizations, such as SCAMPI [23], ISO 15504 [17] and CBA-IPI [12], and improvement models such as IDEAL [21] have been developed. This interest in software improvement in large enterprises is now being extended to small and medium enterprises. However, the problem is the high implementation cost, independently of the company size [24]. Because models have been developed for large enterprises, only a few Small and Medium software Enterprises are aware of them. In Spain, in April 2006 there were almost 3 million Small and Medium Enterprises (SMEs) that accounted for 99.87 % of all companies; 10% of which are software enterprises (see Table 1). With this information we were able to determine the importance of SMEs at the macroeconomics level.

It is expected that the application of the questionnaire to an organization's PMP team can provide useful information related to the current state of the processes and

Table 1. Characteristics of Spanish enterprises (Source: DIRCE 2006)

Micro-enterprises (1-20)	Small (21-50)	Medium (51-250)	SMEs (1-250)	Big (250 and more)	Total
2.722.003	88.173	25.599	**2.835.775**	8.533	2.844.308
95,7%	3,1%	0,9%	**99,7%**	0,3%	100%

indicate those PMP that require immediate attention. Data derived from the question-naire can help to identify the people who implement some PMP in order to incorpo-rate them into the SPI effort. Finally, the questionnaire could be used as a data collection instrument for a more extensive appraisal method such as SCAMPI [23].

3   The Capability Maturity Model Integration for Development

As CMMI official documentation indicates: *"Major systems development today often requires integrated engineering activities and components. Many organizations have found several models to be useful: SEI's Capability Models (Software, Software Ac-quisition, Systems Engineering, People, etc.), EIA/IS 731.1 (SECM), ISO 9000, ISO 14000, etc. While independently useful, the models had significant overlaps and re-dundancies, some contradictions and inconsistencies, different levels of detail, and poorly described or non-explicit interfaces. These issues lead to inefficiency in proc-ess improvement program implementation and benchmarking. Capability Maturity Model Integration (CMMI) practices and structure attempt to minimize the issues with multiple models. The CMMI project work is sponsored by the U.S. DoD, specifi-cally the Office of the Under Secretary of Defense, Acquisition, Technology, and Lo-gistics (OUSD/AT&L). Industry sponsorship is provided by the Systems Engineering Committee of the National Defense Industrial Association (NDIA). Organizations from industry, government, and the SEI joined forces to develop the CMMI Frame-work, a set of integrated CMMI models, a CMMI appraisal method, and supporting products"* [29].

According to SEI, *"CMMI is a process improvement maturity model for the devel-opment of products and services. It consists of best practices that address develop-ment and maintenance activities that cover the product lifecycle from conception through delivery and maintenance. This latest iteration of the model as represented herein integrates bodies of knowledge that are essential for development and mainte-nance. These, however, have been addressed separately in the past, such as software engineering, systems engineering, hardware and design engineering, the engineering "-ilities," and acquisition"* [29]. The prior designations of CMMI for systems engi-neering and software engineering (CMMI-SE/SW) are superseded by the title "CMMI for Development" to truly reflect the comprehensive integration of these bodies of knowledge and the application of the model within the organization. CMMI-DEV provides a comprehensive integrated solution for development and maintenance ac-tivities applied to products and services.

The CMMI-DEV official report indicates that: *"CMMI for Development V1.2 is a continuation and update of CMMI V1.1 and has been facilitated by the concept of CMMI "constellations" wherein a set of core components can be augmented by addi-tional material to provide application-specific models with highly common content. CMMI-DEV is the first of such constellations and represents the development area of interest".* There are six capability levels; numbered 0 through 5 (see Figure 2). Each capability level corresponds to a generic goal and a set of generic and specific prac-tices providing a framework for organizing the process improvement steps [29].

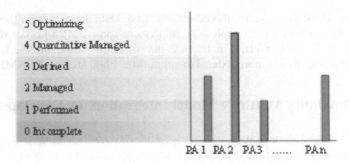

Fig. 2. CMMI-DEV Capability Levels

3.1 Model's Structure

According to [29], *"CMMI models are designed to describe discrete levels of process improvement. The capability levels and generic model components focus on building the organization's capacity to pursue process improvement in multiple process areas. Using capability levels, generic goals, and generic practices, organizations can improve their processes, as well as demonstrate and evaluate their progress as they improve. Capability levels in continuous representation provide a recommended order for approaching process improvement within each process area. For each process area, a capability level consists of related specific and generic practices that, when performed, achieve a set of goals that lead to improved process performance. Furthermore, generic practices provide "institutionalization" to ensure that activities related to the process area will be effective, repeatable, and enduring".*

In continuous representation, a capability level profile is a list of process areas and their corresponding capacity levels. This profile is used by the organization to track its capacity level by process area. The profile is an achievement profile when it represents the organization's progress for each process area while ascending the capacity levels. Alternatively, the profile is a target profile when it represents the organization's process improvement objectives. An achievement profile, when compared with a target profile, enables us not only to track the organization's process improvement progress, but also to demonstrate the organization's progress to management. Maintaining capacity level profiles is advisable when using a continuous representation. Before using a CMMI model for improving processes, the organization must map its processes onto CMMI process areas. This mapping enables it to control process improvement by helping it track the organization's level of conformity to the CMMI model. Every CMMI process area is not intended to map one to one with the organization's processes [29].

4   The Project Management Practices

PMP cover project management activities related to planning, monitoring, and controlling the project. All the causes of project failure analyzed on section 1 can be mapped onto process areas of CMMI-DEV Level 2 (see Table 2).

Table 2. A cause vs. process area comparative table

Cause	CMMI-DEV process area
"Software projects are cancelled or exceed the schedule"	Project Planning
"Software projects are abandoned or their costs are excessive"	Project Planning / Project Monitoring and Control
"Software projects fail due to their poor quality"	Product and Process Qualiy Assurance
"Poor communication of project status, and lack of historical information"	Project Monitoring and Control / Supplier Agreement Management
"Software does not cover all the requirements for which they were created"	Requirements Management
"Software must be modified frequently and is difficult to maintain"	Configuration Management

Table 2 provides a bird's-eye view of the process areas included in the assessment questionnaire. The principal aim in the selection of these process areas is to cover all causes of failure and provide an evaluation result to improve deficient practices. The process areas shown in Table 2 are in CMMI-DEV's capability Level 2.

5 Data Collection Instruments: An Overview

This study has been defined by taking into account the generic SPI model defined by ISPI (Institute for Software Process Improvement Inc.) with four stages (commitment to appraisal, assessment, infrastructure and action plan, and implementation). Their objectives are similar to those of the IDEAL model [21] from the SEI. It must not be forgotten that this study focuses on phase 2 of the SPI Model: *The Software Process Assessment.*

There is a wide number of data collection instruments that can be used for appraisals: questionnaires, surveys, interviews, and reviewing documentation, each having its own advantages and disadvantages. One of the commonly used techniques is a questionnaire. This is mainly because they can be applied to many people, they are cost effective, non-invasive, provide quantitative data, and results can be analyzed promptly [13]. However, it is important to mention that this technique lacks precision and also is easily open to misinterpretation. Questionnaires can be classified into *open* and *closed questions*. An open-question provides more information than a closed one. The complexity of analyzing data provided by open questions, however, is higher than those in closed-questions [32]. Moreover, a closed-question provides less information but its results can be more easily analyzed and are obtained faster than with the open one. Consequently, for this research a questionnaire was developed using closed questions as the main instrument for collecting appraisal data.

In order to propose a new instrument for collecting appraisal data, a review was performed of the questionnaires available in the literature. The first questionnaire to be reviewed was the SEI' Maturity Questionnaire [33]. The major disadvantage with this questionnaire is that it was developed for the SW-CMM model and cannot, therefore, be applied as it is to the CMMI-DEV model. Furthermore, the maturity questionnaire provides little information about the PMP because it focuses on the maturity of the process without paying attention to finding the weakness of the practices. Another disadvantage is that this questionnaire is limited in the number of responses that can be selected: *Yes, No, Does not Apply* and *Don't Know*. In fact, there are only two options - Yes and No, because Does not Apply and Don't Know are used to validate the application of the questionnaire. Using the maturity questionnaire limits the information to two extreme ends: Yes, if the practice is performed and No if the practice is not performed. Therefore, it does not leave room for intermediate points. There are, for example, no options to pick up cases where practices are performed but rarely documented or when they are not documented at all. This type of question cannot be addressed with the options provided in the Maturity Questionnaire.

Questionnaires with limited answer options may provide limited or misleading information. For example, a project sponsored by the SEI "CMMI Interpretive Guidance Project" supports this argument [9]. The questionnaire was applied to more than 600 people and the results report the following:

"We are not providing the results of the Generic Goals and Practices and Specific Process Areas sections of the Web-based questionnaire in this preliminary report. In both of these sections, there were no radio buttons and therefore the responses provided were in the form of specific comments. Many of these specific comments contain little information. For example, responses such as 'none' or 'no' were common" [9].

However, in one question of the same project, the SEI used five possible responses: *Almost always, More often than not, Sometimes, Rarely if ever* and *Don't know*. As a result, more distributions of the types of responses were obtained (see Figure 3). The report does not explain, however, the reasons why this methodology was not used in the same way for specific and generic practice questions.

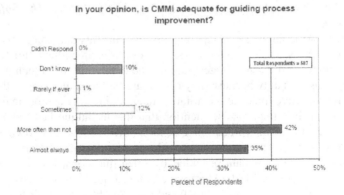

In your opinion, is CMMI adequate for guiding process improvement?

Fig. 3. Example of answer distribution

The report of the Process Improvement Program for the Northrop Grumman Information Technology Company [23] proposes a Questionnaire-Based Appraisal with seven possible responses: *Does Not Apply, Don't know, No, about 25% of the time, about 50% of the time, about 75% of the time,* and *Yes*. This work proposes more response granularity. It does not, however, explain how to apply this questionnaire to the PMP. Another disadvantage is that this report used the SA-CMM as a reference model and it focuses on the Software Acquisition process.

Another study reviewed was the software improvement model proposed by the ISPI. This model was used by [5] and [6] in their research. For the appraisal stage, they proposed a questionnaire structure using five types of responses: Always when the practice is documented and performed between 100% – 75% of the time, More often when the practice is documented and performed between 74% – 50% of the time, Sometimes when the practice is not documented and is performed between 49% – 25% of the time. Rarely when the practice could be documented or not and is performed between 25% - 1 of the time. And Never when the practice is not performed in the organization.

The response granularity is similar to that of Marciniak and Sadauskas [22] and provides more information about the current state of practices. This study only provides general information about the process without covering the PMP in full detail and without proposing precise actions for process improvement. Moreover, this questionnaire was designed for SW-CMM.

The last study reviewed was the questionnaire proposed by Cuevas and Serrano [10]. This study proposes an assessment methodology based on a questionnaire to identify which practices of the *requirements management process* are performed but not documented, which practices require to be prioritized and which are not implemented due to bad management or unawareness. Cuevas's questionnaire is based on CMMI v1.1 and only covers the requirements management process.

In summary, the questionnaires reviewed here are deficient in their design and do not obtain relevant information. Furthermore, there is no evidence of a questionnaire that addresses the PMP in detail and there is no evidence of a questionnaire that covers both generic and specific practices.

6 An Alternative Data Collection Instrument: The PMP Two Phase -Questionnaire

Based on the previously reviewed literature, a two-phase questionnaire is proposed. The questionnaire uses closed questions and limits the number of possible responses to seven. These are organized as follows:

- Five level-perform-answers: *Always, Usually, Sometimes, Rarely if ever,* and *Never*. These will enable us to know the extent to which each practice is performed.
- Two validity-answers: *Don't Know* and *Not Apply*. These will be used to appraise the validation of the questions, to validate the correctness of the question, and to check the syntaxes of the questions.
- Additional information spaces (*Comments*) to extract supplementary background information. It is mandatory to write some comments when checking any of the validity-answers.

Each possible response has a unique interpretation and indicates the performance level of a PMP as described in Table 3.

The level-perform-answers determine the percentage in which each practice is performed. This varies from 'Never' with a value equal to 0, 'Rarely if ever' with a value equal to 1, 'Sometimes' with a value equal to 2, and 'Usually' with a value equal to 3, and 'Always' with a value equal to 4. The validity-answers don't have numerical value. Giving a specific weight to each response will enable us to easily analyze the results of the evaluation and to identify which practices are common within the whole organization and which ones are not performed at all.

Table 3. Perform Level Classification

Possible Answer	Perform Level	Description
Always	4	*The activity is documented and established in the organization. It is always realized, between 75 and 100% of the time, in organization software projects*
Usually	3	*The activity is established in the organization but rarely documented. It is usually realized, between 50 and 75 % of the time, in organization software projects*
Sometimes	2	*The activity is weakly established in the organization. It is realized sometimes, between 25 and 50 % of the time, in organization software projects*
Rarely if ever	1	*The activity is rarely performed in the organization. It is rarely realized, between 1 and 25 % of the time, in organization software projects*
Never	0	*The activity is not performed in the organization. No person or group performs the activity in the organization.*
Don't Know		*The person is not sure how to answer the question.*
Not Apply		*The question is not applicable to the organization.*
Comments		*This space is for elaborating or qualifying one's response to a question, and it is mandatory when one selects Don't know or Not Apply options.*

6.1 Questionnaire's Structure

The questionnaire proposed here has been based on the two types of practices established by the CMMI-DEV and is divided into two phases. The first-phase is related to specific practices while the second-phase is related to generic practices. Another reason of this division is to differentiate the type of audience to whom it is applied.

The first-phase is aimed at employees who implement the process and is based on the specific practices from PMP of the CMMI-DEV [29]. This phase is divided into six process areas that will be performed to achieve a well established project management process:

- *Project Planning:* The purpose of Project Planning is to establish and maintain plans that define project activities.
- *Project Monitoring and Control:* The purpose of Project Monitoring and Control is to provide an understanding of project progress so that appropriate

corrective actions can be taken when the project performance deviates significantly from the plan.

- **Requirements Management:** The purpose of Requirements Management is to manage the requirements of the project products and product components and to identify inconsistencies between those requirements and project plans and work products.

- **Configuration Management:** The purpose of Configuration Management is to establish and maintain the integrity of work products using configuration identification, configuration control, configuration status accounting, and configuration audits.

- **Process and Product Quality Assurance:** The purpose of Process and Product Quality Assurance is to provide staff and management with an objective insight into processes and associated work products.

- **Supplier Agreement Management:** The purpose of Supplier Agreement Management is to handle the acquisition of products from suppliers.

- **Measurement and Analysis:** The purpose of Measurement and Analysis is to develop and sustain a measurement capability that is used to support management information needs. We include this process area because it is assumed that all processes must be measured and controlled.

The second-phase is aimed at higher-level management such as general managers, system managers, software managers, or team leaders, and is based on the generic practices from the PMP of the CMMI-DEV [29]. The application of this phase aims to find those activities for managing the software projects whether they are institutionalized or not and if they can support a managed process. A managed process is a performed (Level 2) process that has the basic infrastructure in place to support the process. It is planned and implemented in accordance with policy; it employs skilled people who have adequate resources to produce controlled outputs; it involves relevant stakeholders; it is monitored, controlled, and reviewed; and it is evaluated for adherence to its process description. To determine if a PMP is institutionalized, it is necessary to perform the following activities:

- Adhere to organizational policies.
- Track a documented project plan.
- Allocate adequate resources.
- Assign responsibility and authority.
- Train the affected people.
- Be placed under version control or configuration management.
- Be reviewed by the people affected.
- Measure the process.
- Ensure that the process complies with specified standards.
- Review the status with higher-level management.

It is expected that the cross analysis of the responses of both questionnaires will enable us to know those PMP practices that have been covered by the software team and that have been spread throughout the organization as an institutionalized process.

Similarly, this cross analysis can help us to identify other issues related to the combination of both phases of this questionnaire.

7 Conclusions

Though CMMI and ISO/IEC 15504 have exploded onto the market as models to follow when organizations try to apply process improvements, there are many organizations that are still not using these models. The CMMI is considered to be one of the best known models that focus on software process improvement for achieving quality software. The CMMI-DEV, however, is relatively new, so there is not much research written about which data collection instruments can be employed when using the CMMI-DEV approach. This research, therefore, developed an instrument to evaluate the current status of project management practices. The data collection instrument developed for the appraisal is a two-phase questionnaire.

The questionnaire proposed here is divided into two phases. This division is mainly due to the fact that the CMMI-DEV clearly differentiates between specific practices and generic practices. As well as this, another reason for the division into two phases is because each section is applied to a different domain of people. The specific-practices-phase refers to the series of steps that have to be followed to perform the PMP. Furthermore, it will be applied to those employees who implement the PMP. The generic-practices-phase refers to the maturity and institutionalization of the PMP. Institutionalization implies that the process is ingrained in the way the work is performed. In the same way, institutionalization implies the steps that need to be followed to ensure that the specific practices are spread throughout the entire organization. This phase will be applied to the employees who manage the PMP. Most of the literature has focused on which practices need to be implemented to improve a given process but has barely focused on explaining how to implement these practices. Identifying only those practices which need to be implemented is not sufficient, and the description steps of how to implement them are also required for a successful SPI program. In view of the foregoing, our future research efforts will focus on developing a methodology to implement the CMMI-DEV PMP practices on SMEs internal processes. The PMP two-phase questionnaire represents the first step in this research. The next step is related to the validation of the questionnaire. For this purpose, the questionnaire will be experimented on 26 SMEs through a project funded by the Spanish Ministry of Industry, Tourism and Trade. Our future research will concentrate on proposing the use of questionnaires for the PMP related to Levels 3 and 4 of the CMMI-DEV. This research advocates the idea of defining and implementing an "organizational repository of assets" where our questionnaires could be selected for any SMEs according to their needs.

Acknowledgement

This paper is sponsored by ENDESA, Everis Consulting Foundation and Sun Microsystems companies through "Research Group of Software Process Improvement in Latin America".

References

1. Bach, J.: Enough about process: what we need are heroes. IEEE Software 12(2), 96–98 (1995)
2. Brewerton, P.: Organizational research methods. SAGE, London (2001)
3. Brock, S., Hendricks, D., Linnell, S., Smith, D.: A Balanced Approach to IT Project Management. In: Proceedings of SAICSIT, ACM Publications, New York (2003)
4. Brodman, J., Johnson, D.: Project Planning: Disaster Insurance for Small Software Projects. In: Proceedings from SEPG 2000: Ways to Make Better Software, March 20-23, 1999, LOGOS International, Inc., Seattle, Washington (1999)
5. Calvo-Manzano, J.A., Cuevas, G., San-Feliu, T., De-Amescua, A., Arcilla, M.M., Cerrada, J.A.: Lessons Learned in Software Process Improvement. The European Journal for the Informatics Professional IV(4), 26–29 (2003)
6. Calvo-Manzano, J.A., Cuevas, G., San-Feliu, T., De-Amescua, A., García, L., Pérez, M.: Experiences in the Application of Software Process Improvement in SMES. Software Quality Journal 10(3), 261–273 (2002)
7. Cairó, O.: Proyecto KAMET II. Instituto Tecnológico Autónomo de México (2004)
8. Carreira, M., Román, I.: Estimación del Coste de la Calidad del Software a través de la Simulación del Proceso de Desarrollo. Revista Colombiana de Computación 2(1), 75–87 (2002)
9. CMMI Interpretive Guidance Project: Preliminary Report (CMU/SEI-2003-SR-007): Software Engineering Institute, Carnegie Mellon University, Pittsburgh, PA (October 2003)
10. Cuevas, G., Serrano, A., Serrano, A.: Assessment of the requirements management process using a two-stage questionnaire. In: Quality Software, QSIC 2004. Proceedings of Fourth International Conference on Software Quality (September 8-9, 2004)
11. Dove, R.: Value Propositioning - Book One - Perception and Misperception in Decision Making. Iceni Books (2004)
12. Dunaway, D.K., Masters, S.: CMM-Based Appraisal for Internal Process Improvement (CBA IPI). Method Description, Technical Report CMU/SEI-96-TR-007, Carnegie Mellon University, Software Engineering Institute, Pittsburgh (1996)
13. Gillham, B.: Developing a Questionnaire. Developing a Questionnaire, London, New York (2000)
14. Hadden, R.: Effective Planning and Tracking for Small Projects. In: SEPG Conference, Datatel, Inc. (2002)
15. IBM: Gestión de Proyectos TIC en la Seguridad Social. Asociación Internacional de la Seguridad Social. Asociación Internacional de la Seguridad Social. Ginebra (2004)
16. ISO/IEC 12207:2002/FDAM 2: Information Technology – Software Life Cycle Processes. International Organization for Standardization: Geneva (2004)
17. ISO/IEC 155504-2:2003/Cor.1:2004(E): Information Technology – Process Assessment – Part 2: Performing an Assessment. International Organization for Standardization: Geneva (2004)
18. ISO/IEC TR 15504:1998(E): Information Technology – Software Process Assessments. Parts 1-9. International Organization for Standardization: Geneva (1998)
19. Jones, C.: Why Flawed Software Projects Are Not Cancelled in Time. Cutter IT Journal 16(12), 12–17 (2003)
20. Jones, G.: Software Engineering. John Wiley & Sons, Inc., New York, NY (1990)

21. McFeeley, B.: IDEAL: A User's Guide for Software Process Improvement. Handbook, CMU/SEI-96-HB-001, Software Engineering Institute, Carnegie Mellon University (February 1996), http://www.sei.cmu.edu/pub/documents/96.reports/pdf/hb001.96.pdf

22. Marciniak, J.J., Sadauskas, T.: Use of Questionnaire-Based Appraisals in Process Improvement Programs. In: Proceedings of the Second Annual Conference on the Acquisition of Software-Intensive Systems, Arlington, Virginia, USA, p. 22 (2003)

23. Members of the Assessment Method Integrated Team: Standard CMMI® Appraisal Method for Process Improvement (SCAMPI), Version 1.1, (CMU/SEI-2001-HB-001). Pittsburgh, PA, Software Engineering Institute, Carnegie Mellon University (December 2001) (2006), Descripción técnica disponible en: http:// ww.sei.cmu.edu/ pub/ documents/ 01.reports/pdf/01hb001.pdf

24. Mondragón, O.: Addressing Infrastructure Issues in Very Small Settings. In: Proceedings of the First International Research Workshop for Process Improvement in Small Settings, CMU/SEI-2006-SR-001, pp. 5–10 (2005)

25. Oktaba, H.: MoProSoft: A Software Process Model for Small Enterprises. In: Proceedings of the First International Research Workshop for Process Improvement in Small Settings, CMU/SEI-2006-SR-001, pp. 93–100 (2005)

26. Pino, F., García, F., Piattini, M.: Revisión Sistemática de Procesos Software en Micros, Pequeñas y Medianas Empresas. Revista Española de Innovación, Calidad e Ingeniería del Software 2(1), 6–23 (2006)

27. Pressman, R.S.: Software Engineering: A Practitioner's Approach, 5th edn - European Adaptation. McGraw-Hill, New York (2004)

28. Programa para el Desarrollo de la Industria Software (ProSoft): Avances al 1er semestre del 2004. Portal de la Industria del Software. Disponible en: www.software.net.mx

29. Software Engineering Institute: CMMI for Development (CMMI-DEV, V1.2). CMU/SEI-2006 TR-008, Software Engineering Institute, Carnegie Mellon University (2006)

30. Standish Group International: Extreme Chaos. The Standish Group International, Inc. (2001)

31. Standish Group International: 2004 Third Quarter Research Report. The Standish Group International, Inc. (2004)

32. Yamanishi, K., Li, H.: Mining Open Answers in Questionnaire Data. IEEE Intelligent Systems 17(5), 58–63 (2002)

33. Zubrow, D., Hayes, W., Siegel, J., Goldenson, D.: Maturity Questionnaire (CMU/SEI-94-SR-7). Pittsburgh, PA, Software Engineering Institute, Carnegie Mellon University (June 1994) (1994), http://www.sei.cmu.edu/pub/documents/94.reports /pdf/sr07.94.pdf

Using Practice Outcome Areas to Understand Perceived Value of CMMI Specific Practices for SMEs

Xi Chen and Mark Staples

NICTA, Australia Technology Park, Eveleigh, NSW, 1430, Sydney, Australia
School of Computer Science and Engineering, University of New South Wales, Australia
`xi.chen@nicta.com.au, mark.staples@nicta.com.au`

Abstract. In this article, we present a categorization of CMMI Specific Practices, and use this to reanalyze prior work describing the perceived value of those practices for Small-to-Medium-sized Enterprises (SMEs), in order to better understand the software engineering practice needs of SMEs. Our categorization is based not on process areas, but on outcome areas (covering organizational, process, project, and product outcomes) and on the nature of activities leading to outcomes in those areas (covering planning, doing, checking, and improvement activities). Our reanalysis of the perceived value of Specific Practices for the CMMI Level 2 Process Areas shows that SMEs most value practices for working on project-related outcomes, and for planning and doing work on product-related outcomes. Our categorization of practices will serve as a framework for further study about CMMI and other SPI approaches.

Keywords: SME, Software Process Improvement, CMMI, Specific Practice.

1 Introduction

Software process has attracted increasing attention due to its potential impact on the development and acquisition of software [1, 2, 3, 4]. Software companies have gained benefits from the introduction and application of software process improvement (SPI) and assessment models, such as CMMI [5], ISO 9001 series [6, 7], ISO/IEC 15504 [8], and IDEAL [9]. CMMI [5] is one of the most well-known approaches, and the successful application of CMMI in large organizations has been reported [10, 16] to reduce development cost and risk, and to improve product quality. However, many researchers and practitioners have expressed concerns [11, 13, 14, 15] about the use of CMMI in Small-and-Medium-sized Enterprises (SMEs). Complaints about CMMI from SMEs can include [13] that it results in excessive documentation, interferes with creativity, costs too much, and is too large and complex. A recent study [17] on companies that have chosen to not adopt CMMI reported that small companies often see CMMI as too costly and time-consuming, and that this is a barrier for the adoption of CMMI. Concerns about the use of CMMI by SMEs are recognized by SEI, the owners of CMMI, in their recent efforts to initiate a project on Improving Processes in Small Settings (IPSS) [14].

P. Abrahamsson et al. (Eds.): EuroSPI 2007, LNCS 4764, pp. 59–70, 2007.

Conradi and Fugetta [18], in writing about how SPI approaches can be improved to make them more applicable and relevant to software engineering organizations, call for the business drivers of those organizations to be better understood, and for SPI frameworks to become more goal-oriented. Wilkie et al. [15] believe it is important to better understand the SPI practices in order to develop better appraisal and adoption approaches for SMEs. As SPI researchers, we also think it is critical to understand the business and practice needs of SMEs, in order to increase the relevance and benefits of SPI for SMEs.

Wilkie et al. [15] investigated and appraised the Specific Practices of six process areas in CMMI maturity level 2 within six small software development companies. Wilkie et al. ascribed a measure of "perceived value" of the Specific Practices, based on the activities actually pursued by the companies. This research was important in delivering a more detailed analysis of CMMI at the level of practices, rather than working at the higher level of whole process areas or overall maturity levels. The research provided descriptive results about the actual practices of SMEs. However, the measurement of perceived value of Specific Practices is not an explanatory result – it does not in itself tell us why SMEs value some practices over others.

In this paper we propose a categorization of Specific Practices based on the kind of outcomes achieved by the practices and the nature of the activities contributing to those outcomes. We use this categorization to systematically reanalyze Wilkie et al.'s results, in order to derive a proposed explanation of why SMEs value some Specific Practices more than others.

The remainder of this paper is organized as follows. In section 2, we briefly review Wilkie et al.'s study of perceived value of CMMI Specific Practices. In section 3, we present our new categorization of CMMI practices according to their outcome areas and the nature of their activities. In section 4 we reanalyze Wilkie et al.'s results using our new categorization. We conclude the paper in section 5.

2   Perceived Value of CMMI Specific Practices

Wilkie et al. [15] studied the actual software development practices at six SMEs satisfying Specific Practices in the CMMI Level 2 process areas (excluding Supplier Agreement Management), over a five-month period, using a Class C [19] appraisal method. The companies had all been in the business of developing software for several years, and ranged in size from 8 to 130 software engineers. Of the six companies, none had prior experience of CMM or CMMI, but half were ISO9001 accredited. For each company, Wilkie et al. created a score for each Specific Practice by asking a set of between 1 and 5 questions to identify how well the company met the practice. These scores were averaged over the companies in the sample, and score thresholds were set to classify the practices as having a HIGH, MEDIUM or LOW "perceived value" by the SMEs. The perceived value of these Specific Practices is listed in Table 1 (adapted from [15]). Note that we use an abbreviated name based on the standard CMMI identifiers, defined as followed,

[*Abbreviated Name of Process Areas*] [*Goal Number*].[*Practice Sequence Number*]-[*Capability Level*]

Table 1. Industry perceived value of CMMI Specific Practices

Perceived Value	Specific Practices
High	REQM 1.1-1, REQM 1.2-1
	CM 1.1-1, CM 1.3-1
	PP 1.1-1, PP 2.1-1, PP 2.7-1, PP 3.3-1
	PMC 1.6-1, PMC 1.7-1, PMC 2.1-1, PMC 2.2-1
Medium	REQM 1.5-1
	CM 1.2-1, CM 2.1-1, CM 2.2-1, CM 3.1-1
	PP 1.3-1, PP 1.4-1, PP 2.2-1, PP 2.3-1, PP 2.4-1 PP 2.6-1, PP 3.1-1, PP 3.2-1
	PMC 1.1-1, PMC 1.2-1, PMC 1.3-1, PMC 1.5-1
	PPQA 1.1-1, PPQA 1.2-1
Low	REQM1.3-1, REQM 1.4-1
	CM 3.2-1
	PP 1.2-1, PP 2.5-1
	PMC 1.4-1, PMC 2.3-1
	PPQA 2.1-1, PPQA 2.2-1
	MA 1.1-1, MA 1.2-1, MA 1.3-1, MA 1.4-1 MA 2.1-1, MA 2.2-1, MA 2.3-1, MA 2.4-1

Wilkie et al. concluded with some observations emerging from their appraisal results, including that "…small software companies tend to focus on product quality assurance rather than process quality assurance…"[15 (p. 199)], and that although medium-sized companies do rely more on process, they do not use it as much as suggested by CMMI. In section 4 below, we build on Wilkie et al.'s analysis, using a model of outcomes and activities presented in section 3.

3 Categorization of Specific Practices

CMMI groups its Specific Practices into 25 Process Areas, which are in turn grouped into four categories: Process Management, Project Management, Engineering, and Support. These categories are used to help describe high-level interactions between the Process Areas. CMMI also groups Process Areas by maturity level.

In this paper we present an alternative categorization of Specific Practices. Our purpose is not to "repackage" CMMI, but instead to use our categorization as an analytical tool to generate new views of the content of CMMI, to better understand and support the practice needs of SMEs for software development. In section 3.1 below we describe our top-level category of outcome areas, and in section 3.2 describe a second category of the kind of activities that contribute to outcomes in those areas. Section 3.3 defines and provides examples of activity outcomes within the combination of these two categories.

3.1 Specific Practice Outcome Areas

Our primary category of Specific Practices is defined according to the kind of outcomes they generate. This focus on outcomes is consistent with Conradi and Fuggetta's first thesis on the improvement of SPI that "SPI frameworks should support improvement strategies that focus on goal orientation and product innovation" [18 (p. 95)]. We claim that all the CMMI Specific Practices have the ultimate goal of improving companies' performance in one or more of four outcome areas, namely, organizational outcomes, process outcomes, project outcomes, and product outcomes. In previous research [12], we grouped motivations for adopting CMM-based SPI approaches according to these categories, and two others: customers and people. Our categorization in this paper is inspired from that, now with customer-related outcomes spread into project and/or product outcome areas as appropriate, and with people-related outcomes merged into the organizational outcome area. The definitions for organization, project and product that we use are taken from the definitions in CMMI [5, pp. 620-625]. Some Specific Practices create outcomes that affect more than one outcome area, and so we allow any individual practice to belong to more than one outcome area. Some Specific Practices (such as those in the Measurement and Analysis Process Area) can be applied to outcome of any type.

3.2 Activities for Each Outcome Area

Our secondary category describes the kind of activities performed in a Specific Practice. This was inspired by both the Plan-Do-Check-Act cycle (also known as the Shewhart or Deming cycle), and the "V" software lifecycle.

The Plan-Do-Check-Act cycle [21] is an improvement framework widely used in manufacturing and business. It describes the life of an individual improvement, from the initial "Plan" (identifying the issue and planning the improvement), to "Do" (implementing the planned improvement on a small scale as a study), to "Check" (monitoring and evaluating the study), and to final "Act" (rolling out the improvement based on the results of the study). This model provided initial inspiration for our activity classification. However, we later realized that it is limited in directly describing improvement activities, and does not describe operational development activities well.

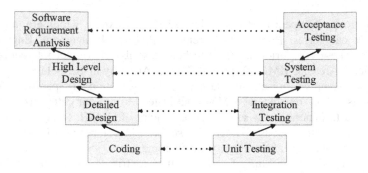

Fig. 1. "V" Software Lifecycle

In software engineering, the "V" software lifecycle is one of the most well known and broadly adopted lifecycle models. It can be seen as a variant of the classical waterfall lifecycle model [20], "bent in the middle", so that design activities cascade down, and verification activities cascade up to correspond with each level of design. It is depicted in Figure 1. The "V" model describes operational development activities, but does not describe improvement activities well.

From the perspective of any individual level in the "V" model, we say that the main types of activity are to "Plan" (planning and specifying the objective), to "Do" (attempting to achieve the objective), and to "Check" (to confirm that the objective does meet its requirements). We recognize working to "Improve" work at this level as another kind of activity, which would encompass all of the activities in the Plan-Do-Check-Act cycle. Figure 2 show our proposed activity cycle.

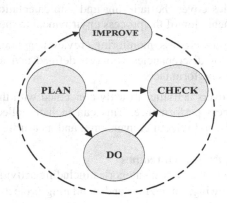

Fig. 2. Plan-Do-Check-Improve model of activity

Some activities relate to planning to check objectives and could be classified in a category "Plan to Check" which could be added to Figure 2 on the dashed line in the centre of the figure. However, we have chosen to classify these practices into "Plan", because sometimes plans for doing and checking work are hard to separate, and because having a small number of outcome areas can provide a clearer view.

3.3 Combining Outcome Area and Activity Categories

In this section we describe the combination of our two categories of outcome area and activity, and give examples of each kind of activity contributing to each outcome area.

3.3.1 Working on Organizational Outcomes

Organization-Plan. means management activities for organizational planning for outcomes such as those related to the creation of strategies, budget, and planning for resourcing, staff, and training. This includes establishment of policies and values that provide fundamental rules for organizations.

Organization-Do. covers activities for the operation of organization. Examples include maintaining the work environment, maintaining awareness of current and emerging technologies, establishing incentive mechanisms, and delivering training.

Organization-Check. includes monitoring, analyzing, and assessing the status, structure, and operation of the organization and its performance relative to its goals.

Organization-Improve. are activities intended to improve the organization's planning, operations, and governance, to improve organizational performance.

3.3.2 Working on Process Outcomes

Process-Plan. includes the definition and selection of processes, as well as providing resources and establishing the environment for process management. Typical outcomes generated by these activities include definitions of an organization's process needs, process definitions, life-cycle model descriptions, tailoring criteria and guidelines, process assets libraries, and process measurement repositories.

Process-Do. activities cover the tailoring and implementation of defined processes, and also the instrumentation of the process environment to monitor the use of process.

Process-Check. covers process monitoring, reviews, appraisals, investigations into the causal reasons for discrepancies between defined and actual processes and the evaluation of process performance.

Process-Improve. covers activities directly concerned with the improvement of process to advance process performance. This can include collecting and analyzing improvement proposals, and selecting, managing, and measuring process improvements.

3.3.3 Working on Project Outcomes

Project-Plan. is one of the largest categories including activities such as:
- Acquiring, reviewing, analyzing, and validating project requirements (including internal and external project constraints). This could include high level "user requirements" (also known as "business requirements"). Activities related to lower-level product requirements are only included in the Product-Plan category, below.
- Determining the scope and schedule, estimation, and resource allocation.
- Predicting skills and knowledge required for the project.
- Assessing and planning mitigations for project risks.
- Determining the types of acquisition to be used for the products to be acquired.
- Collecting and coordinating stakeholders' needs.
- Project acceptance test planning.

Project-Do. is concerned with managing and implementing the project, including:
- Implementing the project plan.
- Managing the involvement of stakeholders.
- Selecting suppliers, establishing and executing supplier agreements.
- Managing requirement changes.
- Enacting risk mitigations if required.
- Establishing the project working environment.

*Project-Check.*activities assess the progress and status of the project, including:
- Monitoring project planning parameters, commitments, project risks data management, project progress indicators, and stakeholder involvement.
- Monitoring relevant supplier agreement and relationships and their processes
- Analyzing the results based on the outcomes achieved.
- Conducting progress and milestone reviews.
- Project acceptance testing.

Project-Improve. activities involve taking and managing corrective actions after finding and analyzing any problems. Other activities include post-project reviews, and synthesizing and recording experiences gained from project to incorporate into organization's experience library for reference in future projects.

3.3.4 Working on Product Outcomes

Product-Plan. includes determining the functional and non-functional requirements of the product, and planning how the product will be constructed to meet those requirements. Examples activities include:

* Establishing, analyzing, and validating system requirements.
* Establishing the configuration management environment and test environment.
* Identifying products to be acquired from suppliers.
* System and software test planning.
* Developing and selecting among alternative solutions.

Product-Do. activities cover the construction of the product, including:

* Developing and selecting among alternative solutions.
* System design, program design, coding, and integration.
* Tracking changes and the creation and modification of configuration items.
* Developing and maintaining product documentation.

Product-Check. activities test whether the product works properly, and include:

* Performing validation and verification
* Identifying inconsistencies between products and requirements.
* Performing configuration audits.
* Analyzing products acquired from suppliers.

Product-Improve. means taking any corrective action (typically redesign and/or recoding in software development) to resolve any issue related to the functionality of the product. Product-Improve also includes activities related to advanced technology improvement to support the organization's product and/or service quality objectives.

4 Analyzing Specific Practices Using Outcome Area and Activity

4.1 Classifying Specific Practices by Outcome Area and Activity

The two authors each independently classified each CMMI Level 2 Specific Practice into one or more of the categories described in section 3.3 above. We then compared our results in a meeting, and came to a joint agreement on points of difference. Table 2 shows the results of this classification exercise.

Note that some Specific Practices address outcomes and cover activities of more than one type, and so are placed in more than one category. For clarity, we have included an outcome area "Any" for Specific Practices that can apply to any outcome area. In CMMI Level 2, these are the Specific Practices in the Measurement and Analysis process area.

An initial observation from this grouping is that the Specific Practices of CMMI maturity level 2 process areas do not focus on organizational outcomes, and have little

Table 2. CMMI Level 2 Specific Practices categorized by Outcome Area and Activity

	Plan	Do	Check	Improve
Process			PPQA 1.1-1 PPQA 2.2-1	PPQA 2.1-1
Project	PP 1.1-1, PP 1.2-1 PP 1.3-1, PP 1.4-1 PP 2.1-1, PP 2.2-1 PP 2.3-1, PP 2.4-1 PP 2.5-1, PP 2.6-1 PP 2.7-1, PP 3.1-1 PP 3.2-1, PP 3.3-1 REQM 1.1-1	PP 3.1-1 PP 3.2-1 PP 3.3-1 REQM 1.2-1 REQM 1.3-1 REQM 1.4-1 REQM 1.5-1	PMC 1.1-1 PMC 1.2-1 PMC 1.3-1 PMC 1.4-1 PMC 1.5-1 PMC 1.6-1 PMC 1.7-1	PMC 2.1-1 PMC 2.2-1 PMC 2.3-1
Product	CM 1.1-1 CM 1.2-1 PP 1.2-1 REQM 1.1-1	CM 1.3-1 CM 2.1-1 CM 2.2-1 CM 3.1-1 REQM 1.3-1 REQM 1.4-1	CM 3.2-1 PPQA 1.2-1 PPQA 2.2-1 REQM 1.5-1	PPQA 2.1-1
Any	MA 1.1-1 MA 1.2-1 MA 1.3-1 MA 1.4-1		MA 2.1-1 MA 2.2-1 MA 2.3-1 MA 2.4-1	

focus on process outcomes – their primary focus is instead on project outcomes and product outcomes. This observation is consistent with the view in CMMI that level 2 processes are characterized for projects and are managed – the process areas in level 2 include basic project management process and also supporting processes for project management and product development.

4.2 Re-analysis of the Perceived Value of Specific Practices for SMEs

After classifying Specific Practices using the new categorization, we factored in Wilkie et al.'s [15] results. Table 3 presents the combined view of Table 1 (Wilkie et al.'s results on the perceived value of Specific Practices) and Table 3 (our classification of Specific Practices by Outcome Area and Activity).

Table 3. Combining Cateories of Outcome and Activity

	Perceived Value	Plan	Do	Check	Improve
Process	High				
	Medium			PPQA 1.1-1	
	Low			PPQA 2.2-1	PPQA 2.1-1
Project	High	PP 1.1-1, PP 2.1-1 PP 2.7-1, PP 3.3-1 REQM 1.1-1	PP 3.3-1 REQM 1.2-1	PMC 1.6-1 PMC 1.7-1	PMC 2.1-1 PMC 2.2-1
	Medium	PP 1.3-1, PP 1.4-1 PP 2.2-1, PP 2.3-1 PP 2.4-1, PP 2.6-1 PP 3.1-1, PP 3.2-1	PP 3.1-1 PP 3.2-1 REQM 1.5-1	PMC 1.1-1 PMC 1.2-1 PMC 1.3-1 PMC 1.5-1	
	Low	PP 1.2-1, PP 2.5-1	REQM 1.3-1 REQM 1.4-1	PMC 1.4-1	PMC 2.3-1

Table 3. (*continued*)

Product	High	CM 1.1-1 REQM 1.1-1	CM 1.3-1 REQM 1.2-1		
	Medium	CM 1.2-1	CM 2.1-1 CM 2.2-1 CM 3.1-1	PPQA 1.2-1 REQM 1.5-1	
	Low	PP 1.2-1	REQM 1.3-1 REQM 1.4-1	CM 3.2-1 PPQA 2.2-1	PPQA 2.1-1
Any	High				
	Medium				
	Low	MA 1.1-1 MA 1.2-1 MA 1.3-1 MA 1.4-1		MA 2.1-1 MA 2.2-1 MA 2.3-1 MA 2.4-1	

From Table 3, we can see that SMEs do not perceive that the CMMI level 2 practices related to process outcomes are highly valuable, but that some project and product outcomes are highly valuable. For the product outcomes, SMEs tend to perceive the activities for planning and developing as being more relevant than those for checking and improving the product. In order to derive a more detailed explanation of the reason why SMEs find some Specific Practices more valuable than others, we have looked at the work products associated with the practices. We present this analysis for the project and product outcome areas in Table 4 and Table 5 respectively.

Table 4. Analysis for the Project Outcome Area

Activity	SMEs Do (High Perceived Value)	SMEs Don't (Low & Med. Perceived Value)
Plan	• Estimating the scope, budget and schedule of the project • Establishing a plan for the project obtaining commitment for project plan • Obtain a correct understanding and concise and complete description about the requirement	• Preparing estimation in terms of effort, cost, resources, risks, especially in work products, task attributes, needed knowledge and skills
Do	• Obtaining relevant project participants' commitment both to the requirement and plan.	• Reconciling work and resource levels at the beginning of the project • Reviewing the plans as projects evolve • Testing and validating project work against requirements • Managing changes of requirements, as well as their bidirectional traceability
Check	• Reviewing progress and milestones	• Monitoring project planning parameters, commitments, risks, and stakeholder involvement • Managing data
Improve	• Analyzing problems and issues before taking corrective actions	• Managing corrective actions

Table 5. Analysis for the Product Outcome Area

Activity	SMEs Do (High Perceived Value)	SMEs Don't (Low & Med. Perceived Value)
Plan	• Obtain a correct understanding and concise and complete description about the requirement • Identifying configuration items	• Preparing estimation in terms of effort, cost, resources, risks, especially in work products, task attributes, needed knowledge and skills • Establishing a configuration management system
Do	• Creating or releasing baselines of work product for further development	• Controlling configuration items • Establishing configuration management records
Check		• Performing configuration audit • Objectively evaluating work product • Managing to identify inconsistencies between product and requirement • Establish records, such as evaluation logs, quality assurance reports, status reports of corrective actions, and reports of quality trends etc.
Improve		• Communicating and ensuring resolution of noncompliance issues • Reporting corrective action, evaluation • Foreseeing quality trends

For activities supporting project outcomes, we can see from Table 4 that SMEs are interested in estimation at the project level, but are less interested in more detailed estimation activities that might nonetheless support overall project estimation. SMEs are interested in obtaining commitment to the project from stakeholders, and in conducting progress and milestone reviews, but are less interested in detailed management and monitoring tasks that might nonetheless support project control and progress, such as reviewing plans, reconciling estimated resource demands with actual resources, and managing changes to requirements. When problems or issues arise in the project, they are more interested in analyzing those problems than in managing subsequent corrective actions.

For activities supporting product outcomes, we can see from Table 5 that SMEs are interested in understanding and documenting requirements. SMEs are interested in initially identifying configuration items and in finally creating release baselines, but are less interested in the detailed control and recording of changes to configuration items. Although SMEs have an interest in testing and validating project work overall, they are less interested in the details of product-level quality monitoring and assurance.

Broadly, we claim SMEs tend to be interested in the "high level" activities of project management and product planning and development, but are less interested in the more detailed practices that may support those high level activities.

5 Conclusion

We have developed two categories to classify SPI practices according to the outcome areas influenced by the practices, and the nature of the activity performed in the practices. We classified the Specific Practices of CMMI Maturity Level 2 process areas (excluding Supplier Agreement Management). We have used this classification to systematically reanalyze Wilkie et al.'s results on the perceived value of those Specific Practices by SMEs. Based on the result and analysis, we can conclude that SMEs tend to focus on high-level project-related outcomes and on planning and doing work on product-related outcomes, rather than being process-focused. When developing software products, they try to ensure projects progress as planed and meet their deadlines. However, some activities that are intended to support project and product outcomes are lacking, especially for estimation, evaluation, verification, and validation.

Work is still needed in order to help SMEs to improve their software process. Our new framework may be used to better understand SMEs' needs, which may be more variable than large organizations. The development of approaches to tailor standards such as CMMI to meet the requirements of specific organizations is still a challenging topic, both for small and large companies.

Research is still needed to investigate the costs and benefits of implementing individual Specific Practices. In order to mitigate their risk of project failure and improve product quality assurance, SPI researchers should consider changing or providing alternative practices for Specific Practices with medium or low perceived value, to reduce the costs of those practices without significantly reducing their benefits.

We will conduct future research to further validate and apply our practice categories, to better understand relationships between existing SPI approaches, and to develop outcome-based approaches for tailoring and adopting improved software engineering practices.

Acknowledgements

NICTA is funded by the Australian Government's Department of Communications, Information Technology, and the Arts and the Australian Research Council through Backing Australia's Ability and the ICT Research Centre of Excellence programs.

References

1. Diaz, M., Sligo, J.: How Software Process Improvement Helped Motorola. IEEE Software 14, 75–81 (1997)
2. Basili, V.R., McGarry, F.E., Pajerski, R., Zelkowitz, M.V.: Lessons Learned From 25 Years of Process Improvement: The Rise and Fall of the NASA Software Engineering Laboratory. In: Proceedings of the 24th International Conference of Software Engineering, pp. 69–79 (2002)
3. Haliey, T.J.: Software Process Improvement at Raytheon. IEEE Software 13, 32–41 (1996)
4. Humphrey, W.S., Snyder, T.R., Willis, R.R.: Software Process Improvement at Hughes Aircraft. IEEE Software 8, 11–23 (1991)
5. Chrissis, M.B., Konrad, M., Shrum, S.: CMMI: Guidelines for Process Integration and Product Improvement. Addison Wesley, Boston, MA, USA (2003)
6. ISO 9001:2000: Quality Management System – Requirement. International Organization for Standardization, Geneva, Switzerland (2000)

7. ISO/IEC 90003: Software Engineering – Guidelines for the application of ISO 9001:2000 to computer software. International Organization for Standardization, Geneva, Switzerland (2004)
8. ISO/IEC 15504:2005: Information technology – Process assessment, Part 1-5. International Organization for Standardization, Geneva, Switzerland (2005)
9. Gremba, J., Myers, C.: The IDEAL(SM) Model: A Practical Guide for Improvement. In: Bridge, Software Engineering Institute (SEI), Pittsburgh, PA, USA (1997)
10. Reifer, D.J.: The CMMI: it's formidable. The Journal of Systems and Software 50, 97–98 (2000)
11. Desharnais, J.M., Laporte, C.Y., Abouelfattah, M.M., Bamba, J.C., Renault, A., Habra, N.: Initiating Software Process Improvement in SMEs: Experiments with Micro-Evaluation Framework. In: Proceedings of the SWDC-REK International Conference on Software Development, Reykjavik, Iceland (2005)
12. Niazi, M., Staples, M.: Systematic Review of Organizational Motivations for Adopting CMM-based SPI. Technical Report PA005957, NICTA (2006)
13. Turgeon, J.: CMMI on the Sly for the CMMI Shy - Implementing Software Process Improvement in Small Teams and Organizations. Presentation in SEPG (2006)
14. Improving Processes in Small Settings (IPSS): white paper, the International Process Research Consortium (IPRC). Software Engineering Institute, Pittsburgh, PA (2006)
15. Wilkie, F.G., McFall, D., McCaffery, F.: An Evaluation of CMMI Process Areas for Small-to Medium-sized Software Development Organizations. Software Process: Improvement and Practice 10, 189–201 (2005)
16. Gibson, D.L., Goldenson, D.R., Kost, K.: Performance Results of CMMI-Based Process Improvement. Technical Report, Software Engineering Institute, CMU (2006)
17. Staples, M., Niazi, M., Jeffery, R., Abrahams, A., Byatt, P., Murphy, R.: An Exploratory Study of Why Organizations do not Adopt CMMI. Journal of Systems and Software 80(6), 883–895 (2007)
18. Conradi, R., Fuggetta, A.: Improving Software Process Improvement. IEEE Software, 92–99 (July/August 2002)
19. SEI: Appraisal Requirements for CMMI, Version 1.1. Technical Report CMU/SEI-2001-TR-034, Software Engineering Institute, Pittsburgh, PA (2001)
20. Royce, W.: Managing the Development of Large Software Systems. In: Proceedings of IEEE WESCON, pp. 328–338. IEEE Computer Society Press, Los Alamitos (1970)
21. Shewart, W.A.: Statistical Method from the Viewpoint of Quality Control. Dover (1986)

SPI with Lightweight Software Process Modeling in a Small Software Company

Paula Savolainen, Hanna-Miina Sihvonen, and Jarmo J. Ahonen

Department of Computer Science, University of Kuopio
P.O. Box 1627, FI-70211 Kuopio, Finland
{paula.savolainen,hanna-miina.sihvonen,jarmo.ahonen}@uku.fi

Abstract. In small growing software companies, it is important to pay attention to software process improvement (SPI) in order to be successful and competitive in both domestic and foreign markets. However, limited resources and lack of knowledge about process culture may hinder the improvement efforts in small companies. In this paper, we present development activities done in a small growing software company in order to establish basis for SPI. Familiarizing to processes and SPI is done by modeling company's processes using a lightweight software process modeling technique. The modeling combined with external consulting provides the company with capability to visualize their processes and to identify the problems in the processes. The improvement activities have been triggered by pointing out the problems. In the presented case, the company has independently implemented quite significant improvements for identified problems by acquiring needed knowledge and by implementing new tools to support workflows.

1 Introduction

Small software companies (SC)[1] play in important role in the software industry, because they are innovative, exploit new technologies, create job opportunities and keep established firms on their toes as described in [1] [2] [3] [4]. Some of these innovative SCs seek constantly new business opportunities and new market areas. In countries where domestic software markets are quite limited, such as Finland, the SCs with desire to grow and pursue greater turnover are compelled to become international. Rapid growth implies increasing the personnel, creating new job descriptions, coping with cultural differences and business opportunities. SCs face the inevitable challenge of modifying their processes to match new and changing circumstances [5]. They are forced to notice the importance of processes and improving them, in order to become competitive and successful on international market. On the other hand, improved processes may result in expanding staff, new international sales, and pressure for more intensive release schedules.

However, introducing the concept of software process improvement (SPI) in SCs may not be possible, because the organization's maturity can be low. Organization

---

[1] A common abbreviation used for small companies with less than 50 employees [6].

P. Abrahamsson et al. (Eds.): EuroSPI 2007, LNCS 4764, pp. 71–81, 2007.

structure is often informal, implicitly defined processes evolve based on daily work and actions may not be planned beforehand [7]. Work is trust-based thus not often formally documented, and there is lack of knowledge about process culture. In addition, there is often lack of resources, skills, experience, and qualified and SPI motivated staff. Due to the reasons listed above, it can be very challenging for SCs to establish an efficient and competitive process culture and furthermore, concurrently manage the growth. One possibility to start preparations for SPI is to make processes visible by modeling them.

In this paper, we describe development project activities done in a small rapidly growing software company. In this case, CMMI, ISO 15504, CBA-IBI or other massive SPI approaches were not suitable choices, because they are designed for large organizations and require specialized SPI personnel. Instead, we chose to combine and adapt lightweight process modeling techniques [8] [9] that conform to characteristics required from a model used in SCs [10] [11]. The techniques are easy to use, flexible, applicable, and adapt to SCs limited resources. Usage of this combined modeling technique enables to visualize processes, to identify the flaws and problems in the process and deficiencies of knowledge and skills. Furthermore, more importantly using this lightweight modeling and carrying out related activities, promotes future formal SPI with measures and techniques that best serve the company's own operations. In this paper, we present our experiences of using a lightweight process modeling technique in familiarizing a small software company with SPI by visualizing their software development process and identifying problems in the process.

2 Objectives and Context

In this development project, the objectives were to explore how the lightweight process modeling contributes to small software company's SPI activities and how the process modeling can be initiated in a small low maturity software company.

The development project was carried out in a small growing Finnish software company. The company has been involved in the development project was founded at the beginning of 2000. The employees were also founders and part owners of the company. In the beginning, there were less than 10 employees, but the personnel expanded quite fast to 15 employees. By the end of 2006, there were 20 employees and during 2007, the company has estimated to hire 10 employees more. Despite earlier and planned growth, the company is still a SC and likely will be SC for some years.

The company started on domestic market. During past two years, the company has steadily expanded its operations to three foreign countries and will expand foreign business further during 2007. The company's offices are distributed around Finland and abroad. The company is now divided in two separate companies. Another company concentrates on product development and other one on sales and marketing.

The organization and hierarchy of the company are not clearly defined, though an informal structure exists. The company's management concentrates only on business decisions and running the company. The software development team and other employees work independently and the communication with management is informal and is done in ad hoc manner. The development team's varying work assignments and situations have an influence on employees' work methods. However, they have established working practices though those are not documented in detail. A considerable amount of knowledge and skills that the employees possess is tacit knowledge, which is not generally distributed within the company. This has inflicted on blocks in information flows. The growth of the company has increased the awareness of need for SPI and establishing process culture.

3 Process Modeling Technique and Practical Implementation

In this case, we needed a modeling technique, which conforms to SCs limited resources. The technique itself serves as a tool for the company in order to analyze their own work in a structured manner and initiate discussion about their processes. We apply the techniques described in [8] and [9], which we use for modeling and making the process, its roles, and information flows visible. The techniques were chosen because they are flexible, easy to learn, understandable for non-experts and require minimal resources. We have combined and applied the techniques as follows:

- First Phase
  - Model the information flows of selected process with wall-chart technique
  - Analyze the gathered information and define the problems and points of improvement
  - Create an electronic version of the information flows
  - Inspect and approve the electronic version
  - Analyze and enhance the approved model
- Second phase
  - Model the selected process with wall-chart technique
  - Analyze the gathered information and define the problems and points of improvement
  - Create an electronic version of the process and its phases
  - Inspect and approve the electronic version
  - Analyze and enhance the approved model
- Third phase
  - Inspect the results and plan follow-up

The phases are carried out in chronological order. The first phase is now completed. In the first phase, the aim was to create an information flow diagram of the selected process. This information flow diagram describes who participate in the process and in what roles, and determines the information flows between the roles Problematic information flows were marked with red. By analyzing the diagram and by discussing with the employees, the problems of passing information from role to another can be perceived and analyzed. The discussions also assist in discovering deficiencies of knowledge and skills that relate to roles participating in the process. In the second phase, the aim is to make the actual process visible by defining the process phases in detail and define problems that relate to the process and its phases. In the third phase, the aim is to evaluate the modeling process, inspect the results, and plan future SPI activities.

Each phase includes modeling sessions, which are carried out as follows. Researchers, in this context referred as consultants, attend each modeling session.

They instruct the modeling technique to company's employees who participate in sessions, and guide and follow through the session. The employees participating in session are those who are involved in the process, which will be modeled. Modeling sessions last about three to four hours. Each modeling session functions also as a checkpoint for assessing what changes may have occurred.

The software process modeling sessions of the first phase began in February 2006. In the first phase, we have carried out three software process modeling sessions and had consulting meetings with the company's employees after each modeling session. In meetings, the training needs were discussed, prioritized, and defined them as described in [12] to support the company's independent SPI initiatives. The company has freedom to decide what problems they want to concentrate on and how to prioritize them. The company is also in charge of what improvement actions and steps will be taken. In order to carry out the necessary improvements, the employees are entitled to focused training and consulting through the development project, described in [13]. Taking advantage of training and actually implementing corrective measures is the company's responsibility. However, these measures are discussed with employees and consultants at the beginning of new modeling session.

3.1 The First Modeling Session

The first session was carried out in February 2006. There were three consultants guiding the session and five employees from the company's software engineering group, each responsible for different areas of software development process. First, the aim of the session was explained and the concept of process discussed and defined. Second, the employees were familiarized with wall-chart technique, and the main features of the modeling technique were explained. Third, the employees were instructed to choose the process that they wanted to model. They chose their software development process for modeling, which is the core activity of the company. For this most important and critical process from company's point of view, all roles, and information flows were modeled.

All participating employees were actively involved in modeling and there was much discussion and interaction between them. They noticed and pointed out the problem of acting various roles. In SC, one employee has many roles and responsibilities and due to this, he or she should be able to assess the process and information flows from different perspectives. Despite this, there was not much disagreement about the roles or information flows between them and the problem areas were quickly identified. As an output from the first session, a wall-chart, an electronic diagram of the wall-chart and a draft text document describing roles and information flows were produced.

3.2 The Second Modeling Session

The second session was carried out in August 2006. Between the first and second session, the employees had a chance to inspect and approve the information flow model from the first session. There were two consults guiding and three employees participating in the session. The model from first session had been approved unchanged. However, the participating employees wanted to specify the modeling to software product development process. The wall-chart model was recreated to represent the roles and information flows of the software product development process.

The second session was easy to follow through, because the employees were already familiar with modeling technique and had already thought through the roles and information flows of the process. It was essential for the employees to go through the modeling and analyzing the wall-chart in tight collaboration with the consultants. Their motivation to proceed with the modeling and improvements had remained and even increased. As an output from the session, a new version of the wall-chart, an electronic diagram of the wall-chart, and a formal detailed text document describing roles were produced.

3.3 The Third Modeling Session

The third session was carried out in February 2007. Between the second and third session, the employees had a chance to inspect and approve the electronic version of model created from second session wall-chart. The model had been approved with slight modifications. The aim in the third sessions was to revise and enhance the approved model. There were two consultants and two employees attending to the session. However, during the session, analyzing the existing information flows, new problems occurred from the flows that had been considered functional.

There was no modeling with wall-chart included in the third session. Concentration was on extracting detailed information about the information flows, both problematic and functional ones, in the electronic wall-chart diagram. Each information flow and related roles were analyzed individually. Information flows, their contents and way of distribution, were defined in detail. The enhanced electronic version of the wall-chart was inspected and approved. As an output from the session, a formal document describing information flows was produced.

4 Key Points and Identified Problems

In this section, some of the noteworthy key points from the sessions are presented and the most important identified problems of the process are described at general level. These are summarized in Table 1.

In the first session, it was extremely important to create a confidential relationship between the consultants and employees, and among the employees themselves. The employees were able to recognize the roles quickly and there were not many conflicts about the roles. Concluding from this, the daily work in the company is reasonably organized and responsibilities in the process are defined at some level. However, adding the information flows between roles caused hesitation, but the problems that related to those were readily highlighted. The most problematic information flows concentrated on the critical design and implementation phase. Some noteworthy problems were related to project management. For example, the company had previously worked on only few projects simultaneously and now the growth has enabled to work on several projects at the same time, which has caused problems in resource management and the working hours follow up has been inadequate. Requirements and design documents are structured but the contents and the depth of documentation are fuzzy. There were also problems related to testing assignments and especially testing documents. Managing customer requirements was considered a problem, since the requirement documents were too detailed and exhausting to read.

Table 1. Key points from sessions and problems at general level

	Key points	Problems at general level
Session I	• Confidential relationship • Software development process chosen for modeling • Identified roles and information flows of the process • Identified problem spots • Problem area in critical design and implementation	• Project management • Managing requirements and design documents • Testing • Managing customer requirements • Working hours follow-up
Session II	• Software product development process specified for modeling • Clearly better structured and specified view of the software development process • Identified problem spots • Software process improvement manager (SPIM) • Product manager	• Managing requirements and design documents • Managing customer requirements • Assignments between some roles unclear • Documentation maintenance
Session III	• Understanding distribution of work and what matters need attention • All roles identified • All information flow identified • Process visibility • Tacit knowledge to explicit knowledge	• Managing requirements and design documents • Managing customer requirements • Assignments between some roles unclear • Product manager's role • Documentation maintenance • Undistributed tacit knowledge

In the second session, the employees specified the modeling to concern their software product development process and a new information flow diagram was created. Participating employees were already familiar with the modeling technique and the session was carried out smoothly. The model was better structured in the design and implementation phase. Concluding from this, the employees had given thought to the process between the sessions. However, even though the whole model was clearly more structured than the previous one, the process itself was not stabilized, some problems remained, and new ones occurred. The employees pointed out the importance of making the roles and their responsibilities clear for themselves. Some new roles had emerged, though the distribution of work between new roles is not yet completely defined. Two of the roles will have significant impact on the process. First role is a software process improvement manager's role (SPIM), whose responsibility is to assess current practices and to explore what actions can be taken for improving processes. Second role is a product manager's role, whose responsibility is to manage customer requirements in the future. The problems in managing the requirements and design phase's documentation and the exhausting customer requirements documentation remained. In this session, the document maintenance was identified as a problem.

In the third session, one of the most important points the employees highlighted, was the need for converting the tacit knowledge of their common work methods to explicit knowledge. The distribution of organization to different geographical locations will bring further problems, if formal and documented working methods do not exist. The interfaces between companies' units need to be defined accurately, so that there would not be blocks on information flows and the employees would have a common way to communicate and work in a distributed organization. The third session was very important for revising the roles and especially the information flows in order to produce a well-defined and clear document of what these contain. The mere information flow modeling and specifying roles was valuable from the employees' perspective for visualizing their process. The process flows were also at this point becoming structured for the employees, and the point where the actual process modeling can begin was reached. There were still problems in the depth of documentation in definition stage, the assignments between some roles are not clear, document maintenance is not adequate, and the product manager for managing the customer requirements is not yet role of which some person would be in charge of.

5 SPI Actions Taken

As the process has been recognized, the improvement actions can be taken. The company is in charge of the improvement actions and the actual implementation. The company carries out the SPI activities the way that best suits their schedule and serves their business goals. The motivation for improvements is strong and it compensates the common SPI barriers and failed success factors presented in literature [14] [15] [16] [17] [18] [19]. The development project is used for supporting the SPI by modeling the process, by consulting and by organizing needed training for improvements.

The development project has encouraged the company for taking certain improvement steps, but additionally improvement actions have been carried out unprompted. Nonetheless, that some problems remain after modeling sessions and new ones occur, the improvements have been done and improvement work carries on. Some major improvements have been done in project management, testing and in documentation. Most recent improvements are related to managing customer requirements and are currently under strict definition. Project management has been improved by enhancing resource management policies and implementing a working hours follow-up system. Implementation of these has been quite successful and has provided clear advantages in project planning, scheduling, and resourcing. Document management and maintenance has been improved by defining document policies and by implementing document management software and document repository. The decisions made in meetings are also documented and followed that those will be carried out by the person in charge and this has improved traceability. Testing has been improved by applying IEEE standards of software testing (IEEE 829, IEEE 1008) and by implementing better software testing tool. Few employees have also qualified their testing capabilities by completing the ISEB foundation certificate in software testing.

Managing customer requirements is ongoing improvement effort, and now there is a clear role and job description for the person who will be in charge of this. For this role, the company is currently hiring new employees. The information documented during the development project has greatly clarified the capabilities and characteristics required from the person for the job. However, for the person in this role, they will need training, and this training is currently under definition. The decision to establish the role of software process improvement manager has also been an important improvement activity that the company has implemented. Now they have a person in charge of evaluating what improvements need to be done. Additionally, the person in this role is highly motivated, has academic and business experience, and can consider the SPI from both perspectives.

The company's employees have attended project management, testing, and technical documentation training, which have supported them in applying the improvements. Additionally, they have acquired general technical training in order to maintain and improve the quality of the products and the whole software process in general. These trainings have covered some of the identified minor process problems too. Altogether, the company has used 52 person-days for training within one year.

It is not possible to carry out a large number of improvements in a short period and it takes several months to implement one improvement effectively [20], as it is in this case too. The company has implemented quite exhausting number of small but significant improvements considering the effectiveness of their software product development process. The improvements have a direct affect to their daily business and indicate a change in work methods. The company has assimilated the importance and benefits of SPI work and established a role of a software process improvement manager. The company has prepared for the problems that growth will inevitably bring. They have the roles and information flows of their software product development process formally documented, thus having better knowledge of what characteristics and capabilities are required from new employees. The current employees have now clarified the process also for themselves and that will facilitate training and including a new employee in the process. They also have observed the need to convert tacit knowledge to explicit knowledge and the need for formal documentation and distribution of knowledge.

6 Discussion

SPI can be exhausting with all assessments, modeling, measuring, evaluating maturity levels and capabilities as presented in literature [20] [21]. SPI is resource consuming in large companies and it is that even more for small companies. SPI models for small companies are often based on some existing model that is originally targeted for large organizations [22] [23] [24] [25]. Furthermore, several factors affect the success of actual implementation SPI [14] [26] [27] and the period during which the SPI activities are carried out can be too short.

In this paper, we have presented case of lightweight software process modeling in a small software company and we have explored the usability of the model. The factors that contributed to success of the process modeling in this case were the initial awareness of the need for improvements and the employees' motivation and commitment to be involved in improvement efforts.

Small companies need some method for systematically going through their processes, work methods, roles, and information flows. However, the tool for this does not have to be a standard oriented and in-depth, since the most important thing is to make processes visible, identify problems in the processes, and initiate the SPI discussions in the company. This enables establishing the process culture and enhancing the SPI awareness. The modeling method has to be lightweight, applicable to current processes and relate improvement goals to business goals. The modeling work done in close cooperation with the company's employees and consultants, forces the employees to think about their own work, work methods, and skill deficiencies.

In presented case, the company has done needed groundwork for future SPI. In the beginning of the development project, the company did not have a clear concept of their information flows and roles of their software product development process. During this project, their knowledge about processes, process flaws and problems, own work methods and internal work distribution have enhanced greatly. The company has determinately followed through improvements for the selected problems. Improvement plans have been initiated by identifying problems using a lightweight process modeling technique, and the company has carried out the improvements with continuous motivation.

The second phase is now beginning with systematic modeling of the selected process. Prior to the development project, the company worked with the "experience and tacit knowledge", but now the process is structured for the employees so that it can be represented formally. The company has achieved the maturity needed for process modeling, the process culture is familiarized, and the selected process is structured. During the first phase, the company was not provided with clear guidelines and instructions what improvements and how they should implement. The second phase concentrates on defining a set of process phases. In the third phase, the improvements can be based on the results from the previous phases and at that point, follow-up and metrics can be used.

References

1. Baskerville, R., Pries-Heje, J.: Knowledge Capability and Maturity in Software Management. Data Base for Advances in Information Systems 30, 26–40 (1999)
2. Wheelen, T.L., Hunger, D.J.: Strategic Management and Business Policy, 9th edn. Prentice-Hall, Englewood Cliffs (2003)
3. Chin In Sing, A.: 10 Factors on Fostering Innovation in Small and Medium-sized Organizations. In: ICMIT 2000. International Conference on Management of Innovation and Technology, pp. 473–478 (2000)
4. Vähäniitty, J., Rautiainen, K.: Towards an Approach Managing the Development Portfolio in Small Product-oriented Software Companies. In: International Conference on System Sciences HICSS '05 (2005)
5. Ward, R.P., Fayad, M., Laitinen, M.: Software Process Improvement in the Small. Communications of the ACM 44, 105–107 (2001)
6. European Commission: Commission Recommendation of 6 May 2003 Concerning the Definition of Micro, Small and Medium-sized Enterprises. Official Journal of the European Union, pp. 36–41 (2003)

7. Järvi, A., Mäkilä, T., Hakonen, H.: Changing Role of SPI - Opportunities and Challenges of Process Modeling. In: Richardson, I., Runeson, P., Messnarz, R. (eds.) Software Process Improvement. LNCS, vol. 4257, pp. 135–146. Springer, Heidelberg (2006)

8. Karjalainen, A., Päivarinta, T., Tyrväinen, P., Rajala, J.: Genre-based Metadata for Enterprise Document Management. In: HICSS'00. International Conference on System Sciences, pp. 3013–3022. IEEE Computer Society, Washington, DC, USA (2000)

9. Ahonen, J.J., Forsell, M., Taskinen, S.: A Modest but Practical Software Process Modeling Technique for Software Process Improvement. Software Process Improvement and Practice 7, 33–44 (2002)

10. Richardson, I.: SPI models: What Characteristics Are Required for Small Software Development Companies? In: Kontio, J., Conradi, R. (eds.) ECSQ 2002. LNCS, vol. 2349, pp. 100–113. Springer, Heidelberg (2002)

11. Richardson, I.: SPI models: What Characteristics Are Required for Small Software Development Companies? Software Quality Journal 10, 101–114 (2002)

12. Sihvonen, H.-M., Savolainen, P.: Towards Improved Software Engineering in Small and Medium-sized Software Companies through Focused Training. In: Proceedings of the 10th IASTED International Conference on Software Engineering and Applications, pp. 346–351 (2006)

13. Sihvonen, H.-M., Savolainen, P., Ahonen, J.J.: The Craving for External Training in Small and Medium-sized Software Companies - A Trigger Effect Towards Software Process Improvement. In: Richardson, I., Runeson, P., Messnarz, R. (eds.) Software Process Improvement. LNCS, vol. 4257, Springer, Heidelberg (2006)

14. Dybå, T.: Factors of Software Process Improvement Success in Small and Large Organizations: An Empirical Study in the Scandinavian Context. In: Proceedings of (ESEC) and SIGSOFT Symposium, Helsinki, Finland, pp. 148–157 (2003)

15. Dybå, T.: An Empirical Investigation of the Key Factors for Success in Software Process Improvement. IEEE Transactions on Software Engineering 31, 410–424 (2005)

16. Lepasaar, M., Kalja, A., Varkoi, T., Jaakkola, H.: Key Success Factors of a Regional Software Process Improvement Programme. In: PICMET'01. Management of Engineering and Technology, p. 432 (2001)

17. Lepasaar, M., Varkoi, T., Jaakkola, H.: Models and Success Factors of Process Change. In: International Conference on Product Focused Software Process Improvement, pp. 68–77 (2001)

18. Baddoo, N., Hall, T.: De-motivators for Software Process Improvement: an Analysis of Practitioners' Views. Journal of Systems and Software 66, 23–33 (2003)

19. Baddoo, N., Hall, T.: Motivators of Software Process Improvement: an Analysis of Practitioners' Views. Journal of Systems and Software 62, 85–96 (2002)

20. Zahran, S.: Software Process Improvement: Practical Guidelines for Business Success. Addison-Wesley, London (1998)

21. Humphrey, W.S.: Managing the Software Process. Addison-Wesley, Reading, Mass (1989)

22. Cater-Steel, A.P.: Process Improvement in Four Small Software Companies. In: ASWEC'01. Australian Software Engineering Conference, pp. 262–272. IEEE Computer Society, Los Alamitos (2001)

23. Allen, P., Ramachandran, M., Abushama, H.: PRISMS: an Approach to Software Process Improvement for Small to Medium Enterprises. In: QSIC'03. International Conference on Quality Software, pp. 211–214. IEEE Computer Society, Los Alamitos (2003)

24. Demirörs, O., Demirörs, E.: Software Process Improvement in a Small Organization: Difficulties and Suggestions. In: Gruhn, V. (ed.) EWSPT 1998. LNCS, vol. 1487, pp. 1–12. Springer, Heidelberg (1998)
25. Calvo-Manzano Villaló, J.A., Cuevas Agustin, G., San Feliu Gilabert, T., De Amescua Seco, A., García Sánchez, L., Perez Cota, M.: Experiences in the Application of Software Process Improvement in SMES. Software Quality Journal 10, 261–273 (2002)
26. Niazi, M., Wilson, D., Zowghi, D.: Critical Success Factors for Software Process Improvement Implementation: an Empirical Study. Software Process: Improvement-and-Practice 11, 193–211 (2006)
27. Niazi, M., Wilson, D., Zowghi, D.: A Framework for Assisting the Design of Effective Software Process Improvement Implementation Strategies. Journal of Systems and Software 78, 204–222 (2005)

A Practitioner Experiment in Understanding Software Process Improvement Using Systems Modular Analysis

Narciso Cerpa[1], Javier Pereira[2], and June Verner[3]

[1] Departamento de Ciencias de la Computación, Universidad de Talca, Curicó, Chile
[2] Escuela de Ingeniería Informática, Universidad Diego Portales, Santiago, Chile
[3] NICTA, Locked Bag 9013, Alexandria, NSW 1435, Australia
ncerpa@utalca.cl, javier.pereira@udp.cl,
june.verner@nicta.com.au

Abstract. Software process improvement (SPI) models can be difficult to understand, principally because they lack visual representations relating concepts to text. Some models do not provide guidelines to help us understand their properties: i.e., their modular structure, the control-regulation configuration of common features in a key process area, and the arrangement of key process areas at each level. We propose Systems Modular Analysis (SMA) as a graphical modelling approach to facilitate understanding of SPI models. Using SMA, we reveal the internal structure of a key process area (KPA) in CMM-SW as a non-redundant configuration of common features. When the Level 2 KPAs of CMM-SW are modelled using SMA, a normative structure which shows a modular and recursive arrangement of process areas is obtained. We conduct an experiment to show how SMA helps in understanding CMM-SW. We conclude that SMA significantly improves understanding of the properties and structure of CMM-SW Level 2.

Keywords: Software Process Improvement, Systems Modular Analysis, Modelling tool, CMM-SW Level 2, Feedback loop structure of KPA.

1 Introduction

Software process improvement (SPI) aims to improve software development processes [16]. Different approaches have been proposed to SPI [3] in particular, the Capability Maturity Model for Software (CMM-SW) [15]. The benefits of implementing CMM-SW in software organizations have been well documented [6]-[8] indicating a sustained reduction of cost, improvement in productivity and quality, reduction in cycle time and increased business value. CMM-SW is characterized by two structures: staged organization of knowledge areas, i.e., key process areas (KPA), and an internal structure of each KPA organized by common features. Some researchers have proposed the idea of scaling CMM-SW in order to have successful SPIs for different project sizes and in different organizations [11], while other studies indicate that implementation difficulties relative to organizations or project sizes are due to wrong interpretations of CMM [8],[14], [17],[18]. CMM-SW can be difficult

P. Abrahamsson et al. (Eds.): EuroSPI 2007, LNCS 4764, pp. 82–93, 2007.

to understand, principally because it lacks visual representations relating concepts to text [1], [13]. In addition, CMM models do not provide guidelines to help us understand its properties [4], [5], [15]: i.e., its modular structure, the control-regulation configuration of common features in a KPA, and the arrangement of KPAs at each level. Once these properties are recognized, several implementation aspects become obvious and alternative configurations become easier to represent and understand.

The literature is scarce on the subject of SPI graphical representations although some techniques have been used in order to show different aspects of SPI models [10]-[12]. In the CMMI models, for example [2], the SEI has included some data flow diagrams to explain how the process areas are related, but these are still very general and do not provide a clear view of the modular structure of the KPAs. However, there are some structural properties which have not been represented to date. Particularly, the requirement for feedback loops in SPI models where its parts make sense only in a control-regulation system. This permits an arrangement of common features facilitating software process management at each level of the SPI model.

In this research we investigate the use of Systems Modular Analysis (SMA) to model an SPI approach in order to facilitate understanding of the configuration of common features of a KPA and the structure of KPAs at each level.

Our specific research question is "Does the use of SMA really facilitate an understanding of the configuration of common features of a KPA and the structure of KPAs at each level for a SPI model.

In Section 2, Systems Modular Analysis (SMA) is introduced, Section 3 is used to represent the modular and feedback structure implied by the set of common features in a generic KPA and in Section 4, an experiment is described which shows that SMA enhances the learning of modular and structural properties of CMM-SW Level 2. Finally, conclusions are provided in Section 5.

2 Introduction to Systems Modular Analysis (SMA)

Systems Modular Analysis represents an organizational activity as a system with two well defined and interrelated components [9]: a technological module, where a transformation is performed; and a steering module, which controls the technological module (see Figure 1). While SMA has extensive semantic definitions, we only reference those appropriate to our model. Concepts in an activity model are defined as follows:

- *Primary and secondary technological flows* represent inputs/outputs to/from the technological module and characterize primary/secondary transformations on it. In Figure 1, a primary technological flow is represented by a thick vertical arrow whilst the secondary technological flow is a thin vertical arrow.
- *Operational flows* are information triggering actions in both types of module; without this type of flow, no transformations or decisions could be made. In Figure 1, an operational flow is represented by a segment-dot vertical arrow.
- *Informative flows* contain useful information for decision making processes; shown by a segmented arrow in Figure 1.

- *Control variables* are goals and objectives defined for technological and steering modules. In Figure 1, they are symbolized by thick horizontal arrows.
- *Essential variables* characterize measures of the technological module's performance; they are quantifiable variables related to defined objectives for the module. In the SMA approach, three kinds of essential variables are set: activity level, cost level and effectiveness. Essential variables are retrieved by the steering module in order to regulate the technological module's behaviour.

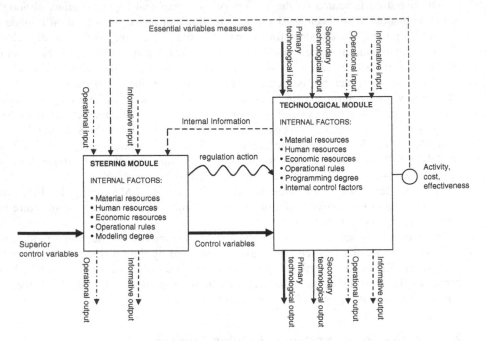

Fig. 1. Activity model in the SMA [9]

- *Regulation* information is used to adjust processes in the technological module as a consequence of deviations as described by the essential variables found among objectives and real performances.
- *Internal factors* are material, human, informative and economic infrastructures indicating resources, and rules to use those resources, available to perform activities in the technological and steering modules.

Let us assume that a KPA is a particular organizational activity. Thus, in terms of SMA, there will be a steering module managing the activity and a technological module carrying out the activity processes. From this point of view, the common features (CF) may be interpreted as follows:

- *Commitments* are of two kinds, those involving the technological module and those involving the steering module. The former are policies set by the manager of the technological module using control variables. The latter are policies and support for the steering module given by a representative at a higher level of an organizational hierarchy.

- *Abilities* are internal factors in the technological or steering module. They are preconditions for implementing a software process; abilities are represented by equipment, personnel and operational rules.
- *Activities* are internal factors in the technological or steering module, and are procedures depending on the operational rules (abilities). Activities are the transformation, regulation and control tasks in both modules.
- *Measurement and analysis*: measurements are performed on essential variables while analysis is the comparative process between the measurement of one essential variable and its associated objectives or standards.
- *Verification*: reviews are established when the steering module performs an inspection on the technological module, retrieving information about internal activities from the technological module; corrective actions defined in a KPA are represented by regulation information (waved arrow in Figure 1). However, audits have not been explicitly considered, although modelling of the structure, organization and behaviour of an activity facilitates a comparison between rules and actual practices.

Additionally, goals are represented in an activity model as the control variables (horizontal arrows in Figure 1) corresponding to goals in a KPA.

3 Modular Structure of a KPA Using SMA

A KPA is a specific well-defined organizational activity. Some best practices defined in a KPA could be placed in the steering module and others in the technological module. In Figure 2, a generic activity model for a KPA has been represented. *Abilities* and *Activities* are embedded in modules whilst *Goals* and *Commitments* are control variables. *Measurement and Analysis* are related to essential variables, representing metrics. Note that *Verification* is constituted by a *Review* task, where the KPA manager inspects implemented practices from a KPA, and a *Correction* task where a corrective (regulatory) action is required.

However, not all KPAs can be modelled by an activity model. Indeed, in CMM-SW the purpose of the Software Project Tracking and Oversight KPA is to help identify and define corrective action when project development practices deviate from the project plan. An activity model meets this requirement through the measurement, analysis and verification cycle. Thus, Software Project Tracking and Oversight does not correspond to an activity, as defined by SMA, but only to the regulation component of an activity model.

An interesting aspect of SMA activity models is the visual representation of the PDCA (Plan-Do-Check-Act) cycles of KPAs such as in a CMM-SW level. Actually, the *Plan* step is clearly modelled by control variables; the *Do* step corresponds to abilities and activities from modules; the *Check* step is related to the regulation process concerning measurement and review flows (segmented arrows in Figure 2); the *Act* step are directives and activities implementing corrective actions based on the results of the Check step.

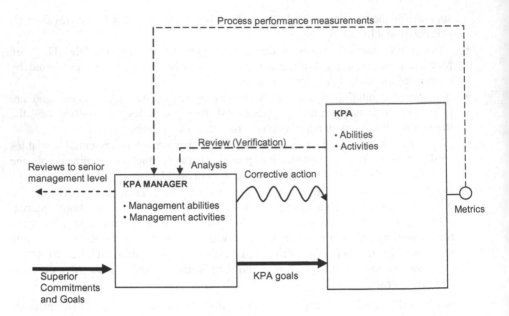

Fig. 2. Using SMA to represent a KPA generic model

3.1 Modelling Requirements Management and Software Project Planning KPAs

Requirements Management involves establishing and maintaining an agreement with the customer in order to set requirements for a software project. This agreement is called "system requirements assigned to software". The agreement is the basis for estimating, planning, executing and tracking software project activities over the software life cycle.

Software Project Planning includes steps for estimating product size and required resources, producing a schedule, identifying and evaluating the software risks and negotiating commitments. Software planning begins with a work order and goals defining and delimiting the software project. In order to create a software project plan, the steps may be iterated. This plan sets the basis for executing and managing project activities. It also includes customer resource agreements, and restrictions of the software project.

In Figures 3(a) and 3(b), two configurations relating Requirements Management and Software Project Planning are shown, both compliant with CMM-SW. Only the control variables and regulation flows have been represented.

In Figure 3(a), both requirements analysis and project planning are coordinated by the software project manager. In Fig 3(b), there are *task leaders* to coordinate and control the respective KPA activities. In CMM-SW, those activities are performed by the software engineering group reporting to the software project manager; the configuration shown in Figure 3(b) clearly takes account of this. Figure 3(b) illustrates the recursive character of the activity models in SMA. It is worth noting that these models are not necessarily equivalent to organizational units, but to processes.

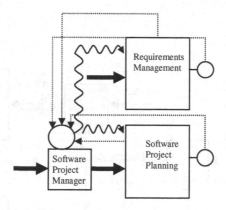

Fig. 3 (a). Relationships between Requirement Management and Software Project Planning KPAs represented by SMA model

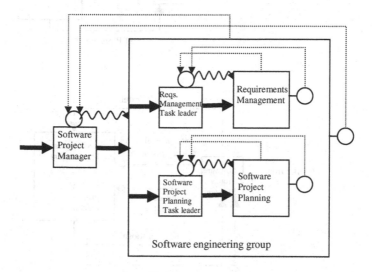

Fig. 3 (b). Relationships between Requirement Management and Software Project Planning KPAs represented by SMA models

In CMM-SW, the software project plan (SPP) is based on the software requirements and is reviewed by a task leader and the software project manager before approval. In Figure 4, part of this process is shown. It begins when a work order is received by the software project manager who sends it to the requirements manager responsible.

These requirements are also reviewed by the software project planning group.In Figure 5, requirements management and software project planning are assigned to the same group and consequently there are no specific task leaders. Thus, the software project manager coordinates both processes. Figure 5 could model a small project where team size does not permit assignment of a specific person as task leader.

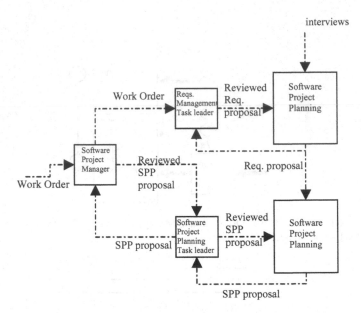

Fig. 4. Software Project Planning (SPP) process model

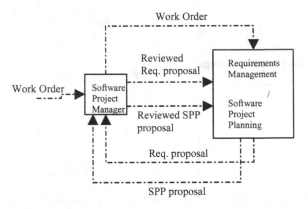

Fig. 5. An example showing the relationship between requirements management and software project planning in small projects

3.2   A SMA Model for the Normative Structure of CMM-SW Level 2

CMM-SW Level 2 KPAs are organized in a normative structure in order to distribute responsibilities, activities and roles. The high level manager coordinates software project development globally in order to solve business conflicts and issues influencing software project life cycle. The project manager coordinates all areas related to product development. The software project manager coordinates engineering activities enabling software product development. The quality assurance manager coordinates quality assurance activities (auditing and reviewing); directly reporting to high level management.

We have a normative structure when relating CMM-SW Level 2 KPAs as shown in Figure 6. The input and output flows have been omitted from modules with only the control variables shown. The software project manager is responsible for requirements management and software project planning tasks.

Software subcontract management, software configuration management and software quality assurance management tasks are assigned to their specific managers. The project manager is responsible for the coordination of affected areas: requirements, planning, subcontracting and configuration, but has no responsibility over quality assurance.

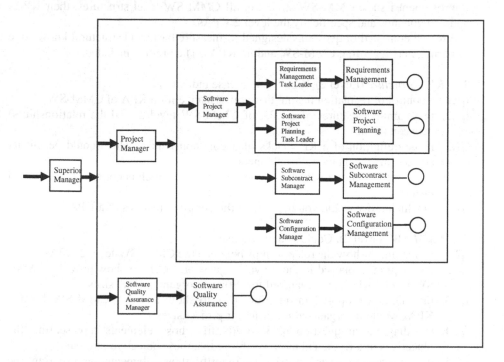

Fig. 6. The SMA normative structure of the Level 2 in CMM-SW

4   Experiment

The aim of this experiment is to test the hypothesis that the SMA modelling approach helps developers to understand the structure and organization of CMM-SW, based on the representation capabilities of the SMA technique.

4.1   Method

We advertised a Software Process Improvement seminar for IT professionals and participants in the experiment were those who registered for the seminar. Participants were thirteen software developers from a variety of organizations starting with different levels of knowledge about CMM-SW. While thirteen software developers may be a small sample in other fields, in this case it is reasonable considering the difficulties encountered in gathering such participants. The aim of this experiment is to compare participant understanding of CMM-SW before and after training in SMA. The experiment consisted of four phases: introduction to CMM-SW (20 minutes); pre-test (20 minutes); introduction to SMA with CMM-SW examples (20 minutes); post-test (same as pre-test) to assess participants structural knowledge of CMM-SW (20 minutes).

The introduction to CMM-SW ensures the same structural knowledge of CMM-SW for all participants. The aspects discussed included general software process improvement issues, CMM-SW structure, all CMM-SW level structures, their KPAs and components, and specifically the level 2 KPAs.

Pre-test consisted of questions designed to measure basic and structural knowledge of participants regarding CMM-SW and its KPAs. The pre-test included:

1. *KPA Structure* (Level 2). Could you please indicate:
q1.1. a control or regulation feature that you visualize for a KPA of CMM-SW.
q1.2. two common features of a KPA of CMM-SW level 2, and the relationship(s) between them.
q1.3. if the definition of a KPA lacks of a common feature which could permit its correct implementation. Which one(s)?
q1.4. if the definition of a KPA has a common feature which is not necessary. Which one(s)?
q1.5. in which order would you implement the common features of a KPA.

2. *CMM-SW* (Level 2). Could you please use:
q2.1. a diagram to show the relationships between the CMM-SW level 2 KPAs
q2.2. the diagram proposed in the previous question (q2.1) to show how the CMM-SW level 2 KPAs are organized for different organizational sizes.
q2.3. the diagram proposed in question q2.1 to show how the CMM-SW level 2 KPAs would be organized for different project sizes.
q2.4. the diagram in question q2.3 to identify those elements representing the objectives of a KPA, and those verifying that these objectives are met.
q2.5. the diagram in question q2.3 to identify those elements representing the relationships between KPAs.
q2.6. the diagram in question q2.3 to identify those elements representing the deliverables of each KPA.

Introduction to SMA consisted of SMA structure, general example, interpretation of CMM-SW's common features, modular structure of a KPA using SMA, and examples. In this phase participants learned about SMA and its potential use.

To measure the structural knowledge of CMM-SW gained by participants after SMA training the same questions were asked in both pre- and post-test. Participants had exactly the same time (20 minutes) to answer all the questions. The answers to questions were evaluated using a seven point Likert scale, where the anchors for the scale are: 1 = no knowledge, and 7 = excellent knowledge.

Introduction to SMA is expected to produce important benefits for the participants. Levels of CMM-SW, common features understanding, and KPA structural knowledge are expected to increase as a result of training. Therefore, the associated hypothesis tested is:

- Null hypothesis - H0: From pre-test to post-test, participants will not have a significant improvement in CMM-SW structural knowledge.
- Alternative hypothesis - H1: From pre-test to post-test, participants will have a significant improvement in CMM-SW structural knowledge.

4.2 Results and Discussion

The variables are the test scores from the pre- and post-tests. Statistical significance is indicated at $p=0.05$. Table 1 shows the median values of the pre- and post-test responses and significance levels (two related samples, i.e. Wilcoxon signed rank test). For each question, we show in bold the higher performance, and significant differences. Overall, the participants show a significantly better structural knowledge of CMM-SW for eight questions during the post-test; as these tests yield p-values of less than 0.05, we reject the null hypothesis.

Table 1. Performance difference for pre- and post test questions

Question	Pre-test Median	Post-test Median	Significance (p)
Q1.1	5	7	0.143
Q1.2	2.	5	**0.005**
Q1.3*	1	1	0.068
Q1.4	1	7	0.149
Q1.5	3	5	**0.026**
Total Q1	1	5	**0.001**
Q2.1*	1	1	**0.041**
Q2.2	1	5	**0.033**
Q2.3	1	2	**0.039**
Q2.4	1	7	**0.007**
Q2.5*	1	1	**0.041**
Q2.6	1	5	**0.016**
Total Q2	1	2.5	**0.000**

* Note: Although the median has not changed, values above the median went from 3 to 5 or 7.

The signed-rank test provides evidence that in general participant levels of structural knowledge of CMM-SW are greater during the post-test than in the pre-test for topics tested. These results suggest that the use of the SMA approach improves software developers' structural knowledge of CMM-SW.

5 Conclusions

We have shown that SMA is a useful tool for modelling CMM-SW Level 2. At the KPA level SMA allows us to:

o understand how common features of each KPA are organized, defining a feedback structure for some KPAs in CMM-SW Level 2;

o   visualize relationships among common features of a KPA;
o   observe that the set of common features is exhaustive, in the sense that we do not
    need other features to implement a control-regulation structure for a KPA;
o   show that common features have well defined purposes without redundancy; all
    the common features are necessary to implement the control-regulation structure;
    each common feature in a KPA is the complement of the others;
o   show that a KPA is organized as a PDCA cycle.

At CMM-SW Level 2, SMA allows us to understand the normative organization of
the set of KPAs; gain a perspective on the multi-layer configuration of management
responsibilities; propose alternate configurations: among the KPAs, for different sizes
of businesses; for different sizes of projects; of control activities in level 2 as
represented by different management layers; as well as visualize the complexity of
communications, regulations and deliverables required to implement the relationships
among the KPAs; and also permit the visual representation of the recursive structure
embedded in the CMM-SW Level 2.

Additionally, SMA models of CMM-SW show that the Software Tracking and
Oversight KPA cannot be represented by a single steering-transformation module pair
because this key area is contained in the regulation components of an activity model.

We show that SMA is a useful modelling tool that helps us understand the structure
of CMM-SW. Practitioners were capable of rapidly understanding the concepts of
CMM-SW and were able to associate them to an activity model of SMA. This is
shown through improvements in performance. We are continuing to use SMA with
practitioners in several software development projects, and in future research we will
use SMA for modelling other SPI models.

Organizations must properly understand the software process improvement model
they intend to implement. Our research shows that using a graphical approach such as
SMA facilitates practitioners understanding of such models.

Acknowledgement. This research has been fully supported by the Chilean grant
FONDECYT 1030785.

References

[1] Brodman, J., Johnson, D.: The LOGOS tailored CMM for small business, small
    organizations and small projects. LOGOS International Inc., Needham, Ma. (1995)
[2] CMMI Development Team: CMMISM-SE/SW, V1.0, Capability Maturity Model
    Integrated for Systems Engineering/Software Engineering Version 1.0. Continuous
    representation, Technical Report CMU/SEI-2000-TR-019, ESC-TR-2000-019 (2002)
[3] Coallier, F.: TRILLIUM: A model for the assessment of telecom product development &
    support capability. Software Process Newletter 2, 3–8 (1995)
[4] Cooper, J., Fisher, M. (eds.): Software Acquisition Capability Maturity Model (SA-
    CMM) - Version 1.03. Software Engineering Institute, Carnegie Mellon University,
    Technical Report CMU/SEI-2002-TR-010, ESC-TR-2002-010 (2002)
[5] Curtis, B., Hefley, W., Miller, S.: People Capability Maturity Model (P-CMM) - Version
    2.0. Software Engineering Institute, Carnegie Mellon University, Technical Report
    CMU/SEI-2001-MM-01 (2001)

[6] Diaz, M., Sligo, J.: How Software Process Improvement helped Motorola. IEEE Software, 75–81 (September-October 1997)

[7] Goldenson, D., Herbsleb, J.: After the appraisal: a systematic survey of process improvement, its benefits, and factors that influence success. Software Engineering Institute, Carnegie Mellon University Technical Report, CMU/SEI-95-TR-009, ESC-TR-95-009 (1995)

[8] Herbsleb, J., Carleton, A., Rozum, J., Siegel, J., Zubrow, D.: Benefits from CMM-based software process improvement: initial results. Software Engineering Institute, Carnegie Mellon University Technical Report, CMU/SEI-94-TR-013, ESC-TR-94-013 (1994)

[9] Mélèse, J.: L'analyse modulaire des systèmes: une méthode efficace pour appliquer la théorie des systèmes au management. Les Éditions D'Organisation, Paris (1991)

[10] Oktaba, H., Irbaguengoitia, G.: Software processes modeled with objects: static siew. Computación y Sistemas. Iberoamerican Journal of Computer Science 1(4), 228–238 (1998)

[11] Orci, T., Laryd, A.: CMM for small organizations, level 2. Umea University, Technical Report UMINF-00.20 (2000)

[12] Orci, T., Laryd, A.: Dynamic CMM for small organizations - implementation aspects. In: Proceedings of European Software Process Improvement Conference, Copenhagen, Denmark (November 7-9, 2000)

[13] Otoya, S., Cerpa, N.: A Small Software Company Attempting to Improve Its Process. In: Proceedings of Ninth International Workshop on Software Technology and Engineering Practice, Pittsburgh, USA (September 1999)

[14] Paulk, M.: Using the Software CMM in Small Organizations. In: The Joint 1998 Proceedings of the Pacific Northwest Software Quality Conference and the Eighth International Conference on Software Quality, Portland, Oregon, October 13-14, 1998, pp. 350–361 (1998)

[15] Paulk, M., Curtis, B., Chrissis, M., Weber, C.: The Capability Maturity Model for Software, version 1.1. Software Engineering Institute, Carnegie Mellon University Technical Report, CMU/SEI-93-TR-024 (1993)

[16] Paulk, M., Weber, C., Garcia, S., Chrissis, M., Bush, M.: Key practices of the Capability Maturity Model, version 1.1. Software Engineering Institute, Carnegie Mellon University Technical Report, CMU/SEI-93-TR-025 (1993)

[17] Software Engineering Measurement and Analysis Team: Process maturity profile of the software community 2001 year end update. Software Engineering Institute, Carnegie Mellon University (2002)

[18] Wiegers, K.: Software process improvement: ten traps to avoid. Software Development Magazine, 51–60 (May 1996)

Organizing Improvement Work: A Longitudinal Case

Jan Pries-Heje[1] and Malene M. Krohn[2]

[1] Roskilde University, Universitetsvej 1, DK-4000 Roskilde, Denmark
janph@ruc.dk, www.ruc.dk
[2] SimCorp, Oslo Plads 12, DK-2100 Copenhagen O, Denmark
Malene.M.Krohn@simcorp.com, www.simcorp.dk

Abstract. Organizing improvement work is a decision that is often made in vain. There is no standardized way to do things that works for every improvement effort. A more contingent approach is needed. Experience from seven years of improvement work at SimCorp shows that different types of improvement work requires different ways of organizing. We identify five ways of organizing for five types of improvement work. We use 9 case studies from SimCorp to show how they fit together. The resulting framework can be used to find a suitable way of organizing for a given type of improvement work.

Keywords: SPI, governance, organizing improvement work.

1 Introduction

How to organize improvement in an organization has been an urgent question ever since organizations started to improve. Badly organized improvement plans may inhibit communication, insulate improvers from practice, and create significant barriers to improvement. A very common answer to the question of how to organize improvement is an SEPG—a software engineering process group—at the core of your improvement organization.

What is an SEPG and what can it do for you? An SEPG should "drive and facilitate" the improvement process in an organization [2]. Humphrey [3, p. 2] states: "The SEPG has two basic tasks that are done simultaneously: initiating and sustaining process change and supporting normal operations". Furthermore, the SEPG should work as a change agent, providing "the energy, enthusiasm, and direction needed to overcome resistance and cause change".

How many people should be involved in improvement? The answer that Humphrey [3, p. 295] gives is that an SEPG should aim at having "full-time assignments to the SEPG of about 2 percent of the software professionals". Furthermore, the SEPG should be led by an experienced and competent manager "with a demonstrated ability to make things happen".

In the literature, the roles and responsibilities for establishing, monitoring, and enforcing process activities is often called the process infrastructure. Zahran [9] distinguishes between (1) A sponsorship role, including budgets and responsibility for benefits, (2) A management role, including guidance and strategies for SPI activities;

P. Abrahamsson et al. (Eds.): EuroSPI 2007, LNCS 4764, pp. 94–105, 2007.
© Springer-Verlag Berlin Heidelberg 2007

(3) A coordination role, providing guidance to the groups or teams carrying out improvement activities; and finally (4) The improvement teams them selves.

Another issue is where to place the ownership of processes. Any process in an organization goes through a life-cycle. It is initiated, described, implemented, and then it needs to evolve continuously maybe for many years. Someone needs to take ownership of all four activities. "Without ownership the process will deteriorate" [9]. Typically the ownership of processes is the responsibility of the SEPG. Zahran [9] has composed a list of tasks that an organization needs to take care of in any effective process environment: (1) Effectively perform the process activities; (2) Maintain and update the process definition; (3) Monitor the process performance; and (4) Implement corrective actions as necessary.

Zahran [9] further argues that an organization should have an improvement framework consisting of a process improvement roadmap, a software process assessment method, process improvement plans, and a process infrastructure.

Caputo [2] emphasize that an SEPG should have not only visible activities such as performing assessments, developing action plans, and defining and implementing processes, but also what she calls "invisible activities", such as redirecting organizational focus towards long-term benefits (of improvement). But none of these tasks can be solved by the SEPG alone. An SEPG "can help managers and engineers focus", but the SEPG "cannot develop an overall perspective without the involvement of the managers and engineers" [2].

The idea that different environments require their own organizational design is not new. Burns and Stalker [1]) argues that in dynamic economic sectors, firms with organic structure are more effective than those with more mechanistic structure. Woodward [7] continues this line of thinking and looks at ways technology and technical complexity shape the organizational structure. And Lawrence and Lorsch [4] explore the connection between conditions in the environment and organizational structure. Thus from this early start, contingency theory was born—building on the assumption that organizations whose internal structures are best fit with the surrounding environments will perform better.

Within IS research the discussion of organizational structure is one of the classic issues. At the core of the discussion is whether one should centralize or decentralize. Centralization has a number of advantages—economy-of-scale, coordination of data and applications, and optimal use of limited resources. But decentralization also has its advantages—a proper and fast response to business needs and the involvement of managers in IT decisions. Willcocks and colleagues [6] talks about five combinations of centralization and decentralization in structuring the IS work in an organization: (1) corporate service, (2) internal bureau, (3) business venture, (4) decentralized, and (5) federal.

More recently Weill and Ross [5] did a study of different ways of organizing what is now called IT governance in an organization. They identify six different ways of organizing IT, ranging from the centralized business, or "IT monarchy", to the totally decentralised "user-driven anarchy", with a federal, feudal, or "IT duopol" organization representing other combinations of centralization and decentralization.

2 Organizing SPI

Having in mind the two ways of organizing work we can ask: In which structure will the SPI tasks perform best, or which structure is most supportive? To begin answering that we derived a characterization of five SPI tasks (inspired by [2], [3], and [9]):

1. Deciding the overall direction of SPI is typically a management task, focusing on the long-term benefits and drivers of SPI, but also covering the invisible activities for influencing culture that Caputo [2] talked about.

2. Creating processes and facilitating process improvement is about building new processes based on careful study and analysis of organizational needs and experiences. One could say that this task is about knowledge elicitation and storage in the form of process descriptions. But it is also about identifying best practices on the one hand and identifying weaknesses in processes on the other.

3. Deploying and implementing processes is about getting people to use the new processes. This often involves change management, handling resistance to change, and helping the users of a process to work in a new and hopefully improved way. It also involves selecting a deployment strategy and deployment means, such as information, communication, training, and evaluation.

4. Monitoring and measuring process performance is about following up and ensuring that the processes actually work and deliver the benefits expected. Process assessments using models such as CMMI or SPICE can be part of measuring process performance. Establishing a metrics program can be another way. No matter what is measured, or how a measurement is made, this task will often provide input for necessary process improvements.

5. Maintaining and updating processes is the major task for most process improvement work. It may take a few weeks or months to create and implement a process, but using the process is often a matter of years. Therefore the most important part of this task is the assignment of ownership—someone in the organization needs to think: "This is my process", and "I am making sure that it is updated and kept alive". Among others, Zahran [9] described the necessity of this process ownership.

Further, we can look at the organization of work. Inspired by Willcocks and colleagues [6] and Weill and Ross [5] we derived five different ways to organize SPI:

A. Centralized SEPG is the classic way of organizing SPI, as recommended by Humphrey [3] and several others. Thus in one organization there is one central organizational unit having sole responsibility for improvement work.

B. Decentralized SPI work attempts to take advantage of decentralization. Positioning oneself close to the customer—the users themselves—is one example. Another way is to dispatch SPI personnel or process consultants to the projects; yet another is to delegate process related tasks to the existing project team.

C. Cross-organizational teams is a strategy for getting people from different organizational units together to share knowledge, prioritize improvements, or solve problems. A team is continuous and a visible entity in the organization, whereas projects are more temporary. A cross-organizational team can be a valuable communication channel and link to the organization for management or a central SEPG.

D. Knowledge agents is a structure built on the fact that key knowledge resides in the minds of people. Therefore it is often recommended to rotate individuals between SPI and traditional IS development, partly to bring new experience into SPI work, but also to bring updated SPI knowledge into development practice.

E. Targeted SPI projects, or Process Improvement Teams (PITs), are also a widely recommended way to carry out improvements in organizations (e.g. [9]). The projects are initiated and completed according to the organization's improvement plan. Depending on the scope of the improvement (and the scope of the project), different competencies are required, thereby calling upon different members of the organization.

3 SimCorp Cases of Organizing SPI

For our research we have used a longitudinal, embedded, single case setting [8]. The research study took place within the Danish company SimCorp. SimCorp delivers standard software for investment management and has more than 30 years of experience in delivering solutions for the financial market. The main product is SimCorp Dimension, developed and maintained primarily by the 200 person IMS Development Department in Copenhagen. SimCorp Dimension is developed in a standardized development life-cycle, releasing a new version of the product SimCorp Dimension every six months. In 1998 SimCorp started using the Capability Maturity Model (CMM) as a guideline and framework for improving the software development processes. In 2000 a group was established to facilitate the SPI work and in 2001 CMM level 2 was achieved.

The study took place during the 10-year period 1998–2007. One of the authors was responsible for SPI in SimCorp for most of that study period. The other author was never involved in any of the improvements reported and was able to look at the organization and the improvement results with neutral eyes. In that sense, it has been an action-research undertaking. Data were collected by the author working in the organization—less systematically in the beginning, and more elaborately and systematically towards the end. In this section, we elaborate the answer to our research question by way of case stories from SimCorp. The case stories describe how various SPI tasks were carried out in different organizational set-ups, and evaluate the respective advantages and disadvantages—how well the chosen set-up supported the different SPI tasks. In total we present nine case stories. The first four concerns what we have called a Centralized SEPG. We will present the cases one by one. Shortly discuss each case after it has been presented, and give a longer more elaborate analysis and evaluation after case 4 as well as after case 9.

3.1 Case 1: Central SEPG/SPI Group Takes Ownership

When SimCorp initiated improvement work based on CMM back in 2000, it was natural to establish one central organisational group to be responsible for the process improvement work. This centralised SEPG/SPI group was established as a staff function within the SimCorp development department, with dedicated employees to perform SPI.

The group's goal was - and is - to facilitate process improvement in the department in other words act as project managers on improvement projects, measure process performance, evaluate best practices, maintain processes, and verify compliance to established standards. Over the years, the group has had between 7 and 11 employees (approx. 5% of total engineering staff), depending on the number of projects running. CMM has been used as a guideline and framework for the process improvements, though the intensity of the focus on CMM has varied during the years due to other large organisational projects. As the improvements were deployed, it was natural that the central SEPG/SPI group took ownership of the deployed processes and standards. An example of this is the process library.

Evaluation of Case 1: The main advantage of establishing an organizational unit is having dedicated persons to perform process improvement work. The ownership of an established organizational process library is clear.

3.2   Case 2: Establishing an SPI Steering Group

When the central SPI group was established at SimCorp, a SPI steering group was also established. The main way of showing management commitment to SPI work at SimCorp was through the steering group. The Director of Development and the head of the Development Department have represented management in the steering group for many years. The head of the SPI group and the head of SQA also participated.

Recently, the steering group has been expanded to better represent all the activities in the development department, as the Application Development manager, System Development manager, Test manager, Product Support manager, and the Planning & Production manager have all joined the steering group. The purpose of the steering group was and is to act as sponsor for the SPI activities in the organisation, and to monitor progress and results of the SPI work. The steering group meets once every month.

Evaluating Case 2, we see that process improvement often represents long-term organizational benefits; it is important that management supports a long-term strategy and prioritizes accordingly. Discussions regarding the overall direction and strategy for process improvement are handled well by an SPI steering group. Furthermore, the steering group makes it possible to demonstrate management commitment and make visible their responsibility for process improvement. And finally, the steering group acts as a continuous management forum for raising issues and discussing process improvement issues.

3.3   Case 3: Central SPI Group to Measure and Follow Up

When the central SPI group was established at SimCorp, it was decided to include the Software Quality Assurance (SQA) function in the group. Two persons have been more or less dedicated to perform SQA over the years, and they have had success with it. The focus of the SQA function was and is to: (1) track the quality of product and processes, (2) perform "supportive SQA", where best practices are shared, and (3) report to management and the organisation.

One way to verify compliance has been to carry out so-called "focused assessments", whereby a specific process area is evaluated and a recommendation for improvement is made. Tracking quality has been implemented by establishing quality checkpoints for the main development phases—planning, development, testing—at which times SQA participates. SQA objectively evaluates the status, and decides with management whether a phase is complete. An important part of this evaluation is standardised measurements.

Measuring process performance has also been an integrated part of the SPI group's work during the years. In the beginning it was very difficult, as processes were immature and limited data existed. But over the years, a metrics programme has been established: a standardised, online collection of measurements used to determine the status of the product's quality, check the progress of the production activities, and perform analysis. SPI members are also encouraged to define new metrics when improving processes.

Evaluation of Case 3: It was an advantage to have the responsibility for developing and maintaining a metrics programme placed in one group, the SPI group. However, input to the metrics programme should come from the organization, because the project managers and management who are supposed to use the metrics in their work must feel comfortable in doing so. CMM knowledge and process focus, which are available in the SPI group, are beneficially used in compliance assessments of the organization. However, it is important that the group's members be continuously informed about the practices in the organization. Because it is an independent group (e.g. independent from the software projects), the Centralized SEPG/SPI group can remain neutral and make recommendations to management on the basis of its own analysis.

3.4 Case 4: Design and Deploy New Processes

In SimCorp the SEPG/SPI group has been responsible, to some extent, for the design and deployment of new and improved processes. This responsibility has been implemented through participation in SPI projects, by participating in cross-organisational teams, and by undertaking the tasks in the SPI group.

The way the SEPG has carried out the design of new processes has been by collecting information about current practices, learning about best practices, designing the process, and having it reviewed.

The SEPG/SPI group has also participated in deployment in the form of frequent communication, "road shows", and the like.

Evaluation of case 4: The people working full-time with SPI possess or develop skills necessary for successful SPI development and deployment, such as communication, change management, and project management skills. From studying best practices and industry recommendations, the SPI personnel have the necessary knowledge for introducing new practices. Of course this knowledge is not exclusively available for SPI personnel, but often they have an external network and have been studying best practices regarding processes. Knowledge of the process library is an advantage when designing new processes that depend on other processes. One challenge is that the Centralized SEPG/SPI group might only have limited knowledge of current practices in the organization and therefore designs a process that is too academic or too difficult to deploy.

3.5 Evaluating the First Four SimCorp Cases

The first four cases concerned different ways of working that all can characterized as Centralized SEPG. If we take the five tasks on "#1 - Deciding the overall direction of SPI" worked quite well for a Centralized SEPG especially after a steering group (Case 2) was established.

For "#2 - Creating processes and facilitating process improvement" it also seems that a Centralized SEPG can do a fairly god job. Especially if one succeeds in attracting knowledgeable and experienced developers to the SEPG group.

However, for "#3 - Deploying and implementing processes" the outcome is not as positive. Case 4 clearly illustrated that processes may become too academic when designed centrally, and that a central group may be too removed to really facilitate the deployment of new processes "in the trenches".

For "#4 - Monitoring and measuring process performance" the combination of a Central SEPG with responsibility for Quality and the use of quality assurance techniques seem to work fairly well as illustrated by case 3.

And then for "#5 - Maintaining and updating processes" we again seems to run into a weakness for a Centralized SEPG. Being central means that you are removed from daily work and it becomes hard to capture the small changes and desires for updating processes. Doing quality assurance means that you often are seen as a control mechanism checking the daily work, more than helping and facilitating. Thus a Centralized SEPG is probably not the best way of organizing the maintenance and updating of processes.

So it seems that a centralized SEPG group is good at providing overall direction, good at creating new processes, but not as effective in deploying processes, and definitely not as good in maintaining and updating processes.

3.6 Case 5: Decentralized SPI Work

We now turn to other ways of organizing SPI work; not using a Centralized SEPG.

The Development department in SimCorp has tripled its size during the past 8–10 years. More specialised functions have been established, such as a Test department, a Product Support department, a Planning and Production group, a SPI group, and more. All departments have grown in size and scope. The growth was made possible by stable growth in SimCorp's business—more customers and also a more complex product. Growth in business, the development organisation, and the system also naturally implies new or improved processes to improve efficiency and quality.

Defining new and improving existing processes has been an integral part of ongoing organisational development, and the responsibility has often been decentralised. For example, the Test department has been responsible for establishing and improving test processes; the Product Support department has been responsible for establishing and improving the support processes, and so on.

When decentralising, the role of the central SEPG/SPI group has been to make sure that the departmental processes are compliant with the established standards; it also is responsible for the overall process improvement plan for the department.

Evaluating Case 5, we see that it is an advantage to place "#3 - Deploying and implementing processes" with the department performing those processes. The advantage comes from the feeling that something close to you is important to you. The knowledge of current practices is right at hand, and is valuable input for further process improvement. Furthermore, the task of deploying improvements is often more effectively performed by the people performing the processes, as they will be able to spot potential pitfalls.

The challenge is to establish and maintain the necessary long-term process focus and "#1 - Deciding the overall direction of SPI" in a department that is often measured on more production related output, such as completed test cases, meeting milestones, and so on. The role of a central SEPG/SPI group can also be difficult to distinguish when the SPI work is decentralized. Top management also often expects and requires standardized ways of following up, and this can be difficult to accommodate when the responsibility is decentralized.

"#2 - Creating processes and facilitating process improvement" is probably difficult to make work in a Decentralized SPI group; again because the main objective is the daily production thus time for creating new processes often becomes second priority.

"#4 - Monitoring and measuring process performance" is definitely not a good task to take on for a Decentralized SPI. The temptation to measure only when the outcome is positive will be too obvious.

Finally, for "#5 - Maintaining and updating processes" the Decentralized SPI group has the advantage of being close to the daily work making it easy to capture the small changes and desires for updating processes. Whether a Decentralized SPI group can find and dedicate the time for maintaining and updating processes is more questionable.

3.7   Case 6: Cross-Organizational Teams to Facilitate Improvement

During the years of SPI work at SimCorp, several cross-organisational teams have been established for support. One goal was to involve more people in the SPI work; another has been to involve practitioners from the organisation.

The Training team, which has existed for seven years as a training council in the department, consisted of approximately 6 members representing Development, Test, Support, and SPI. Their purpose was to (1) to arrange internal courses, (2) to make sure that knowledge is shared in the department e.g. by arranging "Seminars of the month" and "New functionality presentation", publishing "Hints of the month", and (3) maintaining the department's education plan for new employees.

The TAP team (Tools and Practices) existed for a couple of years as a forum whereby ideas and knowledge were shared, and improvements discussed and implemented. The team consisted of a developer from each development team. The purpose of the team was to (1) to collect, suggest, and evaluate ideas for improvement in the development environment and process, (2) to suggest and support the roll-out of procedures affecting the development environment and the development process, and (3) to arrange workshops on specific tools and practices.

3.8   Case 7: Cross-Organizational Teams to Deploy Processes and Take Ownership

As described in Case 6, different cross-organisational teams have been established during the years in SimCorp. For the Training team it was natural to take ownership of the department's training related processes. For some years it has done so successfully thereby implementing improvements. Enabling this was the task of the Training coordinator, located in the department and responsible for the team's activities. The Training coordinator was placed in the central SPI group.

For the TAP team, the situation was a bit different. Because it represents the development processes (design, code, review, unit test), its scope is relatively broad. The TAP team has not taken ownership of any of the processes, although it has been suggested and discussed. However, the central SPI group has successfully used the TAP team to review new or revised processes before deployment, and it has also used the team to do the actual deployment in the development groups.

Evaluating Case 6 and 7: The main advantage of cross-organizational teams is the involvement of practitioners from all over SimCorp in improvement work. Participation in the teams is voluntary, which is a very sound basis for improvement and implies a natural drive. Thus task "#2 – "Creating processes and facilitating process improvement" seems to be well taken care of by a Cross-organizational team.

A Cross-organizational team can be responsible for "#1 - Deciding the overall direction of SPI". In fact the steering group (case 2) could be seen as cross-functional. However, it requires a very special kind of team consisting of (top) managers.

"#3 - Deploying and implementing processes" also works fairly well for a Cross-functional team. There will always be a team member close to each organizational unit ensuring that the deployment takes into account local oddness's. However, it is a challenge to get the cross-functional teams to take ownership of the processes. More successfully, SimCorp experienced that the teams can be used for input and reviewing as they represent different functions in the department. Finally, the team is not necessarily skilled at performing successful deployments—it cannot be expected to find good communication skills, experience with change management, or other attributes itself.

Cross-functional teams are as useless in monitoring themselves as was a Decentralized SPI group. In fact a Cross-functional team may be even worse in doing "#4 - Monitoring and measuring process performance" because the members may start blaming each other to be certain that blame does not come to their own department.

And then for "#5 - Maintaining and updating processes" a Cross-functional team has the advantage of being close to the daily work making it easy to capture the small changes and desires for updating processes. But again it is doubtful whether a Cross-functional team can dedicate the time for maintaining and updating processes.

3.9   Case 8: Rotation Scheme for Knowledge Agents

For some years, SimCorp has had a rotation scheme for the central SPI group: for six months a developer or tester participates in an improvement project with the SPI group, and then returns to his or her own group for six months.

Examples: (1) A concrete SPI project on establishing a unit test framework for the application developers. A developer with programming experience and interest in unit tests is assigned for this task in a 6 months project. (2) To mature the configuration management processes, an experienced developer, responsible for configuration management, is assigned to investigate best practices, document the practices, and make sure that they are CMM level 2 compliant in relation to configuration management. An alternative to this full-time rotation of the SPI group has been to appoint three developers to serve for 10–20% of their time for a six-month period, in order to share best practices and help the less experienced developers with standards, inspections, and so on.

Evaluation of Case 8 on Knowledge agents: The clear advantage of this work set-up is that specialist knowledge from the practitioners is used for process improvement. The practitioners add value to the process improvement work and to the SPI group, and they become positive ambassadors after they rotate back to their own department. A rotation, whereby an individual is moved away from his or her everyday tasks and organizational unit, offers a real advantage, as this person's skills are dedicated to process improvement work. Thus task "#2 - Creating processes and facilitating process improvement" and task "#3 - Deploying and implementing processes" seem to be very well taken care of by Knowledge agents.

A more challenging aspect of this set-up is the ownership of the developed/improved solutions when the practitioner is off to new assignments. Thus for task "#5 - Maintaining and updating processes" Knowledge agents are unsuitable.

As for "#1 - Deciding the overall direction of SPI" we find that Knowledge agents are too fickle and transient to undertake that task.

Finally, for task "#4 - Monitoring and measuring process performance" Knowledge agents may be suitable in that they can come in with their specialized knowledge in another functional department and do good jobs of monitoring and measuring and at the same time pass on some their specialized knowledge.

3.10   Case 9: Targeted SPI Projects

SPI work in SimCorp has traditionally been organised in targeted projects with well-defined scopes, milestones, allocation, etc. The purpose of Targeted SPI projects has been to implement improvements—either within a specific process area or within a specific part of the organisation. Of course, it has been necessary to be flexible in the SPI group when organizing SPI projects, as key personnel from the organization often are requested to participate on these projects.

The SPI group at SimCorp has the following guidelines for Targeted SPI projects:

(1) Establish project with goals, scope, members, and major milestones. (2) Plan activities with tasks, estimates, allocations, and detailed milestones. (3) Provide training using best practices from other companies and studies. (4) Gather data to evaluate current processes in one's own organisation. (5) Develop new and current processes. (6) Pilot new processes and evaluate process performance. (7) Revise the new processes on the basis of pilot study. (8) Implement new processes in full scale throughout the organisation. (9) Monitor, evaluate, and improve processes.

Evaluation of Case 9 (Targeted SPI projects): First, Targeted SPI projects are a structured way to work with improvements. Securing management commitment to a well-defined project is often easier than more ad-hoc improvement tasks. It is also possible to allocate key personnel or persons with the necessary competencies to a project for a shorter or longer period. Furthermore, having project plans and deadlines makes it easier to track progress and follow up on deliverables. Thus task "#2 - Creating processes and facilitating process improvement" seem to be very well taken care of by Targeted SPI projects.

On the other hand, it can be difficult to compete for resources for long-term SPI projects when you are up against shorter-term projects that include delivery to customers. It is also common that the last few activities in a project—such as deployment in the organization, training, following up on the actual improvement—become compromised as new projects start before the old one is completed. Thus task "#3 - Deploying and implementing processes" may be only partly suited for a Targeted SPI project.

Another shortcoming of SPI projects is that they are temporary; project members split up after completion. Therefore it is a challenge to anchor the ownership of the project deliveries (e.g. an improved process). Thus task "#5 - Maintaining and updating processes" is unsuitable for a Targeted SPI project.

As for "#1 - Deciding the overall direction of SPI" we find that a Targeted SPI project is too short-term to undertake that task.

	Deciding overall direction	Creating processes	Deploying processes	Monitoring & measuring	Maintaining
Centralized SEPG	+ [1-4]	+ [1-4]	(+) [1-4]	+ [1-4]	− [1-4]
Decentralized SPI	(+) [5]	(+) [5]	+ [5]	− [5]	(+) [5]
Cross-organizational teams	(+) [6-7]	+ [6-7]	+ [6-7]	− [6-7]	(+) [6-7]
Knowledge agents	− [8]	+ [8]	+ [8]	(+) [8]	− [8]
Targeted SPI projects	− [9]	+ [9]	(+) [9]	(+) [9]	− [9]

Fig. 1. Relationship between SPI tasks (columns) and organizational set-ups (rows). A "+" indicates a well-suited match. A "(+)" indicates partly suited. And a "-"means not suited. In squared brackets are shown from which case(s) the evaluation result is derived from.

4   Conclusion on Organizing SPI Work

In this paper we have analyzed the data from a longitudinal study at SimCorp, seeking an answer to our research question about the relationship between tasks and structure.

We were able to fill out the matrix that these two dimensions distend (see Figure 1), and we were able to come up with recommendations on which organizational forms seem suited for different tasks—at least for our case study organization SimCorp.

Naturally variations of the five organizational set-ups exist. Organizing SPI work in a company is also contingent on different factors, such as company culture, managerial style, and the current economical situation. One way of organizing does not necessarily preclude another, and the different ways may well complement each other. The need for different organizations of SPI work reflects the dynamics in an organization. Nevertheless we believe that our results in Figure 1 can be very useful in other organizations for SPI governance.

References

1. Burns, T., Stalker, G.M.: The Management of Innovation, p. 269. Tavistock Publications, London (1961)
2. Caputo, K.: CMM Implementation Guide: Choreographing Software Process Improvement, p. 319. Addison-Wesley, Reading, MA, USA (1998)
3. Humphrey, W.: Managing the Software Process, p. 494. Addson-Wesley, Reading, MA, USA (1989)
4. Lawrence, P., Lorsch, J.: Differentiation and integration in complex organizations. Administrative Science Quarterly 12, 1–30 (1967)
5. Weill, P., Ross, J.W.: IT Governance: How top performers manage IT decision rights for superior results, p. 269. Harvard Business School Press, Boston, MA, USA (2004)
6. Willcocks, L., Feeny, D., Islei, G.: Managing IT as a Strategic Resource. McGraw-Hill, London (1997)
7. Woodward, J.: Industrial Organization: Theory and Practice, p. 281. Oxford University Press, London (1965)
8. Yin, R.K.: Case Study Research: Design and Methods, 2nd edn., p. 170. Sage Publications, Thousand Oaks, CA, USA (1994)
9. Zahran, S.: Software Process Improvement: Practical Guidelines for Business Success, p. 480. Addison-Wesley, Upper Saddle River, NJ, USA (1998)

An Experiment with a Release Planning Method for Web Application Development

Sven Ziemer and Ilaria Canova Calori

Department of Computer and Information Science,
Norwegian University of Science and Technology,
NO-7491 Trondheim, Norway
{svenz,canovaca}@idi.ntnu.no

Abstract. Web application development is under certain circumstances such as a strong emphasis on time-to-market characterised by the usage of informal and ad-hoc development practices and a lot of tacit knowledge. Here we present an experiment that has been carried out in order to evaluate a recently proposed release planning method for web application development. This method aims at bringing stakeholders together to share knowledge and to decide on a configuration for the next release that satisfies all stakeholders. The method has been evaluated in terms of its effect on factors such as knowledge sharing, understanding, support to reach a consensus and stakeholders satisfaction.

1 Introduction

Developing software systems is a knowledge intensive endeavour, and the quality of a software application is limited by the quality of the knowledge that is available to the development team. Improving the amount and quality of knowledge is therefor a central activity in software process improvement. The first refers to having as much knowledge as possible from multiple stakeholder's, and the later refers to having more precise knowledge. Depending oh the context of a software development project, the knowledge about the development effort will either be explicit or implicit, and quantitative or qualitative. In the case of development projects that apply informal and ad-hoc development practises, and that have a strong focus on time-to-market the knowledge is mostly implicit and qualitative. Improving both the amount and quality of knowledge here is as important as for all software development projects. This can be achieved by using the available tacit knowledge. Bringing the involved stakeholders together and sharing the available knowledge to create a common understanding, is an improvement of knowledge, and a potential first step to systematic software process improvement activities. Sharing knowledge in such an environment involves sharing the opinions, beliefs and expert judgements of the stakeholders.

In a recent paper [1] we presented a method for release planning to be used in web application development projects under such conditions. In order to validate the proposed release planning method and to learn how it works in development

P. Abrahamsson et al. (Eds.): EuroSPI 2007, LNCS 4764, pp. 106–117, 2007.

projects, this method was tested empirically. Among several options, it was decided to use a student experiment. This paper presents the experiment, and the lessons learnt.

The rest of the paper is organised as follows: The background from web application development for the release planning method is given in section 2 and related work is shortly described in section 3. The next sections, experiment definition and goal (section 4), experiment planning and operation (section 5), and the questionnaire and experiment analysis (section 6) are presenting the experiment. The results from the experiments are shown in section 7, and a discussion and further work is presented in section 8. Finally, conclusions are given in section 9.

2   Background

The way web applications are developed depends on such factors as the applications maturity, the number of returning users and the competition with similar web applications. Some web applications have a strong focus on time-to-market, that in some cases can be described as a rush-to-market focus. The development of such web applications can be best described by the usage of informal development practices, the use of implicit and tacit knowledge, by the involvement of a group of stakeholders that have diverse and possibly conflicting interests, and the iterative nature of the development activities [2]. That is not to say that these characteristics can not be found elsewhere, but when the main focus of the development efforts of a web application is on rush-to-market, they constitute a special combination.

Requirement specification and release planning for web application development is in many cases done in an ad-hoc way, with no assessment of the potential

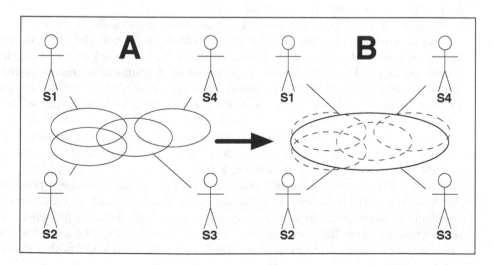

Fig. 1. The diverse knowledge of stakeholders

consequences, of selecting one configuration over another. The focus is on the short-time satisfaction of the stakeholders and not on having a long-time strategy. Even if this may be a common approach with acceptable results, it can result in unbalanced decisions – satisfying only one stakeholder – that turn out to be bad for the web application. In order to be able to assess the consequences of candidate configurations and to prioritise them, a release planning method, that is using the tacit knowledge of all the stakeholders as input, is needed.

The release planning method that is used in this paper is described in [1]. In projects with the aforementioned development practices, stakeholders knowledge is limited to their own involvement and interests in the project (see part A of figure 1). The proposed release planning methods aims at bringing together the knowledge from all stakeholders in a development project and at creating a common understanding among stakeholders reflecting the knowledge of each individual stakeholder. This shared knowledge can be thought of as the union of all stakeholders knowledge (see part B of figure 1).

The communication and knowledge sharing that is expected to be introduced into a development team by the proposed release planning method will thus contribute to increase both the amount and quality of knowledge for the stakeholders that are involved in the decision making on the next release.

3   Related Work

There has been a lot of research into release planning. There is an increasing number of research planning methods published, such as [3], [4], [5] and [6]. In [7] seven existing release planning methods are evaluated with respect to ten dimensions, such as stakeholder involvement, prioritization mechanism, resource constraints, and tool support. None of these methods is designed to use the stakeholders belief and opinion as only input.

There are a few empirical studies on release planning methods. In [8], two case studies of a release planning process are presented. In [9] and [10] the authors present a family of empirical studies to compare ad-hoc based and systematic release planning. The focus of these experiment is on confidence, understanding and trust related to the research planning practise applied. In [11] the authors present an industrial case study to stress the advantages of employing an intelligent decision support system compared with an ad hoc approach. With the proposed system the satisfaction of the stakeholder priorities is maximized, and the time spent in pre-planning activities is reduced and channeled on the delivery process to include more requirements in a release.

There are also some studies on knowledge sharing. In [12] it has been pointed out how important is for multidisciplinary team members working on complex problems to share their knowledge in order to cope with different prospectives on the problem and different individual knowledge and skills. The stakeholders are therefore encouraged to make their beliefs and values explicit. Another study has investigated the motivation factors for knowledge sharing to take place [13]. The result of this study is that two factors – "Development of organisation" and

"Development of individuals" – are the most motivating factors for knowledge sharing to take place.

4   Experiment Definition and Goal

The objective of the proposed release planning method is to facilitate better communication and knowledge sharing between the stakeholders of a small web application development project. The goal of the experiment is to validate if this indeed is the case. The experiment definition – using the definition template based on GQM and shown in [14] – is:

Object of study: The object studied in this experiment is a release planning method, presented in [1].

Purpose: To evaluate the release planning method with respect to:
- understanding of the overall development project situation and of the consequences of potential decisions
- enabling and contributing to increased shared knowledge
- prioritising the requirements and candidate configurations
- reaching a consensus among the stakeholders
- the stakeholders satisfaction after a decision is taken

Quality focus: The quality focus is the stakeholders satisfaction, the increased shared knowledge, better understanding, prioritisation and an easier reached consensus.

Perspective: The development teams point of view.

Context: The context is a student experiment with 63 students, forming groups of 3 or 4 members. The study is conducted as Multi-test within object study.

5   Experiment Planning and Operation

To test the release planning method and to evaluate its effect on knowledge sharing, understanding, reaching a concensus, prioritisation of requirements and stakeholder satisfaction, we decided to create a scenario with a release planning problem and to use groups of students – divided into treatment and control groups – to solve this problem by using either the proposed release planning method (treatment groups) or by using an ad-hoc practise (control group).

5.1   Planning

Context and subject selection. Due to limited resources the experiment is run with volunteer students. They will receive a modest economic compensation to participate in the experiment. After initial contact was made with a student organisation 63 students in their 3rd year of a industrial economy class signed up for the experiment. They all filled in a pre-experiment questionnaire to assess their skills.

The experiment is off-line. A scenario with a release planning task is used and the students take on roles that are described in the scenario. The task is to decide on the next release that can be implemented within a given time constraint and that satisfies all stakeholders.

Hypothesis formulation. Based on this expectation we formulated the formal hypothesis. The hypothesis will be tested for each factor defined in the purpose section of the experiment definition.

H0: The release planning method will not improve the overall development process.
H1: The release planning method will improve the overall development process.

Variables and design. The experiment is a one factor experiment with two treatments. The independent variable is the decision process used and can take on two values: using the proposed release planning method or using an ad-hoc based decision process.

The dependent variables are the degree or amount of (1) shared knowledge, (2) understanding the overall development process, (3) requirement prioritisation, (4) reaching a consensus, and (5) stakeholder satisfaction. These variables are measured with a post-experiment questionnaire.

Instrumentation. The instrumentation of the experiment includes objects and guidelines that are handed out to the subjects. These are (1) a pre-experiment questionnaire to assess the participants skills, (2) general instructions on the experiment, such as a description of the scenario, a requirement list, and a description of each role, (3) a release form, where the groups can write down the release they decided on, (4) a post-experiment questionnaire that is handed out to the groups after the release form has been delivered to the experiment supervisors, and that contains questions used to measure the dependent variables, and (5) an instruction on how to use the proposed release planning method (only handed out to the treatment groups).

Validity evaluation. There is not enough space here to present a full discussion of the validity evaluation. This section is therefore narrowed down to a discussion concerning the construct and internal validity.

Using no method as the second treatment may pose a threat to the validity. It is not possible to control how the control groups are solving their task, whether they use a release planning method or not. But given that the subjects are students in their 3rd year, they will probably have no knowledge about release planning methods, and will just try to solve the problem as best they can. With more experienced subjects – like professional developers and project managers – this could pose a threat to validity, but in the case of our student experiment we believe that it is allowable to ignore this threat.

The members of the the treatment groups are receiving only a short introduction to the release planning method. It is therefore the chance that they may not use the method totally as instructed. This may pose a threat to the internal validity, as not using the method correctly may have an impact on the results. The time that is available for training in a students experiment is limited. To cope with this problem we decided to observe how the students used the method, and in case we observe a misuse of the method we have to consider if this threatens the validity. We were also available to answer questions from the subjects.

5.2   Operation

Sampling: 63 students had signed on to participate in the experiment. We divided them into 20 groups, 10 treatment groups and 10 control groups. Each group had 3 students, with one subject taking on the role as project manager, another as marketing director and a third as programmer. Three groups had to have 4 students, and the fourth subject had to take on the role of a programmer.

The participants filled in a pre-experiment questionnaire, where they answered questions about their skills, experience and preferred role in a group setting. Before the experiment started we decided on what role each participant was to take on. We found this necessary since the subjects were studying industrial economy and only a small number of the students had skills and/or experience in programming and marketing. This way we insured that all subjects had some knowledge of the role they had to play in the experiment and were able to look at the task from the corresponding viewpoint.

We proceeded by drawing for each group a project manager, a marketing director and a programmer. In the end, we had to assign three programmers to three groups, and we did assign groups to them by drawing a group for them. After we had populated the 20 groups, we assigned them either to the treatment group or the control group by chance.

Running the experiment: On the day of the experiment we used two large rooms, one for the treatment groups and one for the control groups. We gathered all students in one room to give them an introduction to the experiment (ca. 15 minutes), and to hand over all handouts. After the control group had left for the other room we gave the treatment groups a 10 minutes introduction to the release planning method and also presented a small example. The experiment took about two hours in total.

When the groups delivered their final release form and the questionnaires, the experiment supervisors controlled that all questions in the questionnaires had been answered. If this was not the case, the subjects were asked to complete the questionnaire.

In the discussion of validity threats we found that using the method in a not intended way may disturb the results. However, observing the students during the experiment showed that they mostly were using the method as intended. We observed cases where groups had small deviations in the use of the method, but we considered them not to be so serious that they posed a threat to the validity of the experiment.

6   The Questionnaire and Experiment Analysis

The questionnaire consisted of 23 statements, divided into five groups, one group for each purpose of the experiment. For each statement the subjects had to express their attitude to the statement. To measure the subjects' attitude we used a five point Lickert-scale [15].

#	Tr group		C group		t-test	Wilcoxon
	X	S²	X	S²	p-value	p-value
1	3.16	0.94	3.41	0.64	0.27874	0.33200
2	3.16	1.21	3.53	0.58	0.12726	0.13900
3	3.48	0.59	3.91	0.67	0.03872	0.03161
4	3.52	0.79	3.72	0.79	0.36935	0.24570
5	2.74	1.60	3.59	0.70	0.00276	0.00421
6	3.03	0.83	3.66	0.81	0.00829	0.00726
7	3.94	0.66	3.88	1.02	0.79391	0.95780
8	4.00	0.53	3.94	0.71	0.75351	0.83800
9	3.32	0.56	3.78	0.50	0.01510	0.01468
10	3.97	0.90	4.28	0.40	0.13016	0.21840
11	3.74	0.53	3.53	0.90	0.32650	0.48600
12	3.84	0.54	3.28	0.60	0.00467	0.00247
13	3.81	0.49	3.56	0.71	0.21569	0.20050
14	3.52	0.72	3.38	0.95	0.54260	0.76450
15	3.94	0.93	3.88	0.69	0.79104	0.61780
16	2.10	0.89	3.38	1.40	0.00001	0.00005
17	2.23	1.05	3.53	1.10	0.00001	0.00002
18	1.94	0.66	2.81	0.87	0.00018	0.00034
19	4.00	0.47	3.72	0.79	0.16352	0.20840
20	3.97	0.70	3.91	0.60	0.76357	0.66380
21	3.23	1.38	2.72	0.72	0.05556	0.09244
22	3.84	0.34	3.47	0.77	0.05350	0.10160
23	3.90	0.36	3.53	0.52	0.02893	0.02518

X = mean value, S² = variance

Fig. 2. Mean value, variance and p-value for each questionnaire item

The data collected using the Lickert-scale are data of type interval scale [16]. This is not a straight forward decision, as there exists several opinions on the measurement scale of data collected by using a Lickert-scale. Some will treat the data collected from a Lickert-scale only as ordinal scale, and some will ask for a Lickert-scale consisting of at least seven points before they will treat data from it as interval scale. Our view is that we find it helpful to treat the data collected by using a Lickert-scale as interval scale. This allows us to use the Student t-test in the analysis. Beyond the argument of measurement scale, we consider it to be pragmatic to use parametic tests on this data. There is a lot of evidence showing that this is a good practice, even if the data is of a so-called non-applicable measurement scale [17].

The responses in the questionnaire were coded (1-dissagree strongly, ..., 5-agree strongly). For every question we calculated the mean value and the variance from all responses both for the treatment groups and for the control groups. Using the mean values, we applied the Student t-test. We have chosen a significance level of 0.10. Given the discussion above, we also chose to perform a non-parametric test, the Wilcoxon test. As can be seen in figure 2, the results were mostly the same.

We have chosen to reject the null hypothesis when the difference is statistically significant for at least half of all questions for each group of questions.

7 Results

The results will be discussed separately for each group of questions. The results for each item from the questionnaire are shown in figure 2.

Understanding: Items 7 – 10 in figure 2.

The results are not what we expected. As can be seen from the results, the control groups perform better then the treatment groups, and thus, the null hypothesis can not be rejected.

The main reason for this result is, in our opinion, the lack of discussions within the treatment groups. They were more focused on using the method (with the provided artifacts) and on using the method correctly. This will be discussed in more detail in section 8.

Shared knowledge: Item 1 – 6 in figure 2.

The results for these items show that the control group performed better then the treatment group. Three out of six questions have a significant difference. The null hypothesis can thus not be rejected. This is – as is the case with the previous topic – not an expected result.

The main reason for this unexpected result is – as for the previous topic – the lack of communication between the group members in the treatment groups. Using the method for the first time, the focus was on using the method and on the requirement list. The control group did not have a method that took away there focus and discussed the importance of requirements and candidate configurations.

We think that the communication between the group members of the treatment group will improve with more experience with using the new method, and by changing the communication pattern in the groups (see section 8).

Reaching a consensus Items 15 – 18 in figure 2.

On all four items the treatment groups performed better, and on three of the items the difference between treatment groups and control groups is significant. Hence, the null hypothesis can be rejected.

There are two possible explanations for this result. First, due the lack of communication there are not so many conflicts, or the conflicts are not really understood. Second, once the requirements and candidate configurations had been assessed, and the mean values had been calculated, finding a common decision seems to be quite straightforward.

Requirement prioritisation: Items 11 – 14 in figure 2.

The results are as expected, as the treatment groups perform better than the control groups. However, only on one item is the difference between the groups significant. The null hypothesis can thus not be rejected.

Using the method made it easy for the treatment groups to prioritise the requirements and candidate configurations. They could simply sort the requirements and configurations according to the assessment they had given to the requirements. However, due to the lack of communication and discussion it seems that the consequences of choosing one candidate configurations over the others were not discussed. The same is true for the written justification of each assessment. The release planning method has simplified the prioritisation process, but has not improved the communication among the stakeholders.

Stakeholder satisfaction: Items 19 – 23 in figure 2.

The treatment groups perform better on all five questions, and the difference between the treatment groups and the control groups is below the 0.1 level on three of the five questions. Therefore, the null hypothesis can be rejected.

The better stakeholder satisfaction in the treatment group most likely stem from the better performance on requirement prioritisation. When all stakeholders can identify their top priorities it is ok to find a configuration that satisfies most stakeholders.

8   Discussion and Further Work

The results of the experiment have been surprising because of the treatment groups performance on understanding and knowledge sharing. Whereas we expected the treatment group to perform better on these issues, in fact the control group performed better. In our opinions there are two contributing factors that could have been controlled if we had been aware of them from the beginning. The first contributing factor is the treatment groups focus on using a new method. The release planning method used in the experiment was unknown to the student volunteers, and they focused mainly on using the method correctly. Whereas the method is meant to be a tool for supporting communication between stakeholders in this type of web application development, using the method correctly became the main activity and focus.

The other contributing factor has been the instrumentation of the experiment. For the convenience of the treatment group, the requirement list received by each student had columns for writing down the assessment and a small justification. Additional columns on the requirement list allowed the project manager to collect all groups members' assessment. Each member of the treatment group worked on his own copy of the requirement list, writing down his assessments and justifications. Bringing the assessments together on the project managers copy became a mere mechanical activity. This is shown as situation A in figure 3.

The result can be improved by introducing two changes to the experiment layout:

- Repeating the experiment with the treatment group using the release planning method two or three times, using a different scenario each time. The students would gain some experience using the method. This should result in a larger focus on the problem to solve and not so much on the method. The

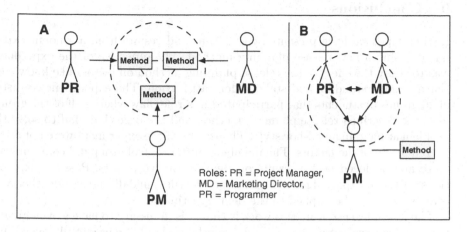

Fig. 3. Communication patterns when introducing a new method

method would become a tool that supports the communication between several stakeholders and enables a better common understanding of the problem to solve.

There is a chance that this may introduce a learning bias on the subjects of the treatment groups. The scenarios will not be so different from time to time, and the students may respond in a way they think is expected from the experiment organisers.

– The instrumentation for the treatment group can be changed by only letting the group's project manager write down the stakeholders assessment and justification. This situation is depicted as situation B in figure 3. The project manager will work sequential on the requirements, and will ask the stakeholders for their assessment and a short justification. This will increase the communication within the group, at least between the project manager and the other group members.

We will conduct two new series of experiments, where the effect of the two suggested changes will be implemented and studied. This will be done in the near future, and will give us some indication on how important the learning effect of using a new software development method will be with respect to the communication of its users, and what effect changing the communication pattern when using a method will have on the results.

Another direction for future work is to study and understand how tacit knowledge is transformed into explicit knowledge in a rush-to-market type of development environment. A general model for Knowledge Sharing is for instance given in [18] or [19]. What practices are enabling knowledge sharing and learning in a web application development project with its short deadlines and informality, and how can they be applied in a practical setting?

9   Conclusions

In this paper we have presented the details and results from a student experiments using a new release planning method. The objective of the experiment was to study the effect of the release planning method on factors like knowledge sharing, understanding and stakeholder satisfaction. The experiment consisted of 20 groups of students that participated in a role play, where half of the groups used the described release planning method and the other half had to solve the problem at hand in an ad-hoc style. The results of the experiment were not as expected for all of the factors. The members of the control group did communicate more and achieved better results on two out of five factors. Possible explanations for the unexpected results have been identified and discussed, together with changes that can be applied to the next experiment.

The lesson learned from this work is that it is necessary to have a even greater focus on how new software engineering methods should be used. Still, even if not all results are as expected, the experiment shows that the use of the proposed release planning method is suitable and that it achieves reasonable results on three out of five factors.

Acknowledgements

We would like to thank our colleagues Tuulikki Gyllensvärd, Tor Stålhane and Jianyun Zhou for their help with the experiment.

References

1. Ziemer, S., Sampaio, P., Stålhane, T.: A decision modelling approach for analysing requirements configuration trade-offs in time-constrained web application development. In: Proceedings of SEKE 2006 (2006)
2. Ziemer, S., Stålhane, T.: Web application development and quality - observations from interviews with companies in norway. In: Proceedings of Webist 2006 (2006)
3. Karlsson, J., Ryan, K.: A cost-value approach for prioritizing requirements. IEEE Software, 67–74 (September/October 1997)
4. Jung, H.W.: Optimizing value and cost in requirement analysis. IEEE Software 15(4), 74–78 (1998)
5. Penny, D.A.: An estimation-based management framework for enhancive maintenance in commercial software products. In: 18th International Conference on Software Maintenance (ICSM 2002), Maintaining Distributed Heterogeneous Systems, Montreal, Quebec, Canada, 3-6 October 2002 (2002)
6. Greer, D., Ruhe, G.: Software release planning: an evolutionary and iterative approach. Information and Software Technolgy 46(4), 243–253 (2004)
7. Saliu, O., Ruhe, G.: Supporting software release planning decisions for evolving systems. In: Software Engineering Workshop, 2005. 29th Annual IEEE/NASA (2005)
8. Karlsson, L., Regnell, B., Thelin, T.: Case studies in porcess improvement through retrospective analysis of release planning decisions. International Journal of Software Engineering and Knowledge Engineering 16(6), 885–915 (2006)

9. Du, G., McElroy, J., Ruhe, G.: Ad hoc versus systematic planning of software releases – a three-staged experiment. In: Münch, J., Vierimaa, M. (eds.) PROFES 2006. LNCS, vol. 4034, pp. 12–14. Springer, Heidelberg (2006)
10. Du, G., McElroy, J., Ruhe, G.: A family on empirical studies to compare informal and optimization-based planning of software releases. In: ISESE '06: Proceedings of the 2006 ACM/IEEE international symposium on International symposium on empirical software engineering, pp. 212–221 (2006)
11. Momoh, J., Ruhe, G.: Release planning process improvement – an industrial case study. Software Process: Improvement and Practice 11(3), 295–307 (2006)
12. Beers, P.J., Boshuizen, H.P.A., Kirschner, P.A., Gijselaers, W.H.: Common ground, complex problems and decision making. Group Decision and Negotiation 15(6) (2006)
13. Ye, N., Zhi-Ping, F., Bo, F.: Motivation factors that make knowldge workers share their tacit knowledge in universities: an empirical research. In: Services Systems and Services Management, 2005. Proceedings of ICSSSM '05. 2005 International Conference (2005)
14. Wohlin, C., Runeson, P., Host, M., Ohlsson, M.C., Regnell, B., Wesslen, A.: Experimentation in Software Engineering: An Introduction. Kluwer Academic Publishers, Dordrecht (2000)
15. Robson, C.: Real World Research. Blackwell Publishers, Malden (2002)
16. Cooper, D.R., Schindler, P.S.: Business Research Methods, 8th edn. McGraw-Hill, New York (2003)
17. Velleman, P.F., Wilkinson, L.: Nominal, ordinal, interval, and ratio typologies are misleading. The American Statistican 47(1), 65–72 (1993)
18. Nonaka, I., Takeuchi, H.: The Knowledge Creating Company. Oxford University Press, Oxford (1995)
19. Argyris, C.: Overcoming Organizational Defences: Facilitating Organizational Learning. Prentice-Hall, Englewood Cliffs (1990)

Defining a Legal Risk Management Strategy: Process, Legal Risk and Lifecycle

Ricardo J. Rejas-Muslera[1], Juan. J. Cuadrado-Gallego[2], and Daniel Rodriguez[2]

[1] Universidad Francisco de Vitoria
[2] Universidad de Alcalá

Abstract. All systems during their lifecycle, no matter how simple, will generate legal implications that need to be managed. The potential cost of an inadequate management of legal aspects can even imply the failure of the project. As a consequence, legal risk management should not only be a major activity of the development lifecycle, but it needs to be performed by qualified personnel following well-defined procedures and standards. However, current software process improvement models do not properly include processes for legal audits and more concretely legal risks management for each phase of the software development lifecycle. Neither in industry related to manage legal risks of software projects is possible to find well-defined and standardised projects. This lack of standardised process means that legal risks are handled reactively instead of proactively. This work presents a process for managing legal risks. It is organised by a series of activities to be performed at each stage of the software development lifecycle to eliminate or minimize the risk of project failures for legal reasons.

Keywords: Legal Risk, Software Process, Software Systems, CMMI, ISO 15504, Software Lifecycle.

1 Introduction

The ever increasing importance of software systems in all economic and social sectors implies an important increment of legal aspects in the software lifecycle.

An inadequate management of such risk can increment the possibility of failure of a project, for example, not having a clear ownership of the product when the product has been developed by a third-party, other cases can related to legal claims by third-parties or even public administrations.

The most important software process improvement and assessment models (CMMI – Capability Maturity Model Integration [1] – or ISO 15504 [2]) do not properly include processes for legal audits and more concretely legal risks management for each phase of the software development lifecycle. Only in CMMI, it is possible to find scattered mentions to contractual or legal aspects in the requirements section.

Neither in industry related to manage legal risks of software projects is possible to find well-defined and standardised projects. Activities performed in this area depend on the perception of the risk by management. Generally such activities do not follow any temporal pattern to systematically perform them but the most common activity

P. Abrahamsson et al. (Eds.): EuroSPI 2007, LNCS 4764, pp. 118–123, 2007.

consists of performing a Due Diligence or legal audit before marketing the product. This lack of standardised process means that legal risks are handled reactively instead of proactively.

This work presents legal audit activities to be performed as part of software process assessment and improvement models. The aim is to provide industry with a framework for efficiently manage legal risks inherent to all software projects. Such a framework allows us to move from a reactive risk strategy to a proactive one.

The organisation of the paper is as follows. Section 2 identifies the most common legal risks involving software projects. In Section 3 is analysed, on the one hand, how risks are treated by major software assessment and improvement processes, and on the other hand, how those are actually managed in industry. Section 4 provides an standardised framework for legal audits to manage legal risks. Finally, Section 5 concludes the paper and future work is outlined.

2 Legal Risks for Software Projects

With the aim of providing a high level view of legal risks and not being completely exhaustive (a comprehensive coverage of all risks is impossible), we provide a Web project as an example. In such type of project, we could find legal risk in the following areas:

2.1 Intellectual Property Area

The design and development of a Web site needs protection in two different ways:

1. As a graphical representation, it is an artistic creation and therefore, it is protected by royalties.
2. As a computer program. it contains source code, e.g., XML HTML, Visual Basic JavaScript, etc. that are also protected by intellectual property rights.

In this area, there are two groups of legal risks:

1. Legal Risks related to the ownership of the product. Deficiencies or the lack of a proper contract with developers can generate claims about its ownership.
2. Legal risks related to the infringement of a third party intellectual property. On the one hand, a Web site can include content or design developed by a third party with their rights. Not acting with caution and ignoring audits to check such infringements can generate legal claims involving expensive settlements and even penal offences.

2.2 Aspects Related to Current Regulations

Designs and contents included in a Web site can violate a large number of juridical regulations designed to protect all kind of activities related to the Web. This can generate legal claims by third parties or penalties by public administration with fines, expedients or even penal actions. These risks can be classified in the following areas:

1. Related to the publication of products or services via Web with the infringement of:

   a. Regulations about advertising.
   b. Regulations about users' rights.
   c. Trading standards
   d. Intellectual property rights

2. In the commercialization of products or services, it is possible the infringement of:

   a. Regulations about electronic business.
   b. General legislations about contracts.
   c. User's rights and obligations

3. In relation data protection, i.e., to how user's personal data are used and treated.

4. In relation to services properly registered, i.e., certain service providing sites must be registered properly by public administrations to carry out the intended business. Not doing so can generate penalties form public administration bodies.

5. Some Web sites and specially those that belong to public administrations must comply with certain level of accessibility defined by the W3C [13] or the European Union.

The previous points highlight the fact of the variety and large possible risks that must be considered when carrying out a software project. Some of those are serious risks that need to be managed properly to avoid the failure of the project.

3 Risk Management in Software Process Assessment and Improvement Models

After commenting the seriousness and importance of a proper management of legal risks in a software project, it is of paramount importance to have procedures and activities defined beforehand to minimize or eliminate such risks. We now analyse how those activities are taken into account by the most important assessment and improvement models, and in particular those related to software engineering. In this analysis we have taken into account the CMMI model [1].

After analysing the CMMI model, we concluded that there is no process area containing legal aspects in a systematic and organised way. There are, however, scattered references to legal aspects of the project mainly in relation to contractual rights and obligations. These references include:

1 Basic Management Process Area: The Supplier Agreement Management process area. This process area consider the assumption in which "*a product component is identified and the supplier who Hill produce it is selected , a supplier agreement is established and maintenance...*", "*The purpose of Supplier Agreement Management is to manage the acquisition of products from suppliers for which there exists a formal agreement.*" and it includes as Specific Goal (SG1) "*Establish Supplier Agreements*".

2   Advanced Management Process Area: Project Management, Integrated Project Management for IPPD. The SG 2 Coordinate and Collaborate with Relevant Stakeholders in the SP 2.2-1 Manage Dependencies establish in its subpractice - 4 point-: *"Review and get agreement on the commitments to address each critical dependency with the people responsible for providing the work product and the people receiving the work product"*.

3   Advanced Management Process Area: Project Management, Integrated Supplier Management. The SG 2 Coordinate Work with Suppliers dedicate the SP 2.3-1 to *"Revise the Supplier Agreement or Relationship"*

4   Engineering, Requirements Management. The SG 1 Manage Requirements include in its points SP 1.1-1 and SP 1.2-2 to *"Obtain an Understanding of Requirements"* and *"Obtain commitment to Requirements"*, respectively.

4   A Legal Risk Management Process

The first step to consider as a process all activities to manage legal risks related to software projects consist of locating such a process in the CMMI scheme; more specifically, we need to define which of the Process Areas could include legal audits.

First, we need to define which category of the CMMI Process Areas (Process Management, Project Management, Engineering and Support) is the most appropriate. After analyzing the scope of each Process Area, we believe that the most suitable place to locate such activities is the Project Management area, as it is defined: *"Project Management process areas cover the project management activities related to planning, monitoring, and controlling the project"*.

The process of legal audit is a set of activities related to both the planning and control of the project. Legal audits are related to planning as it must include activities and resources to minimize legal risks. More concretely, legal audits must include control activities; such activities need to control the legal aspects and avoid any risk during its life-cycle.

The next step, following the categories defined by CMMI v1.1, consists of locating the most suitable Process Area with within Project Management for the legal audits activities. The Process area Risk Management aim is *"to identify potential problems before they occur, so that risk-handling activities may be planned and invoked as needed across the life of the product or project to mitigate adverse impacts on achieving objectives."*

According to this definition, the audit process must be integrated in the process area Risk Management; it complies with its aim, concretely, to identify potential legal problems before they occur. The legal activities and measures must be planned and invoked as needed across the life of the product or project to avoid or mitigate adverse legal impacts on achieving objectives.

Finally, with the objective of structuring the legal audit process in the Risk Management Process Area, it is necessary to divide it into 3 parts following the Introductory Notes:

- *Defining a legal risk management strategy*. It defines a legal audit process for legal risk management inherent to all software projects. A generic definition will consider two main issues: (i) the type of software to be developed because the activities will depend on it (for instance, we will need to carry out different activities depending on if the systems is an invoice system or a Web site); (ii) the software development lifecycle, as it is the cornerstone of all project activities and it will be necessary to locate the legal audit activities.

- *Identifying and analyzing legal risk.* For identifying and analysing the legal risks that can endanger a project, it is also necessary to take into account both the type of software to be developed in technical terms, i.e., its design and development, and its functionality, what the system is suppose to do. These considerations will allow us the identification and posterior analysis of the legal risk related to the project. With knowledge about the technical aspects, it will be possible to identify and associated legal risks, i.e., intellectual property. On the other hand, if we take into account its functionality, we will be able to identify legal risks derived from its use in the market or when the system is in production, for example, legal risks associated with current regulations.

- *Handling identified risk.* As a consequence of the risks that need to be managed, legal audits need to follow a structured process with omnipresence throughout the software development lifecycle. It cannot be an autonomous process but on the contrary, it needs to have relationships with other activities that need to be audited in a proactive way. In this way, once legal risks and the activities have been identified, it is needed to analyse the software development lifecycle, establish its phases and set the legal activities in the most appropriate place. For example, in a project where legal risks related the intellectual property have been identified as a result of subcontracting part of the product, the legal activities related to minimize such risk must be set up in the software lifecycle. In this case, those will be mainly contractual at the beginning of the project (planning) because once the product is being developed; the ownerships of the project can generate legal conflicts.

5 Conclusions and Future Work

In all software projects, a proper management of legal activities is a key area for a successful project. It will mitigate legal risks associated to the project and also it will increment its quality (a project with legal or potential conflicts is a serious defect in terms of quality). However, the most important process improvement and assessment models such as (CMMI o ISO 15504) do not include legal audit processes to manage during the software development lifecycle legal activities. Neither, current practices in industry do manage such issues properly.

This work tries to provide a framework to minimize such risks within the software industry. It presents legal audit activates as an extra process to be implemented in the software assessment and improvement processes inherent to all software processes. Such a way of dealing with risk is a proactive way of instead of reactive. In the CMMI model, the legal audit process should be included as part of Project Management and more concretely, within the Risk Management area.

Future research work will be the detailed description of the audit process in terms of generic and specific goals. Also, the benefits of such audit process will need to be evaluated in a quantitative way.

Acknowledgements

We would like to thank the Spanish Ministry of Science and Technology for supporting this research (Project CICYT TIN2004-06689-C03) and Prof Javier Dolado for his useful comments.

References

1. CMMI-SE/SW/IPPD/SS: V1.1 Capability Maturity Model Integration. CMMISM for Systems Engineering, Software Engineering, Integrated Product and Process Development, and Supplier Sourcing
2. SPICE – ISO 15504: Information Technology - Software Process Assessment
3. Directive 2001/84/EC of the European Parliament and of the Council on the Resale Right for the Benefit of the Author of an Original Work of Art
4. Directive 91/250/EEC of the European Parliament and of the Council on the legal protection of computer programs
5. WIPO International Forum on the Exercise and Management of Copyright and Neighboring Rights in the Face of the Challenges of Digital Technology (1997)
6. Directive 91/250/EEC of the European Parliament and of the Council relating to the approximation of the laws, regulations and administrative provisions of the Member States concerning misleading advertising
7. Directive 98/6/EEC of the European Parliament and of the Council on consumer protection in the indication of the prices of products offered to consumers
8. Directive 97/7/EEC of the European Parliament and of the Council on the protection of consumers in respect of distance contracts
9. WIPO Intellectual Property Handbook: Policy, Law and Use (2004)
10. Directive 2000/31 of the European Parliament and of the Council on certain legal aspects of information society services
11. Directive 97/66 of the European Parliament and of the Council concerning the processing of personal data and the protection of privacy in the telecommunications sector
12. Directive 2002/58 of the European Parliament and of the Council concerning the processing of personal data and the protection of privacy in the electronic communications sector
13. W3C World Wide Web Consortium. Web Site: http://www.w3c.org/

iCharts: Charts for Software Process Improvement Value Management

Román López-Cortijo, Javier García Guzmán, and Antonio Amescua Seco

Computer Science Department
Carlos III University
Avda. Universidad, 30, 28911, Leganés, Madrid (Spain)
rlopez@progresion.net, jgarciag@inf.uc3m.es, amescua@inf.uc3m.es

Abstract. Software Process Improvement Programs provide many benefits to the companies investing in this type of activities. One of the main problems in relation with SPI Value Management consists of the difficulty to convince senior management to invest in this type of programs. This issue is solved by means of benchmarking with successful histories by means of case studies. The information of current of SPI case studies is very heterogeneous, making this task so difficult. This paper presents a technique to formalize the information enclosed in an SPI case study providing an easy access to the relevant information of a SPI case study. Moreover, the results, obtained from its application with pre-existing case studies are provided. This work has been partially supported by the Spanish National Project "Software Process Management Platform: modeling, reuse and measurement" (TIN2004-07083).

Keywords: Software Process Improvement, Improvement Benefits, Improvement Monitoring, SPI value management.

1 Introduction

This paper deals with issues related to determination of the added value obtained as a consequence of a Software Process Improvement (SPI) program.

The continuous process improvement, widely studied in the bibliography [2], [12], [1], [11], [9], [10] is an imperative for the survival and sustainability of software intensive organizations, since the advances of the competitors make be them in a continuous race in which the winner is that one who offers lower prices and greater quality. Therefore, the present question is not why is necessary to improve, because it seems clear that the best organizations are continuously improving [12], obtaining more than satisfactory results [4]. Currently, the most important question is: How to obtain the greater benefit from the investments done in relation with SPI.

One of the main problems in relation with SPI Value Management consists of the difficulty to convince those that must put money and expend resources why (stimulus for change) and how (in what direction) they must put money and expend resources.

Software Engineering Institute (SEI) at Carnegie Mellon University (USA) carried out a study in response to a demand for information on the results of software process

P. Abrahamsson et al. (Eds.): EuroSPI 2007, LNCS 4764, pp. 124–135, 2007.

improvement efforts [8]. This study covered 13 organizations that represent a variety of maturity levels. The results showed that the average yearly cost of software process improvement was $245,000 and the average number of years engaged in software process improvement was 3.5.

This cost is high and the investment period is not short, so these expenditures are very critical to software companies. The senior managers need comprehensive information to decide the resources to employ, to identify the target areas and to estimate the benefits expected.

Case Studies are the most popular tool to obtain the commitment of the senior management to employ the needed resources to begin a SPI program, because show what activities have been done by others and the benefits that were obtained.

Nevertheless, using Software Process Improvement Case Studies, it is difficult compare the experiences from others, because the information, the structure and the indicators (if used) considered in the cases studies are very informal (normally text without indicators, figures (numbers) not well reported), so the usefulness to perform benchmarking activities of these case studies is very limited.

Based on this evidences, it is believed that if SPI case studies were simpler, formalized and rigorous, they will be very useful tools: to achieve the commitment of the senior management for a SPI program; and to serve as standard for documenting and reviewing case studies to the community dedicated to SPI.

In order to study and analyze this hypothesis, the objectives of this research work are:

- To define a technique that show: key success factors, events, improvement investments & actions, values and evolution of improvement indicators and cause-effect information from events and actions to indicators value
- To analyze the feasibility and to define the steps to apply the technique defined to pre-existing case studies.
- To determine the steps apply the technique defined to prepare new case studies.
- To evaluate the usefulness of the technique define in terms of: usefulness of the information provided; difficult to prepare case study charts for new case studies and for pre-existing case studies; and determination of the added value in comparison with traditional case studies

The rest of the paper is structured as follows:

Section 2 presents a state of the art in relation with Software Process Improvement Case Studies, including: a discussion of the case study technique, a classification of types of case studies and a discussion related to how case study techniques has been used describing process improvement programs.

Section 3 provides the definition of iChart Technique, identifying its information elements and the steps to apply the technique by means of the adaptation of pre-existing case studies or the preparation of new case studies.

Section 4 provides examples of the technique application for formalizing pre-existing SPI case studies.

Section 5 discusses the usefulness and added value provided by case study chart technique, identifying the main problems and lessons learned discovered during the application of the technique.

Finally, section 6 presents the conclusions of this research work and next steps.

2 State of the Art

A case study is a particular method of qualitative research. Rather than using large samples and following a rigid protocol to examine a limited number of variables, case study methods involve an in-depth, longitudinal examination of a single instance or event: a case. They provide a systematic way of looking at events, collecting data, analyzing information, and reporting the results. As a result the researcher may gain a sharpened understanding of why the instance happened as it did, and what might become important to look at more extensively in future research. Case studies lend themselves to both generating and testing hypotheses [5].

The types of case studies considered in the bibliography are:

- *Illustrative case studies.* Illustrative case studies describe a domain; they use one or two instances to analyze a situation. Their usefulness in related to the interpretation of other data, especially when the case studies are directed to beginners in the knowledge area.
- *Critical instance case studies.* This type of case studies examines one or a few sites for one of two purposes. A very frequent application involves the examination of a situation of unique interest, not able to be generalized. A second utility is the application that entails the demonstration or testing of a highly generalized assertion in one instance. This method particularly suits answering cause-and-effect questions about the instance of concern.
- *Exploratory case studies.* Exploratory case studies condense the case study process: researchers may undertake them before implementing a large-scale investigation. Where considerable uncertainty exists about program operations, goals, and results, exploratory case studies help identify questions, select measurement constructs, and develop measures; they also serve to safeguard investment in larger studies.
- *Program effect case studies.* This type of case studies is useful to determine the impact of programs and provide inferences about reasons for success or failure.
- *Prospective case studies.* In a prospective case study design, the researcher formulates a set of theory-based hypotheses in relation with the evolution of an on-going process and then tests these hypotheses at a pre-determined follow-up time by comparing these hypotheses with the observed information using "pattern matching" or similar technique
- *Cumulative case studies.* Cumulative case studies aggregate information from several sites collected at different times. The cumulative case study can have a retrospective focus, collecting information across studies done in the past, or a prospective outlook, structuring a series of investigations to be considered for the future.
- *Narrative case studies.* This type of case studies present findings in a narrative format. This involves presenting the case study as events in an unfolding plot with actors and actions.

In SPI value management, analysis based on case studies contributes to the elaboration of a business case with the purpose of determine whether to proceed and how or not with an investment.

SPI case studies usually are a mix between Program Implementation and Narrative Case Studies that are published by means of:

- Specific Technical Reports. Periodically, Software Engineering Institute publishes technical reports including case studies of the Software Improvement Programs reported to SEI [6], [7].
- Papers presented in specialized journals. The main representative of this case studies source is Software Process Improvement and Practice edited by Elsevier.

After an analysis of a great amount of this type of case studies, it can be concluded that, the information provided in the most common case studies is, generally:

- A brief description of the company and software organization
- Improvement objective, but not all the cases and including only qualitative information
- An imprecise description of the result obtained as a consequence of the improvement activities
- A fuzzy chronology of the improvement activities
- A brief description of the improvement activities performed

In the most part of cases, there is not any information related to the initial operational model of the software organization.

As a conclusion of the analysis of SPI case studies, it can be concluded that more formalization would be very useful to perform benchmarking activities.

3 Definition of iChart Technique

iChart is a technique that pretends to formalize the information enclosed in an SPI case study and present all the elements related to SPI value management in way that enables a rapid reading and performing benchmarking and comparison activities based on an standardized (or common) information between the cases to be considered.

The definition of the technique has to parts:

- The specification of the information required to formalize a SPI case study by means of iCharts.
- The sequence of steps to prepare an iChart by means of analyzing existing SPI case studies or gathering information from on-going SPI programs.

A) Information elements of an iChart
An iChart has two sections:

1. Context Information
   The context information is an organization description sheet including information related to: Number of employees, Range of turnover, Business sector, Capability Level before and after the improvement program, the reference model to determine the capability level and the process areas affected by the improvement program.

Moreover, information related to improvement objectives must be provided by means of a textual description.

Finally, information regarding to the human and technical resources employed in the improvement program should be provided by means of a textual description.

2. Chart

The chart section provides information related to:

- Indicators measuring the benefits obtained from the process improvement, including:
  - Measures and unit
  - Evolution over the time (textual and graphical): Previous to the process improvement, at the moment when the improvement program begun and several times, during the execution of the improvement program
- Activities performed in the scope of the improvement program by means of a Gantt chart with the same time scale than the indicators graphic, including:
  - Identification of the scope of the activity
  - Identification of the beginning and ending dates of the activity

B) Process to create an iChart

iCharts can be elaborated in several circumstances. Currently, they have been applied using two types of information sources: a document describing a SPI case study or from an on-going case study. The steps to prepare an iChart using both information sources are presented below.

B.1) A document describing a Software Process Improvement Case Study

The steps to elaborate iCharts using existing case studies are:

1. The purpose of the first reading is to extract the information related to the improvement journey. In order to elaborate this improvement journey, it is necessary to:
   - Establish the time scale regarding to the improvement program: months, trimesters or semesters.
   - Identify the activities performed by means of a work brake down structure.
   - Infer the information relative to the beginning and ending dates of the activities.
   - Identify the milestones or important dates in relation with the improvement program.

2. The second reading is oriented to search for the information related to the improvement benefits based on indicators.
   In order to compile this information, it is necessary to:
   - Identify the indicators used to determine the improvement results and benefits
   - Identify the improvement objectives. In case of having enough information in the case study, it is necessary to link the improvement objectives and the indicators provided
   - Identify the values of the mentioned indicators

In some circumstances, the case study text does not provide enough explicit information, but good deductions can be done. In several case studies, neither explicit nor implicit information is provided, so these case studies are not apt to be formalized by means of iChart.

B.2) Using data compiled during an on-going SPI program

In this case, the information is compile as the improvement program advances. The most important milestones required to gather iChart information are:

1. During commitment phase, it is necessary to gather information related to: improvement objectives; improvement action plan, including activities (with the beginning and ending dates), milestones and important dates that will configure the improvement journey; and indicators to measure the results and benefits obtained as a consequence of the improvement activities.

    This information is not always available at this stage, but it should be identified at this moment or as soon as possible from this moment.

2. During diagnosis phase, it is necessary to gather information related to:
    -   Initial values of the indicators defined (only, if enough information is available).
        So, it is important to select indicators that can be stated (without a huge effort) at the beginning of the improvement program
    -   Information regarding to the actual activities performed (updated set of activities performed with their beginning and ending dates) and milestones and important dates, in order to update the improvement journey

3. During improvements implementation and deployment, it is necessary to gather information related to:
    -   Periodic values of the indicators defined
    -   Information regarding to the actual activities performed (updated set of activities performed with their beginning and ending dates) and milestones and important dates, in order to update the improvement journey

4. When the improvement program finishes and it is being evaluated, it is necessary to obtain the final indicators figures and actual improvement journey

The main purpose of this paper is to show the added value of iCharts technique versus SPI text case studies. We had worked in new SPI initiatives where iCharts were employed as a technique for controlling the results obtained in the project, but due to space restrictions its presentation is not included in the paper.

4 Application of iChart Technique

The iChart technique has been applied by paper authors for formalizing many SPI case studies and for compiling information of on-going SPI programs in order to present periodic reports to senior management.

On order to show the results obtained from the application of iChart technique, several cases from [6] have been selected.

The selection of SPI case studies from [6] was decided because these SPI case studies can be obtained free of charge, so the readers of this paper can check easily how the authors apply the method and the results obtained. For this purpose, for each case study considered, it is provided the reference to the text in SEI's report, a list of the items used to prepare the iChart and the iChart obtained. Only the chart is provided, so the contextual information of each case study is not described due to space restrictions. If considered necessary, this information is available for each case in the original document from SEI.

A) iChart Example: 3H Technology

As case study information says: *"3H Technology (3HT) is an information technology company offering a wide range of products and technical services. These include performing custom software development, systems integration, and product implementation".*

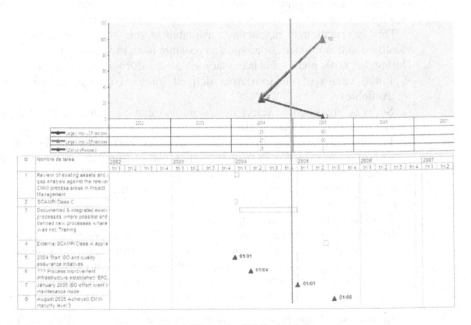

Fig. 1. iChart for 3H Technology

The 3HT had no real experience with process improvement prior to starting its ISO and quality assurance initiatives. The CMMI based program was initiated as a way to deploy continuous improvement activities stated in the quality policy of the company.

The information provided in this case study is related to Project Planning, Project Monitoring and Control and Risk Management.

The most useful information provided in this SPI Case Study to prepare iChart was:

- Process Improvement History section (see page 32 at [6]) that provides information related to improvement phases and the temporal scale of the case study.
- CMMI Based Improvement section (see page 32 at [6]) that provides information related to the main stages of the program, but not detailed

information is provided. This information can be deduced by means of text interpretation.

- Performance Results section (see page 33 at [6]) provides quantitative results related to the level of implementation of generic and specific practices of the process areas considered (Project Planning, Project Monitoring and Risk Management).

The final iChart including the improvement journey and benefits assessment based on indicators is shown in figure 2.

B) iChart Example: Motorola GSG China

As case study information says: *"the primary business of the GSG China Center is to provide software development services and solutions to other Motorola business units. GSG China's products include various embedded systems in cellular, network system, and other telecommunication devices"*.

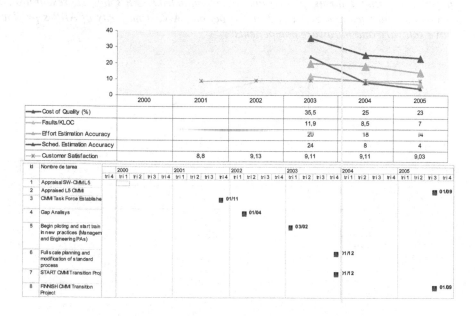

Fig. 2. iChart for Motorola GSG China

One of Motorola GSG China was to achieve the CMM maturity level 5 (that was satisfied), but with the publication of CMMI, the fulfillment of the maturity requirements specified by this reference model was the new objective to achieve.

The information provided in this case study is related to Project Planning, Project Monitoring and Control, Requirements Management, and Verification.

The most useful information provided in this SPI Case Study to prepare iChart was:

- Process Improvement History section (see page 47 at [6]) that provides information related to improvement phases and the temporal scale of the case study.

- CMMI Based Improvement section (see page 48 at [6]) that provides information related to the improvement journey, including general information on the resources and efforts spent in the improvement program.
- Performance Results section (see page 49 at [6]) that provides information related to improvement benefits based on indicators (cost of quality, errors rate, effort estimation accuracy, schedule estimation accuracy, and customer satisfaction).

The final iChart including the improvement journey and benefits assessment based on indicators is shown in figure 2.

C) iChart Example: ABB

As case study information says: *"ABB is a leader in power and automation technologies. It enables utility and industry customers to improve performance while lowering environmental impact. ABB's products help operate utilities, process industries, manufacturing plants, and other industries. ABB has representation in over 120 countries and employs 110,000 people. A vast majority of ABB's products have software and hardware components".*

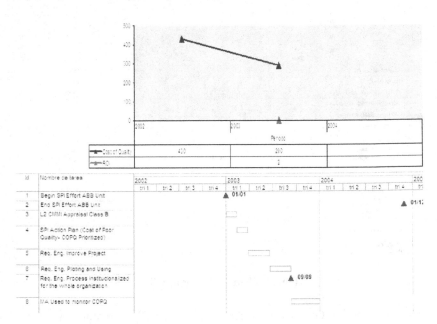

Fig. 3. iChart for ABB SPI case study

The ABB software and systems process initiative process improvement (ASPI) group addresses processes for the full product life cycle (systems and software process initiatives), but the information provided in this case study is related to Requirements Development, Requirements Management and Measuring and Analysis processes.

The most useful information provided in this SPI Case Study to prepare iChart was:

- Process Improvement History section (see page 38 at [6]) that provides information related to the temporal scale of the case study.
- CMMI Based Improvement section (see page 38 at [6]) that provides information related to the improvement journey.
- Performance Results section (see page 40 at [6]) that provides information related to improvement benefits based on indicators (cost of quality and Return on Investment).

The final iChart including the improvement journey and benefits assessment based on indicators is shown in figure 3.

5 Evaluation of iChart Technique

The evaluation of iChart technique is performed in terms of its usefulness and its added value in comparison with already existing techniques for documenting SPI case studies. Moreover, problems found by the authors during the application of iChart Technique and lessons learned gathered from the experience are also presented.

5.1 Evaluation of Usefulness and Added Value

Case study chart provides the most relevant information for benchmarking related to targets and benefits of process improvement programs.

Although, the most part of current SPI case studies have a predefined format (Background (Organization Background, Process Improvement History), CMMI-Based Process Improvement, Results Performance), this format is very generic and the content of each section is heterogeneous, being to much complicated by means of a simple reading exercise, to have a common insight of case study.

In this sense, iChart provides a formalization basis to provide homogeneous information of SPI based on objective evidences. Moreover, iChart provides an easy way to compare different SPI initiatives in the same or different organizations.

ICharts also can be used as a tool to benchmark SPI case studies, because schedules are completely comparable. In order to compare indicators, it is essential that two iCharts indicators will be comparable, concretely, they will express measures of the same type; i.e.: investment or organizational performance indicators, etc.

Finally, it is important to mention that authors have applied this technique during the Initiating Phase of a SPI program. The main benefits if its use in this phase were related to:

- Enable senior management to understand the need for software process improvement (SPI), commit to a SPI program, and define the context for SPI.
- Recognize and understand the stimulus for improvement.

5.2 Problems Found and Lessons Learned

The main lessons learned and problems found during iChart application are:

- It is difficult to become an idea of all the history of the case without a first reading for being introduced to the whole case study. The greater effort consists of "finding out" the chronology of events and activities. The iCharts help to order the main SPI activities or events.

- It is difficult to locate in the time the events and to relate them to the improvement indicators to become an idea of the times of maturation and consolidation of the improvements. In this sense, the authors are developing inside a SPI value management framework to isolate causes and effects, using Activity Based Costing models. In other ongoing SPI programs, the authors used cause-effect diagrams adapted to iCharts (Ishikawa diagrams, fishbone diagrams). It is important to indicate, that in the case of translating existing SPI case studies to iCharts, if the original case study does not provide base information, of course, this cause-effect relation cannot be derived;
- Sometimes, it is difficult or impossible to make a graph of the Results Performance. Moreover, the Results Performance is very heterogeneous from case to case.
- Those derived from not having the suitable tool. For the first cases, Microsoft Project was used for describing the project journey and Microsoft Excel was used to compile and present information related to indicators.

Currently, there is a software tool available to apply iChart technique, which main functionalities are:

- Creation an SPI improvement program, including the introduction of the iChart contextual information, that is: type of organization, dimension in terms of employees, types of software-services provided, Organization's SPI Objectives and indicators measuring the consecution of the improvement objectives
- Management of the evolution of the improvement programs, including information related to actual activities executed during the improvement program and temporal evolution of the indicators selected.
- Information search capabilities in order to find case studies with similar types of organization; improvement objectives or indicators to measure the benefit of the improvement program.

The functionalities that will be available at the next version will be related to simulation and capabilities to compare SPI programs.

6   Conclusions and Future Work

iChart technique to formalize the information enclosed in an SPI case study. This technique has been applied to formalize the information of several pre-existing SPI case studies.

iChart technique can be used as a tool to validate the quality of a software process improvement case study provided by a company.

Moreover, iChart has been applied to create new SPI case studies and it can be very useful as a simple and costless way to create standardized SPI case studies.

A validation of the application of iChart technique has been performed and authors have concluded that this technique provides the key information required by senior management to analyze other initiatives in order to take decisions related to: the investments required by an improvement program; and the benefits that can be obtained. This key information is: summarized information of the history of the SPI program; hey success factors of the SPI program; most relevant events of the SPI program; improvement investments and actions; and cvlues and evolution of improvement indicators.

The future research works in this area are directed to design a framework for SPI value management that will enable to:

- Increase the understanding and transparency of cost, risks and benefits resulting in much better informed management decisions.
- Increase the probability of selecting investments that have the potential to generate the highest return.
- Increase the likelihood of success of executing selected investments such that they achieve or exceed their potential return.
- Reduce the surprises relative to SPI cost and delivery, increasing business value, reducing unnecessary costs and increasing the overall level of confidence in SPI.
- Reduce the risk of failure, especially high-impact failure.

References

[1] CMMI Product Team: CMMI for Development, Version 1.2, CMU/SEI-2006-TR-008 (Agosto 2006)
[2] Cuevas Agustín, G.: Gestión del proceso software. Editorial Centro de Estudios Ramón Areces SA (2002)
[3] Capell, P.: Benefits of Improvement Efforts. SEI SPECIAL REPORT CMU/SEI-2004-SR-010 (Septiembre 2004)
[4] Ferguson, P., et al.: SEI TR- 99-TR-027. Software Process Improvement Works! AIS (1999)
[5] Flyvbjerg, B.: Five Misunderstandings About Case Study Research. Qualitative Inquiry 12(2), 219–245 (2006)
[6] Gibson, D.L., Goldenson, D.R., Kost, K.: Performance Results of CMMI-Based Process Improvement. SEI TECHNICAL REPORT CMU/SEI-2006-TR-004 (August 2006)
[7] Goldenson, D.R., Gibson, D.L.: Demonstrating the Impact and Benefits of CMMI: An Update and Preliminary Result. SEI SPECIAL REPORT CMU/SEI-2003-SR-009 (Octubre 2003)
[8] Herbsleb, J., Carleton, A., Rozum, J., Siegel, J., Zubrow, D.: Benefits of CMM-Based Software Process Improvement: Initial Results (CMU/SEI-94-TR-013). Software Engineering Institute. Carnegie Mellon University (August 1994)
[9] ISO/IEC 15504-4:2004: Information Technology. Process Assessment. Guidance on use for process improvement and process capability determination (2004)
[10] ISO/IEC 12207: Information technology- Software life cycle processes
[11] McFeeley, R.: IDEAL: A User's Guide for Software Process Improvement (CMU/SEI-96-HB-001, ADA305472). Software Engineering Institute, Carnegie Mellon University, Pittsburgh, PA (1996)
[12] Mutafelija, B., Stromberg, H.: Sistematic Process Improvement using ISO 9001:2000 and CMMI. ArtechHouse Pub. (2003)

Organizational Learning Through Project Postmortem Reviews – An Explorative Case Study

Torgeir Dingsøyr[1], Nils Brede Moe[1], Joost Schalken[2], and Tor Stålhane[3]

[1] SINTEF Information and Communication Technology
[2] Vrije Universiteit Amsterdam
jjp.schalken@few.vu.nl
[3] Department of Computer and Information Science,
Norwegian University of Science and Technology

Abstract. A central issue in knowledge management and software process improvement is to learn from experience. In software engineering, most experience is gathered in projects, which makes project experience a prime source for learning. Many companies conduct postmortem reviews, but we have found few companies that analyze the outcome of several reviews to facilitate learning on an organizational level. This paper reports an explorative study of what we can learn from analyzing postmortem review reports of twelve projects in a medium-size software company.

1 Introduction

Knowledge management has received much attention in the software engineering field during the past years, as a promising field for software process improvement with focus on increasing quality and decrease costs in software development.

Software process improvement has its roots in bottom-up improvement philosophies like total quality management, which has been tailored to software engineering in the Quality Improvement Paradigm [1], and in top-down standardization approaches like the ISO 9001 and the Software Engineering Institute's Capability Maturity Model [15].

A common factor in knowledge management and software process improvement is to learn from past successes and failures in order to improve future software development. Experience Factory [2] has been a central term in focusing organizational learning on improving software development processes.

Most companies that develop software organize the development in projects. In the Experience Factory, the projects are seen as the main arena for learning, and experience which appears in the projects is to be shared with other projects. Experience from completed projects can be collected through postmortem reviews [5] or project retrospectives [11].

Postmortem reviews can have a learning effect on an individual level, team-level and also on an organizational level. There are few empirical studies addressing the organizational level [6].

P. Abrahamsson et al. (Eds.): EuroSPI 2007, LNCS 4764, pp. 136–147, 2007.

1.1 Organizational Learning and Postmortem Reviews

Garvin defines a learning organization as "an organization skilled at creating, acquiring, and transferring knowledge, and at modifying its behavior to reflect new knowledge and insight" [9]. Huber gives advice on what managers can do to make their organizations more "learning" [10]:

- Learn from experience - systematically capture, store, interpret and distribute relevant experience gathered from projects; and also to investigate new ideas by carrying out experiments.
- Use a computer-based organizational memory - to capture knowledge obtained from experts to spread it throughout the organization.

One way to collect experience from projects is to perform postmortem reviews [3, 5]. By a postmortem review, we mean a collective learning activity which can be organized for projects either when they end a phase or are terminated. The main motivation is to reflect on what happened in the project in order to improve future practice – for the individuals that have participated in the project and for the organization as a whole. The tangible outcome of a meeting is a postmortem report.

Researchers in organizational learning sometimes use the term "reflective practice", which can be defined as "the practice of periodically stepping back to ponder on the meaning to self and others in one's immediate environment about what has recently transpired. It illuminates what has been experienced by both self and others, providing a basis for future action" [16]. This involves uncovering and making explicit the results of planning, observation and achieved practice. It can lead to understanding of experiences that have been overlooked in practice.

1.2 Related Work

Most work on organizational learning or knowledge management in software engineering address technical systems for distributing experience in an organization [6]. There is little work on the effects of gathering experience on software development issues over time.

Schalken et al. [17] reports on an analysis of 55 postmortem reports from an information technology department of a large financial institution with 1500 employees in The Netherlands. The 55 postmortem reports were selected from more than 600 evaluation reports on completed projects based on how the projects scored on a selected set of success criteria. The work reports candidate relationships between project characteristics and project success criteria.

Dingsøyr et al. [7] studied the difference between experience reports and postmortem review reports in two medium-sized companies in Norway. They found that the postmortem reports and the experience reports documented very little of the same experience. Experience reports written by project managers tended to focus on contract issues, design and technology, while the postmortem reports tended to focus more on experience related to implementation, administration, developers and maintenance.

The rest of this paper is organized as follows: We first describe the research questions, the research method, data collection and data analysis. Then we present findings from our explorative study, and finally discuss our research questions and conclude.

2 Research Questions and Method

The research reported here is an explorative case study [21] of twelve projects in a medium-size software company. We ask the following research question: what can we learn from analyzing postmortem reports that are accumulated over time? More specifically, we ask:

1. What characterizes the projects selected for postmortem review?
2. Do information sources provide consistent information about the projects? If not, how can this be explained?
3. Do we get similar results when analyzing data about projects with different perspectives? If not, how can the discrepancies be explained?
4. Which challenges should be considered when analyzing postmortem data from an academic perspective and from an industry perspective?

We now describe the company chosen for the study, what data we collected and how the data was analyzed.

2.1 The Case Company

Kongsberg Spacetec AS ("Spacetec") of Norway is one of the leading producers of receiving stations for data from meteorological and Earth observation satellites. Spacetec has expertise in electronics, software development and applications. 80% of the 60 employees in the company have a master's degree in physics or computer science.

A change from engineering projects to developing generic products through internally financed and managed projects, and the fact that several of their big projects had problems, motivated Spacetec to focus on learning from experience. The company has conducted postmortem reviews since 2000.

2.2 Data Collection

The data used in this paper are collected from twelve software development projects which were finished between 2000 and 2005 at Spacetec. The projects that are analyzed are not a random sample of the company's projects, but projects singled out because they had cost overruns – 8 to 155 percent, see Table 1.

We have used three data sources which we briefly describe:

Postmortem review reports. Three of the reports were written by researchers participating in carrying out the review, while nine were written by the company's quality department. In Table 1, the project overrun is given as a percentage, size is either large (>5000 h) or medium (<5000, >1000), duration in years and we have indicated whether we have an extensive (long) or brief (short) postmortem report. The postmortems were carried out after project completion for 10 projects, and after finishing the main part of the project for the remaining two projects.

Three of the postmortem reports were long reports written by researchers (17-23 pages). The researchers used the following, postmortem review process [3]:

• Use the KJ [18] process for brainstorming to identify what went well and what when wrong in the project.

Table 1. Projects selected for postmortem review

#	Overrun (%)	Project size	Duration	Report
1	99	Large	3Y	Short
2	31	Large	3Y	Short
3	155	Large	0,5Y	Short
4	8	Large	0,5Y	Long
5	15	Large	1Y	Short
6	100	Large	1Y	Short
7	114	Medium	1Y	Short
8	85	Large	1,5Y	Short
9	18	Large	3Y	Long
10	23	Large	2Y	Short
11	79	Medium	1Y	Long
12	79	Large	4Y	Short

- Root cause analyses [19] to identify the root causes for the most important reasons for success and for failures.
- Prioritize improvement actions based on the results from the root cause analysis.
- Write a postmortem report, summing up all important points. In addition, the meetings were taped and transcribed as part of the report.
- The report was reviewed by all participants and misunderstandings were corrected.

Nine reports were written by the company's quality department. They wrote short reports (3-8 pages) and their process differed in that they:

- Only collected the negative experiences, because of the project sample and time limitation.
- Did not tape the meeting and later make a transcript.
- Did not circulate the postmortem report for commenting and to correct possible misunderstandings.

Questionnaire-based evaluation. This was sent to two members of the quality department as well as the person responsible for all software projects, and the person responsible for the software products. This was done in order to get an opinion on the project quality as perceived from these roles. We asked them to rank the projects according to the following factors: Strategic importance, Customer satisfaction, Software quality and Software productivity. In addition, we asked them to indicate what they thought was most important in the project: Quality, productivity or customer satisfaction. We also gathered information on the project size, duration and project cost overrun.

Workshop. This was done with five persons from the company, who were either from the quality department, or project managers from the projects who also had participated in one or more projects as developers. All participants had participated in one or more postmortem reviews on the selected projects.

In the workshop we asked them to express which events or "project factors" they thought occurred most frequently in the projects under study, and which factors would correlate with productivity, overrun, quality and customer satisfaction. Further, we asked them what they thought would be the dominant factors within a classification framework for analysis: "knowledge", "management", "deliverables", "people effects" and "process effects". Finally, we asked each participant to comment on the correlations between causes and effects found in a statistical analysis on project factors and success factors.

2.3 Data Analysis

To analyze the data from the postmortem reports, we chose to 1) Code the reports into a predefined set of project factor categories and 2) analyze the most occurring factors through a bottom-up qualitative analysis, inspired by grounded theory [20]. We describe these two steps in the following:

Step 1: To code the data from the postmortem reviews, we used a predefined framework inspired by McConnel [14], which covers most topics that are relevant in a postmortem review.

We coded all negative project factors from the postmortem reviews by the categories listed in the coding framework (axial coding). Each review was coded by two researchers independently, and we discussed disagreements until we reached consensus on the coding.

This coding resulted in a matrix with project factors and occurrences in projects. We combined this matrix with success factors from the quality department and from the questionnaire-based evaluation.

Step 2: For factors that happened in more than nine projects in our sample, we did a bottom-up analysis of the text by importing the text into the NVivo tool for analysis of qualitative data and used open coding. Based on the researchers' experience and knowledge, both of software development in general and of this special company, each of the main categories were split up into five to ten new categories. During the coding process, some of the items in the postmortem reports were moved from one main category to another.

3 Results

We now present the key findings from our explorative study. First we present findings from the quantitative analysis and then the qualitative analysis:

3.1 Quantitative Analysis

Qualitative information from postmortem reports was combined with quantitative information, which was obtained separately from the company. As the company had no formal metrics program in place, we relied on subjective measures to get an insight into the quantitative performance of each project. From the development manager, product manager and the QA staff (2 employees), we obtained rankings and ratings of the projects on project focus, strategic importance, customer satisfaction, software quality, and productivity.

A postmortem collects data on many project factors. If we are going to combine these data and, in addition, combine them with other data that the company collects,

Table 2. Projects with project factors, resulting from step 1 of the coding. Projects are ranked by the number of negative project factors registered in postmortem report.

Project #	count of negative remarks	cooperationit.neg	processproductivity.neg	knowledgeeffects.neg	validationtool.neg	hardwarecomp.neg	subcontractor.neg	cooperation.neg	teamstability.neg	validationprocess.neg	qa.neg	tooleffects.neg	commitment.neg	techdesign.neg	requirements.neg	softwaredesign.neg	processoutcomes.neg	effectsqa.neg	peopleeffects.neg	deliverables.neg	management.neg	knowledge.neg	processeffects.neg
11	5						1		1			1						1					1
10	7							1		1		1		1							1	1	1
7	8						1		1			1			1					1	1	1	1
4	9				1					1		1			1				1	1	1	1	1
6	9					1				1		1				1			1	1	1	1	1
9	10							1		1			1				1	1	1	1	1	1	1
2	11							1		1				1		1	1	1	1	1	1	1	1
3	12							1			1		1		1	1	1	1	1	1	1	1	1
8	13							1			1		1	1	1	1	1	1	1	1	1	1	1
5	13								1		1		1	1	1	1	1	1	1	1	1	1	1
1	13								1		1		1	1	1	1	1	1	1	1	1	1	1
12	13								1		1		1	1	1	1	1	1	1	1	1	1	1
SUM		0	0	0	1	1	2	5	5	5	5	5	6	6	7	7	7	8	9	10	11	11	12

we need to use every opportunity to check their quality. Important points to check are for instance whether a participant always records the same information in the same way –intra-rater reliability – and whether different participants record the same information in the same way – inter-rater reliability. If the data that are supposed to agree really do, it increase our confidence in the results, thus increasing the confidence we can have in them and the value they will have when we use them in a decision.

As a basis for this we have used two analysis methods: Kendall's τ [20], which measures inter-rater reliability, and the Krippendorff's α [12, 13], which is a measure of the agreement between two or more classification schemes or classifiers– the intra-rater reliability.

To understand the impact of project characteristics (the project factors) on the failure of projects (as indicated by the success factors), we need to do more than merely collect data. We can gain understanding by studying the regularities in absent project factors and the resulting values for the success factors of these projects.

To study the regularities, we use R to construct a matrix of correlation coefficients between project factors and success factors.

The correlations in Table 3 are based on the factors, as reported by the Quality Assurance staff. Only correlations which are significant at the 5% level are indicated.

We looked at the data from the postmortems for the following success factors:

• Project focus – what was the main aim or goal for this project?
• The satisfaction score – how satisfied were the customer?
• The productivity score – how efficient were the teams when working at the project?
• The quality score – what was the product's quality?

The project focus factor was left out since this measure had neither intra-rater nor inter-rater reliability.

When we look at the customer satisfaction score we find a τ of -0.6, which indicates that satisfaction is an intra-rater reliable score but we find a Krippendorff's α of -0.3, indicating a low inter-rater reliability.

If we instead look at the productivity score we find a τ of -0.5, which indicates that satisfaction is an intra-rater reliable score and a Krippendorff's α of -0.8, indicating a high inter-rater reliability.

Lastly, we look at the quality score. Here we find a τ of -0.8, which indicates that satisfaction is an intra-rater reliable score but a Krippendorff's α of -0.3, again indicating a low inter-rater reliability.

Table 3. Correlation table based on factors reported by the Quality Assurance staff

	Productivity	Overrun	Quality	Satisfaction
1.1 Knowledge *				
Project management			-0.57	
1.2 Cooperation *	0.58			0.49
1.3 Commitment *			-0.57	
1.4 Team stability *				
2.1 Management process *				
Inadequate initial project planning		0.64		
Inadequate contract	-0.42			
Missing or inadequate priorities	-0.52		-0.57	
Inadequate project control		0.46		
2.2 Subcontractor management *				
2.4 Requirements engineering *				
2.5 Technical design *				
2.6 QA *		0.69		
3.1 Validation and Verificaton *		0.50		
4.1 Software design *	-0.51			-0.54
5.3 Hardware components*		-0.50		
A.1 Process outcomes *				
Resources	-0.45			
Low priority				-0.50
Design	-0.45			
A.2 Deliverables *	-0.68			
Internal product quality judged by the		0.77		
Customer relations	-0.45		-0.62	
B.1 Process *				
B.2 QA *			-0.70	
B.3 People *				
Lack of technical skills		-0.46		0.52
Inexperienced project participants		0.52		
Inexperienced project manager		0.45		
B.4 Tooling *	-0.58	0.46		

As investigators, we were curious to know whether the correlations between project factors and success factors, as calculated in Table 3, bear any resemblance on the real state of practice within the company. Unfortunately there is no such independent, objective data about the relationship between project factors (the causes of the problems) and success factors (e.g. productivity and satisfaction). Lacking objective data that can be used to verify the correlation matrix, we take a triangulation approach.

In a workshop at the company, we asked developers and managers to give an independent assessment of the impact of project factors on success factors. We used the results of this workshop to see how well the answers generated by the objective, quantitative approach matched the subjective opinions from the people involved. This comparison leads to a ranking of correlations vs workshop scores, which we compare using correlations.

When we look at the customer satisfaction score the workshop votes for which project factors that are important in order to develop a product that satisfies the customer and compare this to the correlations, we find that factors like management process and requirements engineering both are considered to have a high importance but do not correlate with the customer satisfaction at all.

If we instead look at the productivity score we observe that the workshop votes for which project factors that are important in order to get a high productivity, we find that factors identified by the correlation matrix and the factors identified by the developers have a Kendall's τ of -0.5.

Lastly, we look at the quality score. When we look at the developers' votes for which project factors that are important in order to develop a high quality product and compare this to the correlations, we find that the factor identified by the correlation matrix and the factors identified by the developers have a Kendall's τ of -0.3.

We see from this analysis that only for the success factor productivity the insights of the correlation table match the insights from the workshop. This might be explained by the fact that productivity is a reliable measure (high intra- and inter-rater reliability), whereas satisfaction and quality measures are unreliable.

3.2 Qualitative Analysis

The five categories that were coded in almost all projects (the five factors on the right in Table 2) were analyzed in detail by a qualitative analysis. The categories were "People effects", "Deliverables", "Management", "Knowledge" and "Process effects". In the following, we discuss what subcategories we found in these main categories.

In the material that was coded as "People effects", we found the subcategory "lack of technical skills" to be present in five projects. Further, "people unavailable" was a negative issue in four projects, inexperienced project participants in two and also inexperienced project manager in two projects.

An analysis of the category "Deliverables" revealed that the product quality received a negative evaluation by the customer in two projects, and by the company itself in three projects – two project that had not got a negative customer evaluation. In one project, this was described as "system not ready for delivery". Also, seven projects mention customer relations as a negative issue related to the deliverables, like "the customer expects to get a lot for free".

The category coded as "Management" was split into "inadequate initial project planning" which occurred in six projects. An example of a statement related to this was "not planned for unforeseen expenses and work". "Bad estimation process" also occurred in six projects. An example statement of this is "risk not taken into account when estimating". The subcategories "missing or inadequate priorities" and "inadequate project control" occurred in five projects, "inadequate project management" and "inadequate risk analysis" in four projects, "inadequate contract" in three projects. "Process not followed" occurred in two projects.

A lack of "Knowledge" in the projects was mainly related to project management knowledge. "We lack knowledge on planning" was a statement in one report. This subcategory was found in six of the eleven projects. Knowledge related to technology was seen as a problem in four of the eleven projects, for example "little experience with antenna installation". Lack of knowledge of the customer was seen as a problem in only one project.

For the "Process effects", we found four subcategories. Process effects related to requirements was mentioned in four projects, related to project management in three projects, external relations and resources in two projects and design, low priority and unclear process were negative issues in one project.

When we asked the participant in the workshop to indicate which events (or project factors) they thought would occur most frequently, they ranked them as shown in Table 4, together with the occurrence taken from the postmortem reports. Some factors that occurred frequently in the reports matched the belief amongst the participants: process effects and management and deliverables were among the top in both ratings. However, process outcome, cooperation, team stability and validation process were factors that were believed to be fairly frequent, but only seldomly appeared in the reports.

Table 4. Reported and believed ranking of factors for the selected projects

Event	Report ranking	Workshop ranking	Rank difference
Process effects	1	1	0
Knowledge	1	10	9
Management	3	1	2
People effects	4	10	6
Deliverables	4	4	0
QA effects	6	13	7
Process outcome	7	1	6
Software design	7	13	6
Tech design	9	10	1
Requirements engineering	9	4	5
Tool effects	11	13	2
QA	11	13	2
Validation process	11	4	7
Team stability	11	4	7
Commitment	11	9	2
Cooperation	11	4	7

The workshop participants commented that the large difference for "knowledge" was that the postmortem reports were written at a time when there were many new employees in the company. Another comment was that developing software for space applications, there is always new technology involved, which means that there must always be time allocated for learning. At the time of the workshop "Knowledge" was not seen as a problem anymore, but as a constant challenge in all new projects.

4 Discussion

In this article, our main research question is: what can we learn from analyzing postmortem reports that have accumulated over time? We discuss our research question through our more detailed questions in the following:

1. What characterizes the projects selected for postmortem review?

From the qualitative analysis, we found five main characteristics of the projects selected for postmortem review. All postmortem reports recorded negative experiences related to lack of knowledge, people effects, process effects, deliverables and management (See Table 4).

If we are even more precise and focus on the projects that have the largest cost overruns, we can identify what characterize these projects. According to the statistical analyses on the relation between project factors and cost overrun, the following characteristics/failures lead to the highest cost overrun: inadequate initial project planning, inadequate quality assurance, insufficient validation and verification, poor design and code quality (as noted by internal product quality judged by the workshop or the company's management) and inexperienced project participants.

This can be an important finding in order for the company to focus it's software process improvement initiatives.

2. Do information sources provide consistent information about the projects? If not, how can this be explained?

We compared the results from the qualitative analysis with perceptions of the workshop participants. The following project factors had a short distance in ranking between reports and workshop (2 or less):

• Process effects, Deliverables, Tech design, Management, Tool effects, QA, Commitment

The following factors occurred frequently in the reports, but were not ranked high in the workshop:

• Knowledge, QA effects

The following factors occurred infrequently in the reports, but were ranked high in the workshop:

• Validation process, Team stability, Cooperation

As for the quantitative data, except for productivity, where Krippendorff's $\alpha=0.76$, the other subjective ratings on success factors (quality and customer satisfaction) shows that the data are unreliable. For quality and customer satisfaction, the ratings differ wildly between the different observers. This difference in ratings, or lack in interrater agreement, means that the measurements should not be used.

3. Do we get similar results when analyzing the data with different perspectives? If not, how can this be explained?

There are notable differences between the results of the quantitative analysis and the workshop. Part of this difference might be explained by the fact that the data for the quantitative analysis originated from management, whereas the input for workshop came from both management and developers.

4. Which challenges should be considered when analyzing postmortem data (from an academic perspective and from an industry perspective)?

Having observed the discrepancies in point of view between different stakeholders with respect to project success (such as quality and customer satisfaction) it helps to more clearly define the key success indicators of a project. This will help both in achieving the desired results and in analyzing these results afterwards. If at all possible, we should define objective measurement procedures for quality, productivity and customer satisfaction.

5 Conclusion

We have analyzed twelve postmortem review reports from a medium-size software company in a qualitative and quantitative analysis, focusing on negative experiences. In addition, we have gathered opinions on the projects analyzed through a questionnaire and through a workshop discussion. We have identified some characteristics of the projects selected for postmortem reviews. Qualitative and quantitative findings indicate different characteristics. We have also found that it was little agreement on project success factors, which made statistical analysis challenging.

For the company, we have identified some issues that employees who participated in workshops were not aware of. We have also found that some issues identified in the postmortem reports were no longer relevant. This emphasizes the importance on multiple data sources in software process improvement.

We have found that analysis of postmortem data gives new insight into projects than what company participants think. However, a broad explorative analysis such as we have performed comes with a cost, which is probably too high for small and medium-size software companies. We should seek more efficient ways in analyzing data from larger collection of software projects.

Acknowledgement

This work was supported by the Research Council of Norway under Grant 174390/I40, as a part of the Evidence-based Improvement of Software Engineering.

References

[1] Victor, R.B.: Quantitative Evaluation of Software Engineering Methodology. In: Proceedings of the First Pan Pacific Computer Conference, Melbourne, Australia (1985)
[2] Victor, R.B., Caldiera, G., Dieter Rombach, H.: The Experience Factory. In: Marciniak, J.J. (ed.) Encyclopedia of Software Engineering, vol. 1, pp. 469–476. John Wiley, Chichester (1994)
[3] Birk, A., Dingsøyr, T., Stålhane, T.: Postmortem: Never leave a project without it. IEEE Software, special issue on knowledge management in software engineering 19(3), 43–45 (2002)
[4] Cohen, J.: A coefficient of agreement for nominal scales. Educational and Psychological Measurement 20, 37–46 (1960)

[5] Dingsøyr, T.: Postmortem reviews: Purpose and Approaches in Software Engineering. Information and Software Technology 47(5), 293–303 (2005)

[6] Dingsøyr, T., Conradi, R.: A Survey of Case Studies of the Use of Knowledge Management in Software Engineering. International Journal of Software Engineering and Knowledge Engineering 12(4), 391–414 (2002)

[7] Dingsøyr, T., Moe, N.B., Nytrø, Ø.: Augmenting Experience Reports with Lightweight Postmortem Reviews. In: Bomarius, F., Komi-Sirviö, S. (eds.) PROFES 2001. LNCS, vol. 2188, pp. 167–181. Springer, Heidelberg (2001)

[8] El Emam, K.: Benchmarking Kappa: Interrater Agreement in Software Process Assessments. Empirical Software Engineering 4(2), 113–133 (1999)

[9] Garvin, D.: Building a Learning Organization. Harvard Business Review, pp. 78–91 (July-August 1993)

[10] Huber, G.P.: Organizational Learning: The Contributing Processes and the Literatures. Organizational Science 2(1), 88–115 (1991)

[11] Norman, L.K.: Project retrospectives: a handbook for team reviews. Dorset House Publishing, New York (2001)

[12] Krippendorff, K.: Content Analysis, an Introduction to Its Methodology. Sage Publications, Thousand Oaks, CA (1980)

[13] Krippendorff, K.: Computing Krippendorff's alpha-reliability (2006)

[14] McConnell, S.: Rapid Development: Taming Wild Software Schedules. Microsoft Press, Redmond, WA, USA (1996)

[15] Paulk, M.C., Weber, C.V., Curtis, B., Chrissis, M.B.: The Capability maturity model: guidelines for improving the software process. Addison-Wesley, Boston (1995)

[16] Raelin, J.A.: Public Reflection as the Basis of Learning. Management Learning 32(1), 11–30 (2001)

[17] Schalken, J.J.P., Brinkkemper, S., van Vliet, J.C.: A Method to Draw Lessons from Project Postmortem Databases. Software Process: Improvement and Practice 79(1), 120–131 (2006)

[18] Scupin, R.: The KJ Method: A Technique for Analyzing Data Derived from Japanese ethnology. Human Organization 56(2), 233–237 (1997)

[19] Straker, D.: A Toolbook for Quality Improvement and Problem Solving. Prentice hall International (UK) Limited (1995)

[20] Strauss, A., Corbin, J.: Basics of Qualitative Research, 2nd edn. Sage Publications, Thousand Oaks (1998)

[21] Yin, R.K.: Case Study Research: design and methods, 5th edn. Sage Publications, Thousand Oaks (2003)

Modelling Software Processes as Human-Centered Adaptive Work Systems

Levent Yilmaz

M&SNet: Auburn Modeling and Simulation Group
yilmaz@auburn.edu
Computer Science and Software Engineering
Auburn University
Auburn, AL, USA

Abstract. The lack of conceptualization and inclusion of human, social, and organizational dynamics in software process simulation models is a critical obstacle in (1) exploring the impact of socio-technical dimensions in software development and (2) measuring the performance of software processes. This paper presents a conceptual multi-resolution modeling and simulation framework that delineates various dimensions of organizational behavior as they relate to software development. The framework conceptualizes software development as a transformation system from the perspective of knowledge acquisition and cognitive systems engineering. Explicit distinctions between the strategy, operational, and technical views are clearly presented. Specifically, the paper formulates a preliminary conceptual model and elaborates on design space of the operational and technical views that focus on organizational, social, and human dynamics in process performance modeling and simulation.

1 Introduction

Software processes entail a coherent set of policies, procedures, technologies that are used within an organizational structure to produce and maintain software products (Yilmaz and Phillips 2006). The process involves knowledge acquisition activity phases, during which teams of engineers collaborate and coordinate within the constraints imposed by the management, as well as organizational norms, technology, culture, and policies. The human activity is at the core of the software development practice, as decisions and control actions are not taken by organizations or systems, but rather by a number of decision makers carrying out their activities at various levels and locations within the work system (Constantine 1993) that involves people engaging in activities over time.

Existing simulation-based exploration of dynamics of software processes often involve focusing on flows of products and data through the process using discrete-event and continuous models (Abdel-Hamid and Madnick 1991). However, the lack of conceptualization and incorporation of strategic change, adaptive human, team, organizational, and cultural factors into models of software processes pose special problems:

- *Software processes are goal-directed and adaptive*: In well-adapted software development organizations goals and constraints are often

P. Abrahamsson et al. (Eds.): EuroSPI 2007, LNCS 4764, pp. 148–159, 2007.
© Springer-Verlag Berlin Heidelberg 2007

implicit and embedded in the work practice and norms associated with the organization. Goals vary, requirements change, and employee turnover is common. Hence, in a dynamically changing environment, an effective organizational work depends on self-organizing and adaptive mechanisms that are in place to change properties of the process to meet the current needs.

- *Processes improve over time*: In software development, management frequently modifies the structure and mechanisms of the process to keep some measure (e.g., defect density) related to the relevant performance objective (e.g., reliability) near an optimum. Control of adaptation, however, is distributed across all teams, engineers, and organizational subsystems. A useful and credible model for the analysis of the process and prediction of responses to changes in the circumstances must reflect the mechanisms underlying the evolution of work practice.

- *Software processes are human-centered work practices*: Human actors that manage and coordinate software processes are adaptive and goal-directed agents. What people actually do, how they communicate and collaborate, how they solve problems, resolve conflicts, and learn behavior matters in the outcome of a project. Therefore, simulating human activities requires modeling communication, collaboration, team work, conflict resolution, and tool and technology usage. Decision making strategies and mental models of humans, as well as various forms of team archetypes (Yilmaz and Phillips 2006) influence the performance and effectiveness of software processes.

Given the above observations, the position advocated in this paper is that there is a need for a software process simulation framework that represents not only technical activities, policies, and procedures, but also the resources, preferences, and cognition of staff members, together with functional and social organization and strategic management, all in unified and coherent terms. A cross disciplinary framework should support coordinating findings and models from several fields.

Various researchers have developed alternative work system modeling and design approaches. Business or enterprise process modeling is an active area of research that uses formal specifications of business process to facilitate business process reengineering (Mayer et al. 1998). There exist cognitive modeling frameworks that are based on unified theories of cognition to explore mental processes (Newell 1990). The field of distributed artificial intelligence provided contributions in modeling collaboration of teams of people in complex uncertain environments. Advances in computational organization theory (Carley 1999) enable modeling organizational structure and dynamics in terms of intelligent agent organizations. Such models enable exploring the impact of human and social dynamics on the effectiveness and efficiency of organizations. Human-centered work practice modeling is also advocated to improve fidelity of simulations using activity theory. This paper builds on the observations that depict software development as an adaptive human-centered work system to develop a framework that integrates operational (human, social, and organizational dynamics) and strategic levels in a multiresolution multiaspect multimodeling context. Specifically, the framework presents the conceptualization of the critical elements of each level (e.g., operation, strategic), as well as different aspects that simultaneously co-exist (e.g., social dimension, human behavior dimension, organizational dimension) in the context of software processes.

The rest of the paper is organized as follows. In section 2, an organization-theoretic framework that explicitly delineates the following assumptions is presented: (1) organizational structure, functions, and work activities imposed by the process technology and (2) social work organization. Section 3 focuses on the issues that pertain to modeling human behavior. Finally, in section 4, the paper concludes by discussing potential avenues of further research.

2 Modeling Processes as Human-Centered Work Systems – The Cognitive Systems Engineering Perspective

Software development is a knowledge acquisition activity (Armour 2003) that involves the transformation of the user needs into a software product that realizes the requirements elicited from these needs. Figure 1 depicts the elements of the proposed organization-theoretic framework for software process simulation.

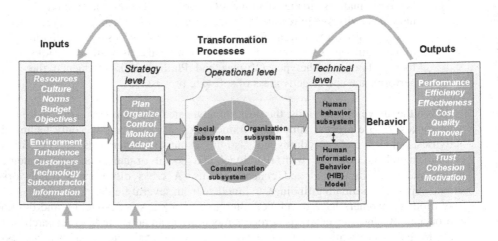

Fig. 1. Organization-theoretic Framework for Software Process Simulation

The transformation processes are influenced by inputs such as resources, the organizational culture (i.e., decision making styles – consensus vs. centralized), norms, values, budget, and objectives. Objectives include product differentiation, innovation, market expansion, and risk reduction. Environmental inputs entail turbulence (e.g., task uncertainty, turnover, requirements change), the impact of customers, technology, and available information regarding the attainment of objectives. The inputs are transformed by a multiresolution process. Three levels interplay to represent the organizational, human, and social dynamics that shape the behavior during software development.

- The *strategy* level can be viewed as the meta-level control mechanism that models the behavior of the management. It is responsible for monitoring, controlling, and adapting the operational level via dynamic model updating. It is also responsible to (re)organize the social and physical structure of the organization.
- The *operational* level consists of three dimensions that collectively model the process, associated activities and tasks, the social and physical structure and interaction in the organization, and the communication mechanism among the actors that carry out the process.
- The *technical* level refers to the human-activity level. In particular, the human activity is based on the Human Information Behavior (HIB) perspective (Wilson 2000) that examines the human behavior in relation to sources and channels of information via information seeking, searching, and uses mechanisms. The knowledge acquisition view of software development in conjunction with the human information behavior model provides an accurate representation of how humans actually work in practice. The HIB model is supported by the human behavior subsystem. Modeling personality traits, cognitive complexity factors (Yilmaz and Oren 2007), as well as affective factors enable representing individual differences to bring variability and credibility to process simulations.

The outputs depicted by the framework include performance metrics such as productivity (e.g., effectiveness and efficiency), project cost and duration, product quality, and turnover. Attitudinal behavior outputs measure engineering team and human cognition factors such as trust, motivation, and cohesion, which further impact the inputs and the transformation processes.

2.1 Operational Level – Organizational Subsystem

The formal organizational subsystem defines such things as specification of workflow, activities, work breakdown and organization structure (including authority), task structure (representation of formal requirements), and job satisfaction. Figure 2 presents the conceptual elements of the organization subsystem of the operational level of transformation system shown in Figure 1. The work domain model specifies the means-ends structure of the process in terms of goals/constraints, abstract functions, general functions, and work activities. The highest level of abstraction in the means-ends structure is the set of constraints and goals, which are the policies that govern the interaction between the work system and its environment. For software development processes, productivity, cost, quality, as well as production within the constraints of the financial resources are potential constraints. Abstract functions of the organizational system in our context denote the representation of concepts that are necessary for allocating resources to general functions and the activities. Departmental functions such as quality assurance, product development, controlling, planning, and human resource management (Abdel-Hamid and Madnic 1990 pp. 22) are abstract functions, for which general work activities are defined. General work functions are at a lower-level of abstraction and are defined in terms of activities and task sequence of groups and individual agents.

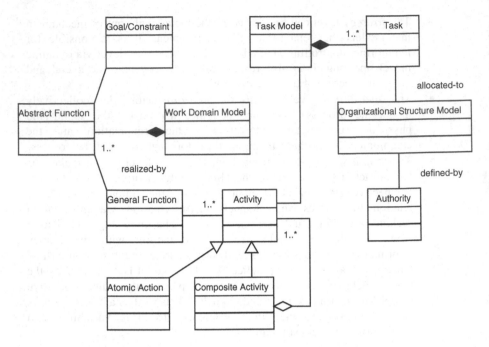

Fig. 2. Conceptual Model for the Organization Subsystem

The organizational structure model depicts the physical form and configuration of the organization. The set of linkages that connect agents, tasks, and resources constitute the structure of an organization. There can be many structures. The authority (e.g., centralized vs. decentralized) and communication structures are the most common ones (Galbraith 1977).

2.2 Operational Level – Social Subsystem

A course-grain and high-level conceptual model for the social subsystem is shown in Figure 3. The focus of the social subsystem is the meta-organization model that specifies the relations between actors, resources, artifacts, tasks, and teams. The relations define multiple networks as shown in Table 1. The meta-organization model specifies the architecture of cooperative work and the criteria for division of work between teams. It is important to distinguish between the work organization (i.e., organization subsystem) perspective and the social organization aspect depicted by the meta-organization model within the social subsystem.

The work domain model of the organization subsystem analyzes and specifies the coordination activities determined by the interaction of control requirements of the work domain and the behavior of teams and engineers. On the other hand, social organization perspective imposed on the interactions among teams and engineers depend on the management style, culture, norms, values, and configuration of the social networks presented in Table 1.

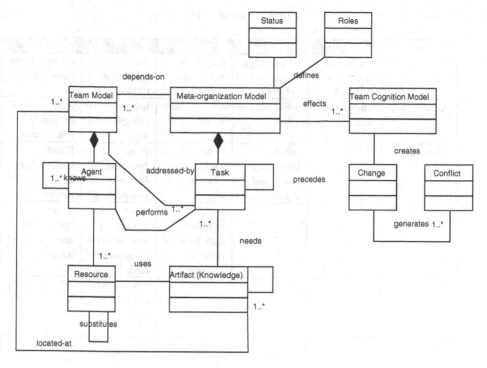

Fig. 3. Conceptual Model for the Social Subsystem

The team model embodies the team composition, structure, and explicit coordination and collaboration styles. Common coordination mechanisms in organization theory are rules, plans, hierarchy, and mutual agreement (Donaldson 1993). Various team archetypes also influence the behavior of teams (Yilmaz and Phillips 2006). The team cognition model incorporates elements such as trust, motivation, and cohesion that are effective in the performance of a software development team. The team cognition mode constitutes mechanisms that suggest specific *changes* and adaptation requests that may cause *conflicts* that have to be resolved by the strategy subsystem of the overall framework. The meta-organization model makes use of *role* and *status* information to improve coordination among teams and update team cognition parameters, respectively. For instance, the role of team leader is critical in allocating a specific task to a team via its leader. Also, the status information assigned to individual agents help assign weights to decisions made by the members of a team to derive a team decision.

2.3 Operational Level – Integration of Organization and Social Subsystems

The operational level can be considered as a distributed control subsystem that serves to a loosely coupled software process simulation that is viewed as a work system. The cooperation among the actors evolves from two directions. The work activities specified by the organization subsystem affect the control activities bottom-up, while

Table 1. Social Networks

	Agents	Knowledge	Resource	Task	Team
	Social interaction network	Knowledge acquisition network	Capacity network	Task allocation network	Employment network
Agents	*who knows who*	*who knows what*	*who has what*	*who is assigned to what*	*who is assigned to what team*
Knowledge		*what knowledge is needed to derive X*	*What knowledge is needed to use Y*	*What knowledge is needed to complete Z*	*What knowledge is located where*
Resource			*what resources can be used with resource Y*	*what resources are needed to complete task Z*	*what resources are located where*
Task				*what task precedes task Z*	*what tasks are performed where*
Team					*which teams work with which teams*

the social organization and its cooperation mechanism propagating top-down. The software development work organization emerges as a result of the interaction between the social practice and management style depicted by the social subsystem and the control requirements of the work domain model. Figure 4 depicts the mechanism by which the interaction ensues. The work activities level at the bottom involves the problem solving activities that carry out the tasks assigned to individual team members. The ways these activities carried out are influenced not only by the constraints of the work-domain model, but also the strategies imposed by the HIB model that is discussed in section 3. The human behavior subsystem affects the performance of individuals by inducing human behavior variability in terms of cognitive, affective, and personality traits and factors. The social interaction control level is driven by the social subsystem of the operational level. The form of communication and interaction styles are governed by the team archetypes, organizational culture, and decision making styles at the social organization level. The structure of the communication net and the content of the communication are based on the functional work organization, and hence they are determined by the control requirements of the work domain. The social interaction control level along with the work activities determines the shape of the coordination of work activities.

Specifically, the constraints of the work domain model (i.e., software process technology) and the structure of the organization (i.e., authority, hierarchy) explicitly

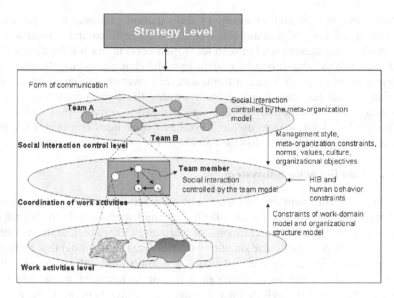

Fig. 4. Integrating Social and Organization Subsystems

delineates how team members need to coordinate to fulfill tasks in accordance with the standards and process guidelines. The management style and social practice of the organization further constrain the flow of information and interaction among team members.

3 The Technical Level

The technical level (HIB and human behavior system) of the proposed framework not only effects the coordination effectiveness at the work activity coordination level (see Figure 4), but also influence the performance of team members, as they carry out work activities.

3.1 Human Information Behavior (HIB) Model

Modeling the activities of humans as they carry out tasks require realistic representations of the domain-independent behavior regarding how humans solve problems in real life. Unfortunately, modeling and simulation of software processes is often done at an abstract level that individual and social work practice involving collaboration, communication, 'off-task' behaviors, multitasking, interrupted and resumed activities, and informal interactions are not captured (Acuna and Juristo 2005; Sierhuis and Clancey 2002). Work activities imposed by the processes can be viewed as knowledge acquisition activities that require engineers to seek, search, use, and synthesize information to derive knowledge (i.e., design constraints and models) that are eventually embodied in the software artifact.

The HIB model (Wilson 2000) elaborates on the common characteristics of information behavior. Information behavior is defined as the human behavior as it pertains to sources and channels of information. *Information seeking* requires interacting not only with computers but also other manual and natural sources (e.g., face-to-face communication between team members) to reach information to satisfy a goal. *Information search* involves micro-level behavior involving the interaction with information systems to locate information. *Information use* consists of mental and physical human acts hat pertain to incorporating the discovered information to one's knowledge-base. Definition of each specific work activity in terms of primitive information seeking, search, use, and synthesis operations constitutes the foundation of the application of HIB within the context of the proposed framework.

3.2 Human Behavior Subsystem

Not every team member performs and interacts the same way. According to personality psychologists (Bem 1983), the fundamental task in human behavior analysis is to translate observations of persons with particular traits behaving in specific manners in particular situations into patterns (assertions) that certain kinds of people behave in certain kinds of ways in certain kinds of situations. Others also emphasized the importance of human behavior in terms of sound and predictable patterns that specify well-defined groups of behavior in relation to groups of situations.

To have a realistic basis to simulate software development, one should consider individual behaviors as part of the human aspect. In this article, we stress the role of cognitive complexity of individuals and its relationship with one of the five traits of human personality, i.e., openness to the success of software teams (Yilmaz and Oren 2007). Even a brief review of the basic concepts of cognitive complexity and openness will cast light on their relevance to the success of software teams.

3.2.1 Cognitive Complexity

In software engineering, as it is the case in many other complex systems, ability of coping with complexity is a fundamental issue and influences the quality of the decisions. As early as 1970s, based on Athey's work (Athey 1976) elaborated on the importance of increasing cognitive complexity of an individual to increase his/her effectiveness in coping with complex situations. Figure 5 (left) shows different levels of information processing of an individual depending on the situational complexity. For a low situational complexity, the individual may need to have low level of information processing to cope with the situation. If the situational complexity increases, his/her information processing level may also increase. However, for each individual there is a critical point beyond which the level of processed information, hence the individual's information processing effectiveness is decreased. After the critical point, an increase in the situational complexity may worsen the individual's ability to cope with complexity.

The information processing curves of two types of individuals, i.e., high and low cognitive complexity individuals are compared in Figure 5 (right) where two important points are shown: First, c_h, the critical point of high cognitive complexity individual is higher than c_l, critical point of low cognitive complexity individual. Thus

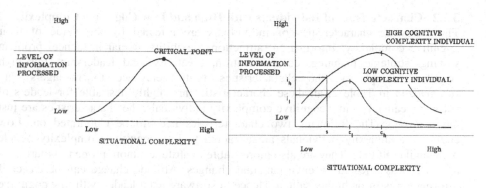

Fig. 5. Relationship between situational and behavioral complexities (Yilmaz and Oren 2007)

increasing the cognitive complexity of an individual –within the applicable limits of course– may increase the range of situational complexity within which he/she can perform effectively. Or depending on the task, it may be advisable to assign an individual with cognitive complexity commensurate with the task. Second, for a given situational complexity, the level of information processed by a high cognitive complexity individual i_h is greater than i_l which corresponds to a low cognitive complexity individual. Additional characteristics of high and low cognitive complexity individuals (with relevance to managers) are summarized in Table 2, based on Streufert and Swezey (1986).

Table 2. Characteristics of high cognitive complexity individuals

Characteristics	High cognitive complexity individuals
Information	More open to new information, search across more categories of information, and rely on their integrative efforts
Problem solving	Tend to search for more information; often less certain after a decision, especially if verification is unavailable.
Strategic planning	Better strategic planners due to: - consideration of more information, from more perspectives, - greater flexibility in considering alternatives.
Communication	More effective at a communication-dependent task. More resistant to persuasive attacks, especially if trained in counter arguments.
Creativity	Able to generate more novel, unusual, and potentially remote views and actions.
Leadership	Show leadership; High integrators in which they are able to relate complex patters of many elements.

3.2.2 Characteristics of Individuals with High and Low Cognitive Complexity

The following characteristics of individuals are affected by the value of their cognitive complexity: information, attraction, flexibility, social influence, problem solving, strategic planning, communication, creativity, and leadership. For high cognitive complexity, the characteristics (with relevance to managers) are summarized in Table 2; all these characteristics are highly desirable for leaders of software teams. For low cognitive complexity individuals, the characteristics are just the opposites. The following two characteristics need to be elaborated on: Low cognitive complexity individuals are attracted to low cognitive complexity people with similar attitude. They are also more stable in attitudes; more prone to polarize on an issue; less affected by environmental changes. Attitude change can be easier if information is made highly salient. Hence, a software team leader with low cognitive complexity may not communicate with colleagues with high cognitive complexity and may not adapt to dynamically changing conditions.

4 Conclusions

Since large and complex software development is inherently an organizational-effort, we need to find ways to understand the influence of alternative organizational structures, strategies, and operational mechanisms on the effectiveness of development processes. Developing simulation models to analyze performance of processes for such large complex system development endeavors require principled development of simulation models. Such principles should embody realistic assumptions that pertain to (1) strategic management of the organization in an adaptive goal-directed manner, (2) organizational structure, functions, and work activities imposed by the process technology, (3) social work organization that reflects the social practice, norms, management style, and culture, and (4) human work activities and behavioral traits.

Future work includes the further development and formalization of the framework. The formalization is expected to lead to development of simulation models of software processes that will explicitly focus on management of human, social, and organizational dynamics. There is an increasing demand for successful software project managers; therefore, efforts are needed to develop management-related knowledge and skills of the future software workforce. As the lower tiers of software and IT work become more commoditized, project management skills, as well as creativity and innovation, will become even more important, particularly in countries that experience the loss of programming work.

References

1. Abdel-Hamid, T., Madnick, S.: Software Project Dynamics: An Integrated Approach. Prentice Hall, Upper Saddle River, NJ (1991)
2. Acuna, T.S., Juristo, N.: Software Process Modeling. p. xix, Springer Science and Business Medias Inc. (2005)
3. Armour, G.P.: The Laws of Software Process: A New Model for the Production and Management of Software. Auerbach Publications (2003)

4. Athey, T.H.: Training the Systems Analysts to Solve Complex Real World Problems. In: Willoughby, T.C. (ed.) Proceedings of the 14th Annual Computer Personnel Research Conference, July 29-30, 1976. The Special Interest Group on Computer Personnel Research (SIGCPR) of the ACM, pp. 103–120 (1976)
5. Bem, D.J.: Constructing a Theory of the Triple Typology: Some Thoughts on Nomothetic and Idiographic Approaches to Personality. Journal of Personality 53, 566–577 (1983)
6. Carley, M.K., Gasser, L.: Computational Organization Theory. In: Weiss, G. (ed.) Multi-Agent Systems: A Modern Approach to Distributed Artificial Intelligence, The MIT Press, Cambridge (1999)
7. Constantine, L.: Work Organization: Paradigms for Project Management and Organization. Communications of the ACM 36(10), 35–43 (1993)
8. Donaldson, L.: Design Structure to Fit Strategy. In: Locke, A.E. (ed.) Handbook of Principles of Organizational Behavior, pp. 291–303. Blackwell Publishing, Oxford (1993)
9. Galbraith, R.J.: Organization Design. Addison-Wesley, Reading (1977)
10. Mayer, J.R., et al.: Framework and a Suite of Methods for Business Process Reengineering. In: Grover, V., Kettinger, W.J. (eds.) Business Process Change: Reengineering Concepts, Methods and Technologies, Idea Group, Hershey, Pa (1998)
11. Newell, A.: Unified Theories of Cognition. Harvard Univ. Press, Cambridge, Mass (1990)
12. Streufert, S., Swezey, R.W.: Complexity, managers, and organizations. Academic Press, New York (1986), http://www.css.edu/users/dswenson/web/Cogcompx.htm
13. Wilson, D.T.: Human Information Behavior. Informing Science, Special Issue on Information Science research 3(2) (2000)
14. Yilmaz, L., Phillips, J.: Organization-theoretic Perspective for Simulation Modeling of Agile Software Processes. In: Wang, Q., Pfahl, D., Raffo, D.M., Wernick, P. (eds.) Software Process Change. LNCS, vol. 3966, pp. 234–241. Springer, Heidelberg (2006)
15. Yilmaz, L., Oren, T.: On Multiresolution Simulation Modeling of Team and Human Behavior for Software Process Design. In: Invited paper. Proceedings of the Tenth World Conference on Integrated Design and Process technology (to appear, 2007)

Performance Comparison of Software Complexity Metrics in an Open Source Project

Min Zhang and Nathan Baddoo

Systems and Software Research Group
School of Computer Science
University of Hertfordshire
Hatfield, UK

Abstract. Software complexity measures are essential aspects of software engineering. Relatively few studies have been conducted to compare the performance of different complexity metrics. This paper describes an experimental investigation, which compares the performance of three different software complexity metrics; McCabe's cyclomatic complexity, Halstead's complexity measures and Douce's spatial complexity, by using data from an Open Source project Eclipse JDT. The results of this investigation indicate that in different situation these complexity metrics show different performance. However, Halstead's effort measure and Douce's spatial complexity are highly correlated, showing bigger correlation coefficient values. This leads us to suggest that because Halstead's complexity measure is more mature and has better supporting tools, it may be a good idea to replace Douce's spatial complexity metric with Halstead's effort measure in practice.

1 Introduction

In this paper we present an experimental investigation into three complexity metrics, McCabe's cyclomatic complexity, Halstead's complexity measures and Douce's spatial complexity, using data from Eclipse JDT Open Source project. Using software measurement to quantify the characteristics of software systems is an essential part of good software engineering. A complexity metric is an important measure for capturing some of these characteristics. By using complexity metrics, software development teams have the capability to indicate potential problems of a software system, guide software testing and estimate maintenance efforts[1]. In the past three decades several software complexity metrics have been introduced[2][3][4][5], but relatively few studies have been conducted to compare the performance of these metrics in order to judge their efficacy at predicting the complexity and performance of software systems. We therefore conducted an investigation to compare the performance of different complexity metrics. We chose the Open Source portal as a source of data because such projects are often developed incrementally over long time scales[6], and their resources are freely accessed. All the data used in this study comes from the Eclipse JDT Open Source project, which is hosted on open source community Eclipse.org.

P. Abrahamsson et al. (Eds.): EuroSPI 2007, LNCS 4764, pp. 160–174, 2007.

In order to couch a succinct hypothesis, we needed to scope a definition for a good metric. In this study, our definition for a good metric is predicated on the following assumptions:

◇ Complexity metrics should indicate Lehman and Belady's law of software evolution, which states that software evolution increase the complexity of a software system[7].
◇ Complexity metrics should have the capability to predict the fault prone modules. The more complex a module is, the more faults are found in this module.
◇ Complexity metrics should capture the fact that the more complex a software module, the more frequently it would be changed.
◇ The proportion of code change may not cause the same proportion of change in the complexity of a software module.

From the above assumptions, we designed studies to test the following hypotheses:

◇ **Hypothesis A:** Software updates lead to positive increase of values of the software complexity metrics.
◇ **Hypothesis B:** Complexity measures of software components have a positive correlation with the number of faults found in these components.
◇ **Hypothesis C:** Complexity metrics of software components have a negative correlation with the time between updates of these components.
◇ **Hypothesis D:** The proportion of complexity metrics changes is not strongly correlated to the proportion of number of lines changes.

To test the above hypotheses, we used data from the CVS system of Eclipse JDT project. We wrote programs to capture this data and calculate the metrics automatically. Finally, we conducted statistical analyses to compare the performance of the complexity metrics. The following is the methodology followed to test each of the hypotheses:

Hypothesis A

CVS version update log is dumped from project's CVS repository. After that, based on the comments information from the log file, log entries about bug fixing updates are picked up for investigation. Then complexity metrics about the selected entries are calculated and statistical analysis is applied to examine whether these updates lead to an increase in positive complexity.

Hypothesis B

Here, we are focused on the relationship between complexity metrics and "number of bugs" measure. Certain versions of software components from Eclipse JDT project are randomly selected for study. On one hand, "number of bugs" measure is calculated by using the information from CVS log file. On the other hand, related source codes are checked out to calculate the complexity metrics.

Finally, a correlation coefficient analysis is performed to study relations between these two variables.

Hypothesis C

Here, we want to establish whether more complex software can be prone to more frequent changes. We randomly choose certain bug fixing updates. The time periods of the bug fixing are captured for investigation. The related source codes are also checked for complexity metrics calculation. At the end, correlation coefficient analyses are conducted to examine which complexity metric indicates negative relationship between these two variables.

Hypothesis D

In the investigation of hypothesis D, bug fixing updates are randomly picked up and the related source codes are checked out from the CVS system. After that, the percentage of LOC change is calculated based on the source codes. Then the percentage of complexity metric value changes about the related source code is also calculated. Finally, based on these two sets of data correlation coefficient analysis is conducted to examine which complexity measures can better support this hypothesis.

The rest of this paper is structured as follows: In Section Two we provide some background to software complexity metrics and review previous studies that have used open source project data in software engineering analysis. Section Three describes our research methods, describing in particular, the experimental design adopted in this study. Section Four presents our results of the study. In Section Five we discuss our results. We conclude in Section Six.

2   Complexity Metrics and Open Source SE Research

There are several software complexity metrics in software engineering, such as McCabe's cyclomatic complexity[2][8][9], which is based on measuring the number of linear independent paths in a software module, Halstead's complexity measures[3] which measures the computational complexity of source code, Douce's Spatial Complexity Metrics[4] and Chhabra's Spatial Complexity Metrics[5], which sees software complexity as the cognitive capability of a program.

2.1   Previous Researches

Several studies have been conducted to study the performance of the above metrics. Curtis et al.[1] conducted a study to investigate the performance of McCabe's cyclomatic complexity metric, Halstead's complexity metrics and the simple line of code measurement. Their results indicate that in small size programs all of these three measures predict the actual efforts well, but in larger size programs Halstead's complexity metrics proved a better predictor than the others.

Gold et al.[10] also examined the performance between Douce's spatial complexity metrics and Chhabra's complexity metrics. Their study showed that Douce's SC spatial complexity was a better predictor of effort than his RC spatial complexity definition and Chhabra's spatial complexity metrics. On the contrary, Douce's RC spatial complexity measure and Chhabra's spatial complexity metric were shown to be unable to capture any more information than the simple line of code measurement.

In this respect, few studies have been performed to compare the performance between McCabe's cyclomatic complexity, Halstead's complexity metrics and Douce's SC spatial complexity. This paper tries to address this question.

2.2 Open Source Projects

Open Source projects have received great attention recently. They are thought of as a fundamentally new way for software development[11]. One of the main features of open source projects is their incremental development. Instead of building the whole software system in one phase, open source projects tend to gradually increase their functionality over a long period[6]. So that, over time, a lot of information about these projects becomes available in Open Source repositories. Also, the project source code and related maintenance data can be freely accessed. This makes Open Source projects a great source for software engineering studies.

Massey, Mockus et al. and Sliwerski et al. have successfully conducted software engineering researches by using the data from open source projects[6][11][12]. In Sliwerski et al.'s research, they investigated the CVS repositories from Eclipse open source project and Mozilla open source project, and found that bug fixing updates can be located by using the CVS comment information. They also developed a method of building links between an open source projects' version control system - CVS - and its bug maintenance system - Bugzilla - to support their experiential researches[12]. This method can act as a guideline for using open source projects data in software engineering research.

3   Research Methodology

In order to examine the four hypotheses listed in the introduction, we conducted three main tasks in this study. The first is capturing data from the CVS repositories; the second is calculating the complexity metrics by using automatic tools; the third is using a statistical tool to analyse the results. We expand on these tasks in the rest of this section.

3.1   Data Capturing

Data capturing is the most important part of this investigation. Although the CVS system is one of the most popular version control systems in software industry, there are still relatively few tools to support extracting information from it for software engineering analyses. Moreover, the analysis tools for CVS system are often built for specific usage and they are difficult to apply to common research[6]. So, in this study, we developed several customized programs to resolve this problem. All of these programs were developed in Java and Apache Ant scripts.

Data Filtering. The first step in capturing data from CVS system is to filter out the useless information. In our studies we focus on the bug fixing updates of Eclipse JDT project. Sliwerski's research[12] found that in Eclipse and Mozilla open source projects source code check in often links with meaningful comments and these comments can be used as filters to pick up useful information. Sliwerski also suggests the following methodology for discovering the bug fixing updates:

1. Translating comments information into list of tokens. There are four kinds of tokens (presented in FLEX syntax).
   - **Bug number:** A bug number is an expression that matches one of the following formats:
     - $bug[\# \backslash t]^*[0\text{-}9]+$,
     - $pr[\# \backslash t]^*[0\text{-}9]+$,
     - $show\backslash\_bug \backslash .cgi \backslash ?id=[0\text{-}9]+$, or
     - $\backslash[[0\text{-}9]+ \backslash]$
   - **Plain number:** A string of digits 0-9.
   - **Keyword:** A keyword matches the following expression: $fix(e[ds])?|bugs?|defects?|patch$
   - **Word:** A word is a string of alphanumeric characters.
2. A comment for bug fixing updates should meet at least one of the following criteria.
   (a) The number is bug number.
   (b) The log message contains a keyword, or the log message contains only plain or bug numbers.

(Source: Sliwerski et al., 2005[12])

In this study, we made two changes in the method suggested in order to improve. Firstly, the rules are changed so that instead of meeting one of the criteria listed in step 2, we only pick up the entries that match both criteria. Also, we dropped entries that contained "copyright" keyword, because we suggest that if the bug fixing updates only change the information about copyright, it is impossible to cause complexity change. After these processes 122 bug fixing updates were located in Eclipse JDT project.

Source Code Gathering. After the data filtering process, a list of file entries about bug fixing updates was prepared. The source code versions before or after these bugs fixed updates were collected for analysis. Consequently, 244 versions of source code were captured in our experiments. We developed a customized program to automatically check out these source code from the CVS repository.

Number of Bugs. The "number of bugs" metric is employed to test hypothesis B. We define "number of bugs" as the total number of bug fixing updates after a certain version of source code.

Time between Updates. For hypothesis C, the definition of "time between updates" measure for a source file is:

$$T_X - T_{X-1} \tag{1}$$

Where X indicates the version number and T_X represents the committing time of version X of a certain source file. If a bug fixing update has more than one source file, the "time between updates" measure of this bug fixing is defined as:

$$\max_{i=1 \sim n} (T_X^i) - \min_{j=1 \sim n} (T_{X-1}^j) \tag{2}$$

Where n is the number of updated files of this bug fixing.

Proportion of Code Change. In this study the proportion of source code change is defined as:

$$diff_{(X-1toX)}/LOC_{X-1} \tag{3}$$

In the above definition, LOC is the number of lines of code measure of a source file; X indicates the version number of the source code; $diff_{(X-1toX)}$ represents number of lines of code either added or altered between two versions. If a bug fixing update has more than one source file, the proportion of code change measure of this bug fixing update should sum up all the proportion of code change measure of each source file in this update.

We do not ignore comment lines and blank lines in the calculation of LOC measure, because in Douce's spatial complexity definition comment lines and blank lines should also affect the complexity values. Consequently, in order to keep constant the calculations of all measures in this study, we include comment lines and blank lines.

The code difference ($diff_{(X-1toX)}$) values were calculated by using the "annotate" function of CVS. Figure 1 shows part of a CVS "annotate" result. Comparing this annotation result with the standard java source files, it can be found that, each line of the result contains three more bits of information. They are the version number of the last modification, author name of the modification and the date of the modification. The code difference measure can be calculated by counting how many version numbers equal current version number in annotation result files.

Proportion of Complexity Metrics Changes. The proportion of complexity values' change of a bug fixing update is defined as:

$$(Complexity_{after} - Complexity_{before})/Complexity_{before} \tag{4}$$

In this formula, $Complexity_{after}$ indicates the complexity measure value of the source codes after bug fixings. $Complexity_{before}$ indicates the complexity value before bug fixing.

```
1.1     (darin  29-Nov-02): public class JavaConsoleTracker implements
                            IConsoleLineTracker {
1.1     (darin  29-Nov-02):     private IConsole fConsole;
1.1     (darin  29-Nov-02):     private StringMatcher fJavaMatcher;
1.2     (darin  03-Dec-02):     private StringMatcher fNativeMatcher;
1.1     (darin  29-Nov-02):
1.1     (darin  29-Nov-02): public void init(IConsole console) {
1.4     (darin  29-Nov-02):         fConsole = console;
1.6     (darins 20-Dec-02):         fJavaMatcher = new StringMatcher("*(*.java:*)", false,
false); //$NON-NLS-1$
1.6     (darins 20-Dec-02):         fNativeMatcher = new StringMatcher("*(Native Method)",
false, false); //$NON-NLS-1$
.
.
.
1.1     (darin  29-Nov-02): }
```

Fig. 1. CVS "annotate" result

3.2 Complexity Metrics Calculation

We used several programs in this study to support metrics calculation.

We used an open source tool JavaNCSS[13] to calculate McCabe's cyclomatic complexity. JavaNCSS is a command line based metrics utility developed by Christoph Clemens. It can measure two standard measures, non-commenting source statements (NCSS) and cyclomatic complexity number (CCN), of java source codes.

Our studies of Halstead's complexity measure focus on its "Effort" measurement. Here, also, we used an open source utility, Lachesis[14], to calculate Halstead's complexity measures.

Spatial complexity studies are based on Douce's simple function spatial complexity definition in this study. Unlike the other two complexity metrics, spatial complexity metric is a new concept in software engineering domain. As a result there are few existing tools to support its calculation. In order to fill in this gap, we developed a program to capture this metric. In this program JavaCC[15] is used as the grammar analysis tools.

Finally, all of the complexity metrics used in this investigation are at the bug fixing level. If a bug fixing update has more than one source file, the complexity value should add up to all the complexity values of the source files.

3.3 Statistical Analysis

Sampling. As discusses earlier, 122 bug fixing updates and 244 version entries of source code were captured in Eclipse JDT project. In order to maintain 95% level of certainty and 5% margin of error, 100 random samples were chosen for the studies on bug fixing updates, such as Hypothesis A and Hypothesis C, and 150 samples were randomly chosen for the studies on source code versions, such as Hypothesis B. The only exception is the study of Hypothesis D. According to our definition of "proportion of complexity change", if the complexity value for a previous version of a source code is zero, then the measure is considered meaningless. This led to some samples being dropped in this study. As a consequence, in order to keep more confidence of our study 110 random samples were chosen.

Correlation Measure. In our studies, Pearson's product moment correlation is chosen as the correlation measure[16]. Microsoft Excel 2003 is employed as a tool for statistic calculation.

4 Results

In this section, we present the results of our studies, outlying how the study results conformed or refuted our hypotheses.

4.1 Hypothesis A

100 random samples of bug fixing updates were investigated in the testing of hypothesis A, Table 1 sums up the number of different change directions for each complexity metric.

Table 1. Numbers of different change directions for each complexity metric

	Positive	Negative	No Changes
McCabe's Cyclomatic Complexity	56	13	31
Halstead's Effort Measure	67	24	9
Douce's Spatial Complexity	64	18	18

Table 1 shows that the numbers of positive changes are much bigger than the negative changes. Moreover, for all of these metrics about 60% of the total numbers of changes are positive. So it can be thought that all of these metrics can support the Lehman and Belady's law[7]. In addition, in this study Halstead's effort measure and Douce's spatial complexity measure show similar results of 67% and 64% positive entries. They all show better performance than the cyclomatic complexity measure, which reports 56% positive entries.

4.2 Hypothesis B

150 random version source code files were selected from the source code pool to test this hypothesis. The results are presented in Table 2.

Table 2 shows that McCabe's cyclomatic complexity measure has a stronger correlation with "number of bugs" measure than the other two complexity metrics; 0.5817 against 0.2848 and 0.3083. Table 2 also shows that all of the correlation coefficient values are significant. From these results, it can be suggested that the cyclomatic complexity metric is best for supporting Hypothesis B. However, it can also be suggested that because the correlation coefficients in all three instance are not very strong, with the highest being 0.5817, it is possible that complexity of software is not the only source of bugs.

Table 2. Correlating Complexity measure with number of bug fixes

	Correlation Coefficient	Significance?	
		$\alpha = 0.05$ sample = 150 min r = 0.1603	$\alpha = 0.01$ sample = 150 min r = 0.2097
McCabe's Cyclomatic Complexity	0.5817	Y	Y
Halstead's Effort Measure	0.2848	Y	Y
Douce's Spatial Complexity	0.3083	Y	Y

4.3 Hypothesis C

100 random samples of bug fixing updates were used to test hypothesis C. Table 3 is a summary of the results of this test.

Table 3. Correlating Complexity measure with time between updates

	Correlation Coefficient	Significance?	Power
		$\alpha = 0.05$ sample = 100 min r = 0.1965	
McCabe's Cyclomatic Complexity	-0.0488	N	0.0077
Halstead's Effort Measure	-0.1146	N	0.0012
Douce's Spatial Complexity	-0.1305	N	0.0007

Table 3 shows that all of the complexity metrics are negatively correlated with the time between updates. However, it can also be found that all of these correlations are weak, and all correlations are insignificant when α equals to 0.05. It means that all this correlations are rejected. For this situation, a power test was conducted to see how confidence to reject these hypotheses without cause type II errors. The results of this power test show that there is a higher probability of correctly rejecting the negative correlation of cyclomatic complexity than the other two complexity metrics, 0.0077 against 0.0012 and 0.0007. So in this case Douce's simple function spatial complexity metric and Halstead's effort measure can be thought as having more significant negative correlations with the "time between updates" measure.

4.4 Hypothesis D

We randomly chose 110 bug-fixing samples from the source code pool to test this hypothesis. According to our definition of "proportion of complexity change", if the complexity value for a previous version of a source code is zero, then the measure is considered as meaningless. Which means that when we calculated the complexity metrics, we dropped the bug fixing updates which had one or more

Table 4. Correlation coefficients for proportion of line changes

	Correlation Coefficient	Significance?	
		$\alpha = 0.05$ sample = 99 min r = 0.1975	$\alpha = 0.01$ sample = 99 min r = 0.2578
McCabe's Cyclomatic Complexity	0.4998	Y	Y
Halstead's Effort Measure	0.4039	Y	Y
Douce's Spatial Complexity	0.4537	Y	Y

complexity values equal to zero from this analysis. This resulted in 11 samples being dropped. We conducted our analysis with the remaining 99.

Table 4 shows the correlation coefficient and significance test results for this hypothesis. Table 4 shows that all the metrics are positively correlated to proportion of line changes. Table 4 also shows that all the correlation coefficients are significant at α values of 0.05 and 0.01, indicating that the correlations are not chance occurrences. However, all the values are between 0.4 and 0.5, which indicates that they are not very strong correlations. We may speculate that even though all of these complexity metrics have correlation with the LOC measure, the change in lines of code is not the only reason for the change in the value of the complexity metric. Also, that complexity metrics can capture more information than the simple LOC measurement. In addition, we find that the differences between these correlation coefficient values are under 0.1, which means that between them there is not much difference in terms of the correlations with proportion changes in LOC. In summary, the above results show that the three complexity metrics studied here can capture more information than the LOC measure, but they do not show great difference between each other.

5   Discussion

In this section we discuss our findings from our study. There are some very interesting findings from the results in Section 4.

Firstly, we found that there are a mixture of weak and strong points for using the three metrics chosen in this study. We found that Halstead's effort metric and Douce's spatial complexity show better performance in hypothesis A and hypothesis C, whilst McCabe's cyclomatic complexity can supports hypothesis B better.

Secondly, we found a common feature amongst the metrics in this study. We found that Halstead's effort measure shows very similar results to Douce's spatial complexity metric in all of the four studies that we carried out. The two metrics show similar results in the testing of all four hypotheses. This leads us to predict that Halstead's measure may be equivalent of Douce's spatial complexity metric. However, in order to support this assumption we performed another experiment to find out whether strong correlation can be found between Halstead's effort measure and Douce's spatial complexity metric. In this experiment we reused the 100 bug fixing samples first used in the studies on hypothesis A and hypothesis C. For each of these bug fixing samples two version source codes were collected giving us 200 source code samples altogether. Then we conducted a cross correlation analysis between the three complexity metrics - McCabe's cyclomatic complexity, Halstead's effort measure and Douce's spatial complexity - using the complexity values obtained for the 200 samples. Table 5 presents the results of this experiment. Figure 2 plot the cross-correlation values.

Table 5. Cross-correlation analysis of three complexity metrics

	Correlation Coefficient	Significance? $\alpha = 0.01$ sample = 200 min r = 0.1818
Cyclomatic complexity vs. Halstead's effort	0.6965	Y
Cyclomatic complexity vs. Spatial complexity	0.7445	Y
Halstead's effort vs. Spatial complexity	0.8686	Y

From Table 5 and Figure 2, we find that correlation between Halstead's effort measure and Douce's spatial complexity metric is the strongest relation. We suggest that this evidence support our initial assertion that the two metrics are equivalent. We further suggest that one of these two metrics with the other would not present too many difference in the values that we obtain for complexity.

We also suggest from our findings that because all of these metrics can be shown to be useful in different situation and because there are no metrics which show significantly better performance than others, it may be a good idea to combine these metrics when we want to show the complexity features of software. Also, although Halstead's effort measure and Douce's spatial complexity metric show similar results in these studies, Halstead's effort measure has longer history and its usability has been validated in several previous studies[1][17]. In this case, we can think that Halstead's effort measure is more mature. In addition, many CASE tools[14][18][19] have been developed to capture Halstead's measure. So it will be prudent to use Halstead's effort measure in place of Douce's spatial complexity measure. Therefore using McCabe's cyclomatic complexity metric and Halstead's effort metric should be a good combination of metrics for capturing the complexity of a software system. But we may have to further exploit this area of research.

Other interesting findings worthy of discussion are as follows:

Why does Halstead's effort measure show strong correlation with Douce's spatial complexity metric in this study? Why does McCabe's cyclomatic complexity show significantly different results from the other two complexity metrics? These are questions that present opportunities for further research, However we may suggest that these symptoms may be caused by their correlations with the size of source code. From the definition of Halstead's complexity metrics, it can be

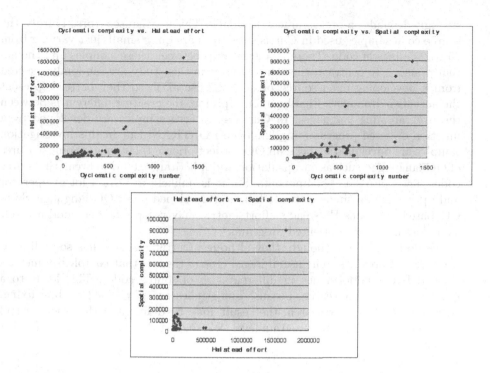

Fig. 2. Cross-correlation analysis of three complexity metrics

found that the value of Halstead's effort measure depends on the numbers of operators and operands of the source code. So when source code size increases, it is most likely to add new operators or operands into the software modules. Consequently, it increases the value of Halstead's effort measure. Similarly, Douce's spatial complexity metric is calculated by summing up the distance between function definitions and function calls. Increasing source code size has great chance to increase the distance. Hence, the value of Douce's spatial complexity metric is also increased. So it may be the internal reason for the strong correlation between Halstead's effort measure and Douce's spatial complexity metric. In contrast, McCabe's cyclomatic complexity is a metric to measure the number of linearly independent paths. To increase the source code size has less chance to increase the number of linear independent paths in a software module. As a consequence, McCabe's cyclomatic complexity shows weak correlations with Halstead's effort measure and Douce's spatial complexity.

We found some differences in the results of our study with the results of Curtis's study[1]. In Curtis's research Halstead's effort measure shows better performance than McCabe's cyclomatic complexity. But in our study McCabe's cyclomatic complexity metrics have better performance in some situations. There are several reasons for this difference. Firstly, in Curtis's research they just focused on the correlation between the maintenance effort and complexity metrics, but in our study several different fields are studied. Secondly, Curtis's research strongly depends on programmers' feedback. This may cause errors. Thirdly, the source code samples used in Curtis's research are quite small, just varying from 25 to 225 lines of code. There is a great gap between these samples and the actual practice. In contrast, the samples used in this study are randomly selected from a developing open source project Eclipse JDT, so they better represent the actual environment. Finally, in our opinion, the greatest different is between the programming languages. In Curtis's research samples are developed by a function oriented programming language FORTRAN. But in this investigation samples are developed in Java, an OO (object oriented) language. Some features of OO languages, such as encapsulation and inheritance, tend to break the source codes down into small components. So, it is unlikely to have a lot of operator and operands in a single software function developed in an OO language. So in OO based programs Halstead's effort metric may not provide as good a result as it does in function oriented programs.

We do need to add though, that although Curtis' research has some limitations, it still provides some useful ideas. One of them is that complexity metrics show different performance in different size of source codes. This leads to a questioning of our research, because our studies are just based on bug fixing. According to Curtis' research, the result may be different if the research had been performed at a total program level. We suggest that this may merit further research.

6   Conclusion

In this paper, we have described a study that compared the performance of three software complexity metrics, McCabe's cyclomatic complexity metric, Halstead's effort complexity measure and Douce's spatial complexity measure. We used data from the CVS version control system of Eclipse JDT open source project. In order ably conduct this comparison, we formulated four hypotheses.

The results of our study show that McCabe's cyclomatic complexity metric, Halstead's effort measure and Douce's spatial complexity show different performance in different situation. In testing hypothesis B, McCabe's cyclomatic complexity shows better performance, however when testing hypothesis A and hypothesis C Halstead's effort measure and Douce's spatial complexity metric seemed better. Furthermore, Halstead's effort measure and Douce's spatial complexity metric appeared to be strongly correlated in this study. When we consider maturity and supporting utilities, we suggest that it should be a good idea to replace Douce's spatial complexity metric with Halstead's effort measure in practice. We also recommend that combining McCabe's cyclomatic complexity metric and Halstead's effort measure to measure software complexity can help to better adjudge the complexity of software systems, than using a single complexity metric.

We plan further research to follow up this study that would include studies that compare the combination of McCabe's cyclomatic complexity metric and Halstead's complexity measure with a single metric to investigate whether such combination can show better performance. We also plan to conduct studies that compare the features of complexity metrics at total project level and single source file level. Finally, we propose a programme of studies to capture internal reasons why Halstead's complexity measure shows strong correlation with Douce's spatial complexity metric.

Biography

Min Zhang is a PhD candidate in the School of Computer Science at the University of Hertfordshire, UK. His research interests include design patterns, refactoring, software metrics and open source software. He received an MSc in software engineering from University of Hertfordshire. He is a member of the Systems and Software Research (SSR) group.

Dr Nathan Baddoo is a senior lecturer in the School of Computer Science at the University of Hertfordshire, UK. He is also a researcher in the Systems and Software Research (SSR) group. His research focuses on human factors in software processes. He holds many publications in this area. Nathan completed a PhD in Motivators and De-motivators in Software Process Improvement, in 2001. His current research interests are in the general areas of software quality, software process improvement and software practitioner motivation. Recent work includes the development of an empirical model of software engineers' motivators and exploratory work on prediction models of software engineers' motivation, using agent-based simulation and fuzzy logic. Nathan is a Programme Committee Chair of EUROSPI 2007.

References

1. Curtis, B., Shepperd, S., Milliman, P.: Third time charm: Stronger prediction of programmer performance by software complexity metrics. In: Proceeding of the fourth International Conference on Software Engineering, pp. 356–360 (1979)
2. McCabe, T.J.: A complexity measure. Software Engineering, IEEE Transactions on 2(4), 308–320 (1976)
3. Halstead, M.H.: Elements of Software Science, Operating, and Programming Systems Series, vol. 7. Elsevier, New York (1977)
4. Douce, C., Layzell, P., Buckley, J.: Spatial measures of software complexity. In: Proc. 11th Meeting of Psychology of Programming Interest Group (1999)
5. Chhabra, J., Aggarwal, K., Singh, Y.: Code and data spatial complexity: Two important software understandability measures. Information and software Technology 45(8), 539–546 (2003)
6. Massey, B.: Longitudinal analysis of long-timescale open source repository data. In: International Conference on Software Engineering. Proceedings of the 2005 workshop on Predictor models in software engineering, pp. 1–5 (2005)
7. Lehman, M., Belady, L.: Program Evolution, Processes of Software Change. Academic Press, London (1985)

8. McCabe, T.J., Butler, C.W.: Design complexity measurement and testing. Communications of the ACM 32(12), 5–9 (1989)
9. McCabe, T.J., Watson, A.H.: Software complexity. Journal of Defense Software Engineering 7, 5–9 (1994)
10. Gold, N.E., Mohan, A.M., Layzell, P.J.: Spatial complexity metrics: an investigation of utility. Software Engineering, IEEE Transactions on 31(3), 203–212 (2005)
11. Mockus, A., Fielding, R., Herbsleb, J.: Two case studies of open source software development: Apache and mozilla. ACM Transactions on Software Engineering and Methodology 11(3), 309–346 (2002)
12. Sliwerski, J., Zimmermann, T., Zeller, A.: When do changes induce fixes? In: ACM SIGSOFT Software Engineering Notes, Proceedings of the 2005 international workshop on mining software repositories MSR '05, vol. 30 (2005)
13. JavaNCSS: http://www.kclee.de/clemens/java/javancss/index.html
14. Lachesis: http://lachesis.sourceforge.net/
15. JavaCC: https://javacc.dev.java.net
16. Black, T.R.: Doing quantitative research in the social sciences: an integrated approach to research design, measurement and statistics. SAGE, London (1999)
17. Jones, C.: Software metrics: good, bad and missing. Computer 27(9), 98–100 (1994)
18. Oman, P.: HP-MAS: A Tool for Software Maintainability, Software Engineering. University of Idaho, Moscow (1991)
19. CMT++/CMTJava: http://www.verifysoft.com/en_halstead_metrics.html
20. Fenton, N.E., Pfleeger, S.L.: Software Metrics: A Rigorous & Practical Approach, 2nd edn. PWS Publishing Company, Boston (1997)

A Methodology for Identifying Critical Success Factors That Influence Software Process Improvement Initiatives: An Application in the Brazilian Software Industry

Mariano Montoni and Ana Regina Rocha

COPPE/UFRJ – Universidade Federal do Rio de Janeiro
P.O. BOX 68511 – ZIP 21945-970 – Rio de Janeiro, Brazil
{mmontoni,darocha}@cos.ufrj.br

Abstract. Continuous improvement of software development capability is fundamental for organizations to thrive in competitive markets. Nevertheless, Software Process Improvement (SPI) initiatives have demonstrated limited results because SPI managers usually fail to cope with factors that have influence on the success of SPI. In this paper, we present the results of a multi-strategy approach aiming to identify critical success factors (CSF) that have influence on SPI. The study results were confirmed by the literature review. The CSF were identified through a combination of qualitative and quantitative analyses of the results of a survey we conducted with SPI practitioners involved in Brazilian software industry experiences. We also identified the relationships of major factors that emerged from the survey. We expect that the major CSF presented in this paper can be used by SPI managers in the definition of SPI strategies aiming to enhance SPI initiatives success.

1 Introduction

Continuous improvement of software development capability is fundamental for organizations to thrive in competitive markets. Nevertheless, Software Process Improvement (SPI) initiatives have demonstrated limited results because SPI managers usually fail to cope with factors that have influence on the success of SPI [22]. Therefore, there is an urge in the SPI field to develop a knowledge-body related to critical success factors (CSF) that affect SPI. Moreover, it is also important to understand how these factors relate to each other and how SPI implementation strategies can be defined, monitored and controlled to provide adequate treatment to critical success factors since the conception of a SPI program and throughout the life of each SPI project [24].

A great number of studies have analyzed SPI initiatives aiming to identify the factors that have positive or negative influence on the success of SPI programs. Despite the fact that many of these studies were conducted following rigorous research methodologies and that statistical significant results are provided, the majority of the studies are context dependent and lack of information on how to generalize the results and

P. Abrahamsson et al. (Eds.): EuroSPI 2007, LNCS 4764, pp. 175–186, 2007.

how to efficiently consider the factors in the establishment of SPI implementation strategies. In this context, we have conducted an empirical study to develop a knowledge-body of factors that influence SPI initiatives in the context of Brazilian software industry. We have used a multi-strategy approach for this study: firstly, by reviewing empirical studies in the SPI field aiming to identify factors that have positive and negative impact on SPI; secondly, by combining qualitative and quantitative techniques to collect and to analyze data related to factors that have positive and negative impact on SPI in the context of Brazilian software industry. The methods and techniques used in this study have been largely applied by other SPI studies aiming to address the same research goal, but focusing on different software industry contexts.

This work is part of a broader investigation of SPI implementation approaches. We are currently examining the requirements for a general SPI implementation approach that supports: (i) the collaboration of SPI managers constituting a Community of Practice in the SPI field; (ii) the development of a knowledge-body of critical success factors that influence SPI initiatives success; (iii) the definition of SPI implementation strategies; (iv) the monitoring and control of SPI implementation initiatives; and (v) the packaging and dissemination of SPI empirical results. In order to provide a computational infrastructure to this approach, we are also integrating Community of Practice Environments (CoPE), Process-centered Software Engineering Environments (PSEE) and Knowledge Management Environments (KME).

The remainder of the paper is organized as follows. Section 2 reviews empirical studies that have investigated factors that influence SPI implementation initiatives and outlines methodological issues of these studies. Section 3 describes the research method of our study. Section 4 discusses the qualitative and quantitative analysis results of a survey we conducted with SPI practitioners involved in Brazilian software industry experiences. We also describe in section 4 the relationship of some of the major factors that emerged from the survey results. Finally, section 5 presents conclusions and points out future work.

2 Background

The focus of the literature review conducted as part of the study presented in this paper is to synthesize empirical results of empirical studies aiming to address the following research question: *What factors, as identified in the empirical studies, have influence on SPI?* Next, we briefly described these studies. The correlations among the CSF identified by each study are presented in the appendix.

Wilson et al. [16] developed a SPI success evaluation framework of questions and validated it with group interviews in seven UK companies in the point of view of developers, supervisors/team leaders, senior managers and SPI coordinator. The authors identified specific questions within this framework that appear to be significant indicators of the difference between the successful and unsuccessful companies.

Baddoo and Hall [17] present findings from a study of SPI motivators involving almost two hundred software practitioners in 13 UK companies in the point of view of developers, project managers and senior managers. From the analysis of the collected data, the authors suggest that SPI implementation can be improved by appropriate management of the common motivators across practitioners groups. Baddoo and Hall

[18] also analyzed the data collected from that study aiming to identify the relationship between motivators that SPI managers should consider when designing SPI implementation strategies. Moreover, the authors reported another point of view of the same survey study focusing on the de-motivators for SPI [19]. We observed that the SPI de-motivators presented by this work are actually representing the lack of presence of the motivators presented in [18] suggesting that some of the motivators and de-motivators can be interpreted as part of the same CSF.

Rainer and Hall [20] report the results of a survey conducted to investigate the CSF that have major impact or no impact on SPI in the point of view of SPI managers of the UK and multi-national companies. The data for the survey was collected from 84 self-administered questionnaires grouped according to the respondent organization appraisal status. The authors identified that organizations with different process maturity capabilities consider different CSF to have major impact on SPI. Rainer and Hall also report the results of another exploratory study aiming to gain more insight into the factors that practitioners think affect SPI [21].

El-Emam et al. [22] presents the results of a study of factors that influence the success of SPI involving organizations that have performed process assessment, and was conducted from 1 to 3 years after the assessment. The study analyzed data extracted from 138 questionnaires according to the respondents' role in the organizations (project level software manager, senior developer, and SEPG manager). Through the application of statistical analysis techniques, the authors identified CSF components that relate relevant factors influencing SPI success.

Niazi et al. [24] present findings of an empirical study of the CSF for SPI implementation with 34 SPI practitioners. The authors identified eight CSF. These findings were confirmed by comparing it with results from a literature survey of CSF that impact SPI. Besides confirming the survey results, the authors identified two new CSF that were not identified in the literature. Niazi et al. [23] also describes a maturity model for the implementation of SPI developed from this study results.

Dybå [25] developed an instrument for measuring CSF in SPI based on data collected from 120 software organizations. The instrument was evaluated and considered to have satisfactory psychometric properties. This instrument is constituted of statements organized in six groups of CSF.

Other important studies conducted to investigate factors that affect SPI are frequently included in the literature review of the studies described above. For instance, Goldenson and Herbsleb [26] conducted a survey with 138 respondents who were involved in 56 CMM appraisals aiming to identify factors associated to both successful and less successful SPI programs. El-Emam et al. [27] analyzed data collected through the ministration of questionnaires in 14 companies involved in SPICE trials. From this study, the relationships of factors to two identified variables of success were investigated. Stelzer and Mellis [28] reviewed experience reports from the literature and case studies of 56 companies that had gone through a successful SPI program. Ten factors that affect SPI success were identified from this review.

Some of the works described above neither distinguish the effect that CSF have on SPI success nor provide concrete information on how to manage the factors. This lack of information in the studies inhibits the consideration of such CSF in the definition and monitoring of SPI strategies. Moreover, the empirical studies that have investigated CSF do not have a uniform interpretation of the concepts related to SPI.

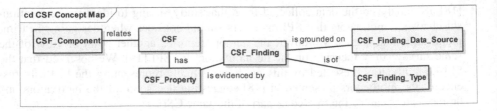

Fig. 1. CSF concept map

Therefore, it is important to define a concept map before investigating factors that affect SPI aiming to compare and aggregate SPI study results and to guarantee that people involved in the studies have the same understanding of SPI concepts. In order to achieve this goal, we developed the CSF concept map depicted in Figure 1.

We initially stated that each instance of *CSF* concept relate to each other in some way that the group of related CSF constitute a *CSF Component*. Considering that CSF is an abstract concept, we related CSF to an observable concept named *CSF Property*. Each CSF Property can be directly evidenced by *CSF Findings*. The CSF Finding must be classified according to the *CSF Finding Type* of evidence it provides (evidence of CSF presence or absence). Since CSF theory emerges from empirical studies, each CSF Finding must be grounded in a *CSF Finding Data Source*. This concept map was used as a framework for identifying and associating the survey study results presented in the next section.

3   Research Method

In order to initiate the study of issues that influence SPI implementation in the Brazilian industry context, we first set out to explore the following research question: *What factors have influence on SPI in the context of Brazilian software industry?*

We also defined a context and scope for the study aiming to answer this research question. The study was restricted to analyze experiences of a selected group of SPI practitioners that participated on SPI initiatives based on software process reference models and standards (like ISO/IEC 12207 [2], ISO/IEC 15504 [3] and CMMI [4]). We were concerned about identifying CSF under two points of view in this study. The first point of view is of SPI practitioners that participated as consultants in SPI projects. The second point of view is of organizations' members involved in SPI projects.

Software development is a complex activity and software process relies heavily on human compliance for its deployment [5]. Considering that software development is social-cultural in nature, any research must provide the basis for interpreting social, psychological and cultural issues [6]. Therefore, we chose the approach Grounded Theory (GT) as the method of investigation of the study for the following reasons: (i) GT is a qualitative technique indicated to study human behavior and organizational cultures, (ii) GT allows theory to emerge based on individual experiences, and (iii) GT provides the techniques for conducting inductive, theory-generating research [5, 7]. The steps executed in this study are described next.

Step 1: Data Collection

The objective of this step is to collect the data necessary for the study. The data was collected through the application of two types of questionnaires aimed to identify factors that have influence on SPI implementation. The first type of questionnaire was sent to a selected group of experienced SPI practitioners that participated as consultants on SPI projects executed by diverse types of Brazilian organizations. The second type of questionnaire was send to members of those organizations that were involved in the SPI projects. The questionnaires did not contain any pre-determined item and the participants filled them out separately. In total, 25 questionnaires were returned containing general descriptions about factors that had influenced the SPI initiatives. These descriptions are the basis from which the theory is grounded.

Step 2: Open Coding

The objective of this step is to analyze the data collected and allocate codes to the text. These codes represent findings of Critical Success Factors (CSF) that have influence on SPI implementation. Since each code can be linked to quotations within the questionnaires, they provide support and rich explanation for the results. In total, 66 different codes were identified through the analysis of the questionnaires.

Step 3: Axial Coding

The objective of this step is to document properties and dimension of codes (CSF findings) identified in the last step. The codes are grouped according to their properties forming concepts that represent categories of CSF. These categories are analyzed and subcategories are identified aiming to provide more clarification and specification. Finally, the categories and subcategories are related to each other. Since the categories are merely descriptions of the data, they must be further developed to constitute the building blocks of the theory. The association between a finding and a CSF property were classified as a finding representing the presence of one CSF property or a finding representing the absence of one CFS property in a specific context of analysis. The list of identified CSF is presented in the appendix along with correlations to previous empirical studies that also identified the same factors as critical. The properties related to each identified CSF are presented in Table 1.

Once we identified all the data related to CSF derived from the coded texts, we continued the axial coding by linking categories (i.e. CSF) at the level of properties and dimensions. The axial coding process proposed by [7] indicates that categories are related to each other along the lines of their properties and dimension. During axial coding we looked for answers to questions such as why or how come, where, when, how, and with what results, and in so doing we tried and uncover relationships among categories. In order to achieve this goal, we applied the multidimensional scaling (MDS) technique to examine the relationships between CFS. MDS is a social science data analysis technique designed to generate a rich visual understanding of human issues [10]. The result of the application of the MDS technique is a set of points in space, arranged in such a way that the distances between the points reflect the empirical relationship, also known as MDS Graph [11]. We also applied the Principal components analysis (PCA) technique [12] to identify the CSF properties plotted in the MDS Graph with statistical significant relationship. PCA provides us a

Table 1. CSF properties

ID	Property	CSF
P1	Existence of acknowledgement politics to SPI collaboration	F1
P2	Frequency of SPI consultants' follow-up during SPI implementation	F9
P3	Degree of changes acceptance	F2
P4	Degree of adequate conciliation of SPI interests	F3
P5	Degree of adequate organization structure	F4
P6	Degree of adequate SPI project management	F5
P7	Degree of adequate SPI push-pull implementation relation	F5
P8	Degree of adequate supporting tools	F6
P9	Degree of adequate processes and procedures	F7
P10	Degree of alignment of SPI implementation with organization strategic goals	F3
P11	Degree of higher management support, commitment and involvement	F8
P12	Degree of SPI consultants' competences	F10
P13	Degree of organization members' software engineering competences	F9
P14	Degree of organization members' commitment and involvement	F8
P15	Degree of trustfulness of organization members in the SPI consultants	F10
P16	Degree of organization members' awareness of SPI benefits	F11
P17	Degree of software and hardware availability to support processes execution	F6
P18	Degree of financial resources availability to SPI	F6
P19	Degree of organization members' time availability to SPI	F6
P20	Degree of organizational internal stability	F4
P21	Degree of SPI institutionalization	F7
P22	Degree of organization members' motivation to SPI	F12
P23	Degree of relationship among organization members and SPI consultants	F10
P24	Degree of people turnover	F4
P25	Degree of organization members' satisfaction	F12

systematic way for identifying a reduced set of CSF components relative to the original set of variables. This reduction facilitates the combination of CSF that relate to the same construct into one composite dimension.

Step 4: Selective Coding
The objective of this step is to integrate and refine the theory. This step involves identifying a core category as a central category to the study and its correlation to other categories. The links between categories and the core category provide the theory. As the core category acts as the link for all other categories, they must relate to it and it must appear frequently in the data [7].

The last steps were executed iteratively for each questionnaire. The objective was to try and emerge the theory since the beginning and constantly comparing it with new data until 'theoretical saturation' has been reached, i.e., were additional data being collected is providing no new knowledge about the categories. This iterative process of collecting, coding and analyzing data whilst simultaneously generating theory is also known as Theoretical Sampling [7]. The 'saturated' categories and the relationships were then combined to form the theoretical framework.

Step 5: Memoing
The objective of this step is to make annotations of ideas, observations and questions that occur during the last steps. These memos may take the form of statements,

hypotheses or questions. The memos annotated in step 4 (Selective Coding) become increasingly theoretical and act as the building blocks for the theory.

4 Qualitative and Quantitative Analysis Results

Once the respondents returned the questionnaires, we extracted the CSF findings from the respondents' statements and proceeded to the application of statistical techniques (MDS and PCA) to derive and aggregate the major CSF. The first step to execute the MDS analysis was to establish a content category dictionary of all CSF properties (presented in Table 1). Next, we created a data matrix based upon how many occurrences of the CSF properties were identified by each participant of the survey. We used the matrices to calculate multivariate correlations between the CSF properties. Finally, we used these correlations to plot the geometric distances between CSF in the MDS Graph.

The PCA technique was applied on the data matrix of CSF properties aiming to identify the properties with statistical significant relationship. By applying the PCA analyses, the properties receive a final loading on each CSF component extracted. These loadings are the correlations between properties and CSF components. The final loading value helps to interpret how "good" the obtained factor loadings are. According to Comrey [13], factor loading value of 0.45 would be considered fair, more than 0.55 is good, those of 0.63 is very good, and those of 0.71 are excellent. In our study we considered 0.55 as the cutoff value given the limited size of sample. The results of the PCA are shown in Table 2. Nine CSF components were extracted from the data analysis. In order to assist in deciding how many CSF components to extract we used the eigenvalue rule. The eigenvalue rule is based on retaining only CSF components that explain more variance than the average amount explained by one of the original items (i.e. CSF components with eigenvalue > 1). Approximately 85% of the variation is explained by these nine CSF components. This is a very good value given the exploratory nature of this study.

We used the extracted factors to construct CSF components. For each CSF component we calculated its Crombach alpha coefficient [14], a measure commonly used to evaluate the reliability of subjective measurement scales. The coefficient can vary from 0 to 1 where 1 is perfect reliability and 0 is maximum unreliability. Nunnally has suggested that for the early stages of research a Cronbach alpha coefficient approaching 0.7 is acceptable [15]. Factor 1 has a Cronbach alpha coefficient of value 0.81 demonstrating that CSF component has a very good reliability. Despite the fact that Factor 2 has too few variables for calculating the Cronbach alpha coefficient, the higher rotated factor loadings of the exploratory factor analysis for this component indicate the higher correlation of Factor 2 variables. Factor 3 has a Cronbach alpha coefficient of value 0.56. Even though this number is not high, the higher rotated factor loadings for this component also indicate the higher correlation of Factor 3 variables. Factor 4 has a Cronbach alpha coefficient of value 0.81 demonstrating that CSF component has a very good reliability. Factor 5 has a Cronbach alpha coefficient of value 0.58. Even though this number is not high, it is actually good for a variable consisting of only 3 variables. These five CSF factors alone explains 65% of total variance which is a very good value given the reduced set of cases analyzed. The

Table 2. Results of the PCA with Varimax normalized as the factor rotation method

CSF Prop	Factor 1	Factor 2	Factor 3	Factor 4	Factor 5	Factor 6	Factor 7	Factor 8	Factor 9
P1	**0.980**	0.072	0.009	0.123	0.043	0.050	0.014	0.044	-0.046
P2	-0.112	0.091	-0.089	0.016	0.242	-0.099	0.055	**-0.818**	0.225
P3	-0.091	-0.135	0.114	-0.026	**-0.811**	0.197	0.026	0.039	0.070
P4	**0.708**	-0.208	-0.259	0.105	-0.046	-0.390	-0.060	-0.131	0.128
P5	-0.033	0.011	0.070	-0.008	0.094	**-0.950**	-0.071	0.023	-0.077
P6	-0.105	**-0.750**	-0.356	-0.096	0.231	-0.249	0.058	0.211	0.155
P7	0.421	0.193	**-0.595**	0.350	0.151	0.156	-0.355	0.025	0.135
P8	0.055	-0.398	-0.262	0.130	-0.004	0.257	-0.211	**-0.582**	-0.332
P9	0.011	-0.279	**-0.612**	-0.436	-0.048	0.103	0.111	-0.220	0.340
P10	-0.079	-0.068	-0.050	0.124	-0.054	0.029	0.006	-0.016	**0.848**
P11	0.174	-0.131	0.055	**0.840**	0.052	0.059	-0.119	0.030	-0.083
P12	0.033	-0.221	0.137	-0.405	0.136	0.181	0.134	-0.310	0.538
P13	**0.605**	-0.160	-0.282	**0.603**	0.031	-0.002	-0.057	0.041	0.031
P14	0.448	0.255	-0.100	-0.095	-0.479	-0.230	**-0.555**	-0.063	0.033
P15	-0.018	0.158	0.036	-0.057	**-0.678**	0.018	-0.035	0.205	0.004
P16	-0.098	**-0.892**	0.193	0.128	-0.003	0.145	0.096	-0.083	0.090
P17	-0.087	0.054	0.101	0.063	0.079	-0.026	**-0.911**	0.001	-0.075
P18	0.258	0.085	-0.071	**0.814**	-0.006	-0.011	0.060	-0.193	0.156
P19	0.074	-0.440	0.051	**0.594**	0.251	-0.015	0.094	0.535	0.018
P20	**0.980**	0.072	0.009	0.123	0.043	0.050	0.014	0.044	-0.046
P21	0.137	0.110	**-0.621**	0.467	0.114	-0.075	0.312	0.122	-0.005
P22	-0.120	0.206	-0.234	-0.017	**-0.645**	-0.431	0.188	-0.252	-0.170
P23	**0.980**	0.072	0.009	0.123	0.043	0.050	0.014	0.044	-0.046
P24	-0.029	-0.007	**-0.932**	-0.009	-0.017	-0.011	0.016	-0.163	-0.108
P25	**0.980**	0.072	0.009	0.123	0.043	0.050	0.014	0.044	-0.046

Factors 6 to 9 has too few variables to calculate a Cronbach alpha coefficient and do not have high rotated factor loadings of the exploratory factor analysis. Therefore, we consider the Factors 1 to 5 as the major CSF components.

Figure 2 presents the graph of these components and the respective variables as a result of the application of MDS technique on the multivariate correlations calculated for the CSF properties. The major CSF components with statistical reliability identified through the application of PCA are also depicted on the graph.

Factor 1 was labeled "Environment" since all variables measure the organizational environment capability to establish and maintain SPI initiatives. These variables measure if there are favorable conditions for initiating and sustaining an SPI initiative with two points of view: the individual and the organization. The individual measures are related to members' satisfaction and relationship among members and the SPI team. The organization measures are related to conciliation of strategic goals and SPI interests and to organization internal stability.

Factor 2 is labeled "Efficient SPI Implementation Strategy" and indicates that an efficient SPI strategy is concerned on guaranteeing that organization members are aware of the potential benefits that can be achieved by implementing SPI.

We named Factor 3 component as "Solid SPI Implementation" since the variables of this factor measure the solidification of SPI implementation initiatives across the

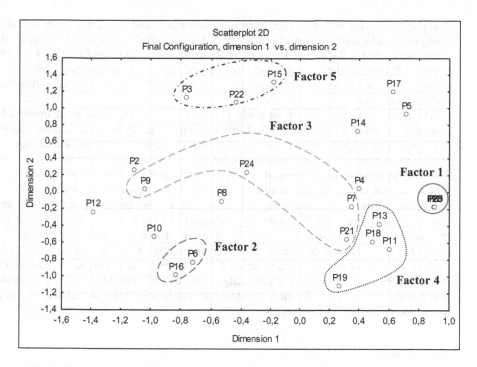

Fig. 2. Graph of major CSF components as a result of the application of MDS and PCA

organization by characterizing the processes and procedures institutionalization resistance degree to organizational structure changes, for instance, people turnover, and to inherent difficulties of implementing SPI in different organizational levels.

Since all variables of Factor 4 component are considered indicators of commitment to SPI, we labeled this factor as "Commitment". A higher management committed to SPI provides adequate financial resources since the conception of an SPI program and throughout the SPI projects. Moreover, a committed senior management guarantees that organization members have adequate competences and available time to efficiently execute process changes.

Factor 5 is termed "SPI motivation and acceptance" and indicates that the SPI team is a facilitator of organization members' acceptance to institutionalization of process changes promoted by SPI initiatives.

It is importance to notice that no analyses have been conducted to identify the type of relationships among the CSF that compound a CSF component. Therefore, we expect to extend the presented work by conducting cause and effect analyses aiming to identify what are the reasons why two or more factors correlate.

5 Conclusions

This paper presented the results of a study conducted with the purpose of identifying critical success factors that influence SPI initiatives in the context of Brazilian software industry. As part of this study, we reviewed the literature related to factors that influence SPI. We also conducted a survey study and applied a combination of qualitative and quantitative methods and techniques aiming to identify the major CSF components that influence SPI success. Although our findings confirm the CSF that impact SPI cited in the literature, we also present a research methodology for investigating CSF that influence SPI adequate to investigate CSF in the context of Brazilian software industry.

The next short-term goal of our studies is to develop and validate an instrument for assessing the readiness of an organization to initiative an SPI program and for predicting the success of SPI implementation based on the results of the presented work. A second short-term goal is to conduct another study to investigate how the influence of CSF can be appropriately managed aiming to increase the success of SPI initiatives. A mid-term goal of our studies is to replicate the study presented in this paper and to apply the instrument for measuring SPI success in a larger context (we expect to analyze approximately 200 SPI initiatives conducted in Brazilian software industries). A pre-requisite for achieving this last goal is to evolve the SPI concept map presented in this paper in a complete SPI ontology aiming to guarantee that people involved in the studies have the same understanding of SPI concepts. As a long-term goal of our study, we expect to construct a knowledge-base of CSF and to develop a computational system to support SPI managers to make decisions aiming to enhance the definition and control of SPI strategies.

References

1. Goldenson, D.R., Gibson, D.L.: Demonstrating the Impact and Benefits of CMMI: An Update and Preliminary Results. SEI Special Report, CMU/SEI-2003-SR-009 (October 2003)
2. ISO/IEC 12207:1995/Amd 1:2002/Amd 2:2004. Information Technology – Software Life Cycle Processes
3. ISO/IEC 15504: Information Technology – Process Assessment. Part 1 – Concepts and vocabulary, part 2 – Performing an assessment, part 3 – Guidance on performing an assessment, part 4 – Guidance on use for process improvement and process capability determination, and part 5 – An exemplar process assessment model
4. Chrissis, M.B., Konrad, M., Shrum, S.: CMMI: Guidelines for Process Integration and Product Improvement. Addison-Wesley, Reading (2003)
5. Coleman, G., O'Connor, R.: Software Process in Practice: A Grounded Theory of the Irish Software Industry. In: Richardson, I., Runeson, P., Messnarz, R. (eds.) EuroSPI 2006. LNCS, vol. 4257, pp. 28–39. Springer, Heidelberg (2006)
6. Berstelsen, O.W.: Towards a Unified Field of SE Research and Practice. IEEE Software, 87–88 (November/December 1997)
7. Strauss, A., Corbin, J.M.: Basics of Qualitative Research: Techniques and Procedures for Developing Grounded Theory, 2nd edn. Sage Publications, Thousand Oaks (1998)
8. Dyba, T.: An Empirical Investigation of the Key Factors for Success in Software Process Improvement. IEEE Trans. on Software Eng. 31(5), 410–424 (2005)
9. Niazi, M., Wilson, D., Zowghi, D.: Critical Success Factors for Software Process Improvement Implementation: An Empirical Study. Software Process Improvement and Practice 11(2), 193–211 (2006)
10. Shye, S., Elizur, D., Hoffman, M.: Introduction to Facet Theory. Sage, Thousand Oaks, CA (1994)

11. Guttman, L.: A general nonmetric technique for finding the smallest coordinate space for a configuration of points. Psychometrika 33, 469–506 (1968)
12. Kim, J., Mueller, C.: Factor Analysis: Statistical Methods and Practical Issues. Sage Publications, Thousand Oaks (1978)
13. Comrey, A.: A First Course on Factor Analysis. Academic Press, London (1973)
14. Cronbach, L.J.: Coefficient Alpha and the Internal Consistency of Tests. Psychometrica 16, 297–334 (1951)
15. Nunnally, J.C.: Psychometric Theory, 2nd edn. McGraw-Hill, New York (1978)
16. Wilson, D.N., Hall, T., Baddoo, N.: A framework for evaluation and prediction of software process improvement success. J. of Sys. & Soft. 59(2), 135–142 (2001)
17. Baddoo, N., Hall, T.: Motivators of Software Process Improvement: an analysis of practitioners' views. J. of Sys. and Software 62(2), 85–96 (2002)
18. Baddoo, N., Hall, T.: Software Process Improvement Motivators: An Analysis using Multidimensional Scaling. Journal of Empirical Software Engineering 7(2), 93–114 (2002)
19. Baddoo, N., Hall, T.: De-motivators for software process improvement: an analysis of practitioners' views. J. of Sys. and Soft. 66(1), 23–33 (2003)
20. Rainer, A., Hall, T.: Key success factors for implementing software process improvement: a maturity-based analysis. J. of Sys. and Soft. 62(2), 71–84 (2002)
21. Rainer, A., Hall, T.: A quantitative and qualitative analysis of factors affecting software processes. J. of Systems and Software 66(1), 7–21 (2003)
22. El-Emam, K., Goldenson, D., Mccurley, J., Herbsleb, J.: Modelling the Likelihood of Software Process Improvement: An Exploratory Study. Journal of Empirical Software Engineering 6(3), 207–229 (2001)
23. Niazi, M., Wilson, D., Zowghi, D.: A maturity model for the implementation of software process improvement: an empirical study. Journal of Systems and Software 74(2), 155–172 (2005)
24. Niazi, M., Wilson, D., Zowghi, D.: Critical Success Factors for Software Process Improvement Implementation: An Empirical Study. Software Process Improvement and Practice 11(2), 193–211 (2006)
25. Dybå, T.: An Instrument for Measuring the Key Factors of Success in Software Process Improvement. J. of Emp. Soft. Eng. 5(4), 357–390 (2000)
26. Goldenson, D.R., Herbsleb, J.D.: After the Appraisal: A Systematic Survey of Process Improvement, its Benefits and Factors that Influence Success. Software Engineering Institute, CMU/SEI-95-TR-009 (1995)
27. El-Emam, K., Smith, B., Fusaro, P.: Success factors and barriers for software process improvement: An empirical study. In: Tully, C., Messnarz, R. (eds.) Better Software Practice for Business Benefit: Principles and Experience, IEEE Computer Society Press, Silver Spring, MD (1999)
28. Stelzer, D., Mellis, W.: Success factors of organizational change in software improvement. Software process – Improvement and Practice 4(4), 227–250 (1998)

Appendix: CSF Identified in the Study and Correlations to Previous Empirical Studies

Table 3. CSF and correlations to previous empirical studies

ID	CSF	Previous empirical studies
F1	Politics	El-Emam et al. [22], Niazi et al. [24]
F2	Acceptance to changes	Baddoo and Hall [19], Rainer and Hall [21], Dybå [25], Stelzer and Mellis [28]
F3	Conciliation of interests	El-Emam et al. [22], Niazi et al. [24], Dybå [25], Goldenson and Herbsleb [26], El-Emam et al. [27], Stelzer and Mellis [28]
F4	Organization structure	El-Emam et al. [22]
F5	SPI implementation strategy	Baddoo and Hall [19], El-Emam et al. [22], Niazi et al. [24], Dybå [25], Stelzer and Mellis [28]
F6	Resources	Baddoo and Hall [17, 19], El-Emam et al. [22], Niazi et al. [24], Goldenson and Herbsleb [26], El-Emam et al. [27]
F7	Processes	Wilson et al. [16], Rainer and Hall [20, 21], Niazi et al. [24], Stelzer and Mellis [28]
F8	Support, commitment and involvement	Wilson et al. [16], Baddoo and Hall [17], Rainer and Hall [20, 21], El-Emam et al. [22], Niazi et al. [24], Dybå [25], Goldenson and Herbsleb [26], El-Emam et al. [27], Stelzer and Mellis [28]
F9	Organization members' competences	Baddoo and Hall [19], Rainer and Hall [20, 21], Niazi et al. [24], Dybå [25]
F10	Respect for SPI consultants	Wilson et al. [16], El-Emam et al. [22], Goldenson and Herbsleb [26], El-Emam et al. [27]
F11	Awareness of SPI benefits	Wilson et al. [16], Baddoo and Hall [17, 19], El-Emam et al. [22], Niazi et al. [24], Stelzer and Mellis [28]
F12	Organization members' motivation and satisfaction	Baddoo and Hall [17]

Quality Impact of Introducing Component-Level Test Automation and Test-Driven Development

Lars-Ola Damm[*] and Lars Lundberg

School of Engineering, Blekinge Institute of Technology
Box 520, SE-372 25 Ronneby, Sweden
{lars-ola.damm,lars.lundberg}@bth.se

Abstract. Companies spend significant efforts on testing their products to achieve a sufficient quality level. This paper presents results from evaluating the quality impact of implementing a framework for component-level test automation and Test-Driven Development. The evaluation comprised six projects for two products at a software development department at Ericsson. The paper suggests how an existing measurement approach can be used for evaluating the quality impact of improvements in early phases, i.e. by classifying faults reported on released products after which phase they should have been caught in. Based on this measurement approach, the evaluation determined that the ratio of reported faults in the released products decreased significantly after implementing the framework. That is, the ratio of faults belonging to component-level testing decreased from between 60-70 percent to less than 20 percent in the two studied products.

1 Introduction

Companies constantly seek better processes and tools to shorten lead-time, reduce costs, and improve the quality of delivered products. To ensure that a product has reached a sufficient level, significant efforts are spent on testing and fault removal, commonly at least 50 percent of the total development time [18]. Still, the impact of faults in released software has been estimated to be as much as one percent of the U.S. gross domestic product [20]. Additionally, it is widely recognized that faults are significantly cheaper to find early [24].

A software development department belonging to the telecom provider Ericsson develops component based software to be used in mobile networks. To become better at early fault detection, the department implemented a framework for automated component testing in two products. Additionally, *Test-Driven Development* (TDD) was introduced to further aid in achieving a successful implementation. A previous publication evaluated the impact on the development cost of the framework after one release of each product [11]. The evaluation concluded that the implementation resulted in significant efficiency improvements, i.e. a reduction in the number of faults slipping to function/system test that reduced the development cost. The

---

[*] Is also an employee at Ericsson.

P. Abrahamsson et al. (Eds.): EuroSPI 2007, LNCS 4764, pp. 187–199, 2007.

company also wanted to evaluate the impact the framework had on the quality of delivered products, but that aspect was not yet possible to evaluate at that time. Therefore, the quality aspect is in focus in this paper.

When evaluating the impact of improvements in early phases, e.g. regarding code inspections or unit testing, researchers commonly evaluate the impact on later fault-finding activities such as functional tests [4]. However, the impact on the quality of the delivered product is not taken into consideration. Fig. 1 illustrates the difference between the two perspectives. A reason for why the customer perspective is not commonly evaluated is simply because it is hard to do. That is, much of the research in the area is conducted as experiments where customer deliveries are not made. Additionally, when evaluating the impact on customer faults, the effectiveness of function/system test also influences the number of customer faults, thus making it hard to ensure internal validity. This paper attempts to address these short-comings by not only studying the total number of customer faults but also by sorting them after which phase they should have been found in. Since the implemented test framework was expected to improve the unit/component test phase, special attention was gives to faults related to that phase.

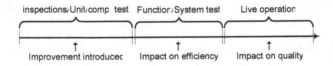

Fig. 1. Early Fault Detection Impact on Efficiency and Quality

As in the previous study [11], a concept called *Faults-Slip-Through* (*FST*) measurement was considered the most appropriate approach for determining the origin of different faults. That is, the FST concept assesses in which phase it would have been most cost-effective to find each fault [12]. However, an adaptation of the method was required for the quality-oriented evaluation performed in this study. Therefore, the purpose of the study was not only to evaluate the quality impact of the implemented framework but also to determine the applicability of using FST measurement for the evaluation. The evaluation comprised six consecutive projects of two products and the studied data includes the faults found in operation and the faults found internally after the product was delivered to customers.

The remainder of this paper is outlined as follows. First, Section 0 provides an overview of related work. Then, Section 0 describes the applied evaluation method and the context of the study. Section 0 presents the obtained results and Section 0 analyzes the results. Finally, Section 0 concludes the work.

2 Related Work

This section describes related work to the study presented in this paper. Section 1.1 presents related work to the implemented framework. Section 1.2 describes possible approaches for evaluating the field-quality impact of improvements in early phases.

2.1 Test-Driven Development and Component Testing

Several widely used techniques for testing units based on their internal structure exist, e.g. path testing, random testing and partition testing [3]. Some unit test techniques implement assertions directly in the product code. *Test-Driven Development* (*TDD*) is one technique that has such an approach [2]. The main difference between TDD and a typical test process is that in TDD, the developers write the tests before the code.

TDD has been successfully used in several cases within agile development methods such as eXtreme Programming (XP) [2]. As described below, a few experiments and case studies on the quality and productivity effects of TDD have been performed. Although the studies have been performed either in experimental settings or as isolated small-scale case studies, some trends have been observed. In [17], TDD had little or no impact on productivity. In [4], the required development time increased by 15 and 35 percent in two studied projects resulting in about 2-4 times lower defect density. The most apparent effect that TDD seems to bring is that it increases the amount of unit testing performed [13][16]. Thus, it is not surprising that at least one study has shown that TDD tends to increase the quality of the developed code [21]. However, neither of these studies considered the impact on customer faults.

Within the area of component testing, several techniques are suggested and implemented [15]. Although, component testing more or less could be managed as ordinary black box testing, some of the more advanced techniques attempt to incorporate the tests in the components more like how unit testing is performed, e.g. using concepts such as XML based component testing [5].

Regarding the variant evaluated in this study, i.e. component-level TDD, little experience exists. Teiniker et al. suggest a framework for component testing and TDD [25]. However, no practical results from applying this framework exist.

2.2 Measurements for Early Fault Detection

Measuring the quality of a delivered product is very hard. In the context of fault detection effectiveness, one can at least in theory compare the number of reported customer faults before and after the introduction of the improvement. However, the result would not be very reliable since the researchers then have to ensure that other quality assurance activities were performed in exactly the same way so that they did not influence the result. In practice, this setup is more or less impossible since industrial environments constantly change.

Several approaches for improving the ability to identify faults early have been suggested and evaluated, e.g. different approaches to code reviews and various test techniques. Such studies commonly evaluate the ability of an approach to find faults in overall [23]. In some cases, they also assess the effect the studied approach had on integration testing before delivery to customers [4], [8], [21]. Studies on the impact early phases have on reported customer faults is however rare, at least when the effects of an implemented approach is studied.

One research area which looks at the relationship between faults and phases is the 'trigger' concept in Orthogonal Defect Classification (ODC) [6]. The idea is basically to classify all faults after the type of review or test activity that should uncover it. For example, one industrial study determined that about one third of all customer faults should have been found in code inspections [1]. However, unit test and integration test activities where not separated to be able to distinguish the degree of fault slippages from unit test activities. Additionally, no matter how defined, fault triggers are very hard to assign to unique development phases [10]. Thus, making them impossible to use for the type of evaluation required in this paper.

Another view of fault origins is to classify them after which phase they were inserted in, i.e. phase containment metrics [19]. In one study, Hevner concluded that 71 percent of the customer faults were inserted in design/implementation [19]. However, from a test perspective, it is not always most cost-effective to find all faults when they are inserted [12]. That is, to distinguish which customer faults should have been found in for example design, unit tests or integration tests, another measurement approach is required. One approach matching these requirements is the approach mentioned in the introduction called *faults-slip-through* (*FST*), i.e. as defined in [12]. The primary purpose of measuring FST is as described in our previous work to make sure that the right faults are found in the right phase, i.e. in most cases early [12]. The norm for what is considered 'right' should be defined in the verification strategy of the organization. That is, if the verification strategy states that certain types of tests are to be performed in different phases, the FST measure determines to which extent the applied verification process adheres to this strategy. This means that all faults that are found later than when the verification strategy stated are considered slips [12].

When having faults classified after when they were found and when they should have been found, it is possible to generate a matrix such as the example provided in Table 1 (the phase abbreviations in the table are defined in Section 1.3). In the table, one can for example see that 30 faults were found in UT that should have been found during reviews in the design phase. The cells with a zero value are cases when a fault in fact should have been found later than when it were. Although this situation is technically possible, it is rare in practice. Further, the Op-Op cell has no value since it in most companies is not okay to find any faults in operation.

From Table 1, it is possible to investigate and calculate relationships between slipping and non-slipping faults in several different ways. In the context of this paper, the values of interest are in the 'Op' column to the right since it is there one can see from which phase each of the faults slipping to Operation should have been found. The FST measurement approach has previously been used for efficiency evaluations, i.e. by measuring slippages between internal test phases [11]. However, its ability to assess the impact on customer faults has never been evaluated.

Table 1. FST matrix

PB PF	De	UT	ST	Op
De	10	30	20	5
UT	0	10	15	3
ST	0	0	15	2
Op	0	0	0	-

*PB=Phase Belonging, PF=Phase Found

3   Method

This section outlines the conducted evaluation including the industrial context of the case study, an overview of the evaluated component test framework, and how to measure the impact of the framework implementation.

3.1 Case Study Setting

The results of this paper are obtained through a case study at Ericsson AB. The department runs several projects in parallel and consecutively. The projects developed software to be included in new releases of existing products used in operators' mobile networks. Each project lasted about 1-1.5 year and had on average about 50 participants. Further, the products were built on a shared platform where the platform provides a component-based architecture and a number of platform components. Thus, the projects built components using the same component architecture and reuse platform components when needed. The components were built in C++ except for a smaller Java-based graphical user interface. Each component contains about 5-30 classes and the components communicate mainly through a common socket connection interface and the data sent between the components are in XML format. In the studied projects, each product had a code base of about 70 *Kilo Lines of Code* (KLoC) and most of the changes in the studied projects were modifications of existing code. Further, the product testing was divided into four phases: *Unit Test (UT)*, *Basic Node Test (BNT)*, *Function Test (FT)*, and *System Test (ST)*. Since the products operate in large mobile networks, verification against other product nodes in the mobile networks is an important part of ST. When ST is completed, the project is considered '*Ready For Acceptance*' *(RFA)*, i.e. the project is ready for customer release. When the test framework was introduced, most functional testing was conducted manually. However, a test automation tool was introduced in some of the studied releases. Section 1.9 discusses the potential impact this tool might have had on the study in this paper.

3.2 Overview of the Implemented Framework

A previous study determined that better tool and process support was needed in the UT phase [13]. In particular, it was concluded that a large reason for insufficient component testing before delivery to integration tests was due to the deadline pressure that commonly occur shortly before the deliveries [9]. During such time pressure, people tend to deliver the code with less quality assurance. To address this problem, a central part of the process change was to introduce component-level Test-Driven Development (TDD).). The reason why TDD could make developers test more is that when writing the test cases before the code it is more likely that the written tests are executed before delivery [7]. From this analysis, a proposal for a framework consisting of component-level test automation and TDD was made [9].

The framework was based on an in-house implemented tool that could send requests to a component's interfaces, i.e. simulating the surrounding components. Commercial tools for TDD such as CppUnit were not applicable since they operate on a class level [9]. The implemented tool provided library routines to use when writing the tests. Then it could control and monitor the execution of the implemented test cases, and finally analyze if the tests passed and log the result in an XML file [9]. Further, applying TDD on a component level meant that some modifications to traditional TDD were required. That is, the test cases were not developed for each class/method but instead for each component interface [9].

The framework was introduced for managing unit level quality assurance of two products, further on denoted as product 'G' and 'S'. This paper evaluates the impact the concept had on 12 months of customer usage in two subsequent releases of each product. The project releases included features with similar characteristics and complexity. Therefore, the releases can be considered comparable. It should be noted that in the first release of one of the products (release 6 of product G as denoted in Section 0), the framework was only partially implemented.

3.3 Evaluation Method

As described in Section 1.2, FST measurements were considered most appropriate to base the evaluation method on. As illustrated in Table 1, the customer faults should be classified after in which phase they should have been found. The general procedure for FST measurements is described in detail in [13], i.e. it applies in the same way for both faults found in development and operation.

As mentioned in the previous section, faults from 12 months of operation from two releases of two products were possible to include in the evaluation. However, some of the reported faults were excluded from the analysis because they were false positives or they did not affect the operability of the products, e.g. opinion about function, not reproducible faults, and documentation faults. The next task in the evaluation was to count the number of real faults reported from each release. Due to confidentiality reasons, the absolute number of faults cannot be provided in this paper. Instead, the number of faults reported in each release are in Section 0 reported as a percentage of the total number of faults from all studied releases of both products. However, as mentioned in Section 1.2, just comparing the number of faults found in different releases is not very reliable when evaluating the impact of a change (even if accounting for size differences). Fortunately, since the implemented concept was supposed to improve a particular test phase (UT), it was possible to measure the amount of fault slippages from UT to customers, i.e. as provided by the FST measure. Thus, to address this major validity threat, the evaluation separates the ratio of FST from specific phases (Section 1.6 illustrates how this was done).

An identified issue with the studied faults was that not all of them were reported by customers, i.e. although they were reported after the project was released to customers, some faults were reported in internal maintenance activities. Although these faults were delivered with the released product as well, their impact could be considered significantly less when not bothering the customers. Therefore, the evaluation needed to distinguish these two types of faults in order to ensure that the right conclusions would be drawn. That is, in Section 0, the faults reported in operation are presented separately as well.

Another possible threat to doing a correct interpretation of the fault distributions is if the size of the evaluated projects differs significantly, i.e. a larger project is likely to report more faults. Therefore, size is also accounted for in the evaluation. However, the most commonly used size measure, i.e. KLoC was not considered reliable enough. That is, KLoC is in overall a poor size measure [14], and the studied projects mostly modified existing code that made the obtained values even less relevant to compare. Function point measurements were not available either. The only remaining size measure considered feasible to use was the effort spent (hours) on implementation and test in each project since that measure was thoroughly tracked. Therefore, the study in this paper accounts for size differences by dividing the number of faults found with the relative effort differences between the projects. The effort-adjusted fault data are presented separately in Section 1.7 so that it is possible to compare them with the unadjusted data in Section 1.6.

4 Results

This section presents the data obtained from the evaluation specified in Section 0. As described in Section 1.5, the measurements below are presented as relative fault distributions divided after which phase each fault slipped from. Section 1.6 presents these distributions and Section 1.7 presents them in the same way except that they are effort-adjusted. Finally, Section 1.8 visualizes the ratio of FST (Faults-Slip-Through) from UT in relation to the total FST. In all figures, the fault distributions are divided after three releases of the two products, i.e. where release R5 of both products serve as a baseline measure before the test framework was implemented. Further, as motivated in Section 1.5, the fault distributions are in the figures below presented first as a total percentage faults found after the date when the project was considered ready for customer delivery (RFA) and then as the percentage of faults reported by customers, i.e. faults found in internal maintenance activities were excluded. Note that faults reported after RFA only regards faults related to the implemented features, all requests for enhancements were handled in new development projects.

4.1 FST to After RFA

Figure 2A presents the distribution for all faults found after RFA. In the figure, the trend for both products is that the number of faults decreased in each release, i.e. due to a decrease in the number of UT faults. The number of FT faults also decreased significantly between 'S R5' and 'S R6'. Figure 2B presents only the faults reported by customers and the trend is similar as in Figure 2A with the exception that 'S R6' had a higher total ratio of customer faults than 'S R5'. When comparing 'S R5' and 'S R6', it is possible to observe that ST caused the increase, i.e. in Figure 2B, the ST part of the 'S R6' column is significantly taller than it is in 'S R5'.

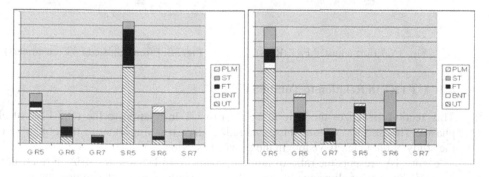

Fig. 2A. FST to after RFA   **Fig. 2B.** FST to Customers

4.2 Effort-Adjusted FST to After RFA

As input to the effort-adjusted FST data, Table 2 shows the relative difference in efforts spent on the studied project. This data is used as input in the figures below. A notable observation in the table is that release 5 of product 'G' was significantly smaller than the subsequent projects. Additionally, release 6 of product 'S' was significantly smaller than the other releases of that product.

Table 2. Effort/project

Project	G R5	G R6	G R7	S R5	S R6	S R7
Relative effort	1.0	2.2	2.1	3.7	1.4	3.2

Figure 3A presents the effort-adjusted variant of Figure 2A, i.e. the fault distribution for all faults found after RFA adjusted according to the relative differences presented in Table 2. The distribution in Figure 3A is similar to Figure 2A with the exceptions that 'G R5' and 'S R6' as expected now have a larger proportion of the faults. As displayed in Figure 3B, the effort-adjusted fault data from customers follow the same pattern as Figure 2B and with the same type of difference for 'G R5' and 'S R6' as in Figure 3A, e.g. almost 60 percent of all faults here belongs to 'G R5'. However, this figure also shows an important effect of adjusting with the effort data, i.e. 'S R6' does not only in total have more faults than 'S R5' - the proportion of UT faults is now also larger in 'S R6'. The reason for this deviation is further discussed in Section 1.9.

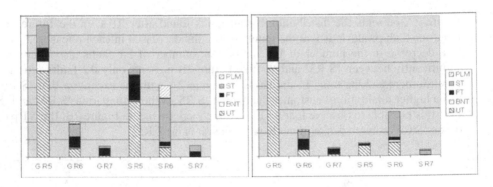

Fig. 3A. Effort-adjusted FST (RFA)　　　　**Fig. 3B.** Effort-adjusted FST (customers)

4.3 UT FST in Relation to Total FST

This section visualizes the ratio of FST from UT in relation to the total FST of all phases. This specific relationship is included since it is important to the objective of the study but not clearly visible in the previous sections.

Figure 4A presents the ratio of fault slippages from UT to after RFA in relation to the total number of slippages to after RFA. As can be seen in the figure, the ratio of

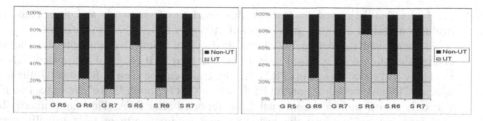

Fig. 4A. UT ratio of total FST (RFA)   **Fig. 4B.** UT ratio of total FST (customers)

UT faults is declining for each release from when the framework was implemented. That is, from about 60 percent in release five to about ten and zero percent in release seven.

Figure 4B presents the same type of distribution as Figure 4A with the exception that only customer faults are included in Figure 4B. In the figure, the ratio of UT faults decreases for each release as in Figure 4A. The only significant difference is that the ratio of UT faults in release seven of product G did not decrease as much.

5 Discussion

This section discusses the results presented in the previous section. First, Section 1.9 analyzes the fault distributions. After that, Section 1.10 outlines potential validity threats and Section 1.11 estimates the cost savings from the obtained improvements.

5.1 Interpretation of the Results

The evaluation results presented in the previous section provided some interesting trends. In overall, the trend was that the number of faults found after RFA decreased after the test framework was implemented. However, some findings require an evaluation in the context of the conducted study to determine whether the positive trend was due to the implemented framework or not.

As could be seen in Figure 2A in Section 0, the fault ratios were in overall declining for each release. However, the trend for customer faults indicated a deviation for release 6 of product 'S'. As mentioned in Section 1.6, ST appeared to cause the most part of the deviation. The reason for this was because in this project ST had problems executing all tests necessary to assure the quality before customer delivery, i.e. due to limited availability of a new technology that the system was supposed to operate together with. This part instead had to be tested more thoroughly together with the first customer. Nevertheless, the ST faults do not explain the whole deviation because as observed in Section 1.7, UT also had fewer customer faults in R5 than in R6 (when accounting for effort differences). In a post-analysis, it could be concluded that the deviation occurred due to problems with the memory checking tools used by the project during UT, i.e. most customer faults that belonged to UT were of this type. Regarding the fact that G R6 only implemented the framework partially (as stated in Section 1.4), it appeared not to have had a significant negative effect. In the fault analysis, it was unfortunately not possible to distinguish which of the faults that belonged to features that used the framework and not. Thus, an evaluation against a control group was unfortunately not possible to perform.

As mentioned in Section 1.3, the studied organization also implemented another change that should be assessed here to, i.e. the increased usage of automated tests in Function Test (in S R6 and in G R7). As especially can be seen in Section 1.7, the tool appeared to have no impact on the FT faults in 'G R7' and in 'S R6' the impact on FT was only significant for the internal faults reported after RFA. This can primarily be explained by the fact that the tests executed automatically at least initially were focused on replacing tests that otherwise would have been executed manually, i.e. not to increase the test coverage.

To conclude, the implemented framework appeared to have a strong positive impact on the amount of faults found after customer release, especially the overall ratio of UT faults decreased significantly for each subsequent release. An interesting implication of this result is that it confirms that it is not only increased test efficiency that is a motive for investing in early fault detection, it can also be used as a motive for decreased maintenance costs and increased customer satisfaction. That is, many faults that are not caught early tend to slip all they way to operation since they are hard to catch in integration tests. The next section discusses possible threats to the validity of the conclusion drawn in this section.

5.2 Validity Threats

The main validity threats concern reliability, internal, and external validity [22].

Reliability. The primary reliability threat regards accuracy of the conducted FST measurements. First, when determining which phase each fault belonged to, all faults were post-validated by one researcher, which thereby minimized the risk for respondent bias, e.g. inconsistent classifications. Additionally, to prevent researcher bias, a test manager and a test leader afterwards analyzed a subset of the classified faults to determine if the classifications were correct. Some incorrect classifications were identified in the post-analysis but it turned out that they tended to even each other out. Another reliability threat relates to the fact that some faults are more severe than others, i.e. they cost more to correct or have a larger negative impact on customer satisfaction. Although not possible to prevent fully, this threat was addressed by sorting out low-severity faults and to distinguish customer faults and other faults reported after RFA.

Internal validity. A major threat to internal validity is whether certain events that occurred during the studied projects affected the fault distribution, i.e. events that the researchers were not aware of. Since the research was conducted in close cooperation with the projects, the awareness of eventual disturbing events was very high. Thus, the major events that could have an impact on the results presented in this paper have been identified and assessed in the paper. Further, since two projects were measured, the likelihood of special events that affected the results without being noticed decreased. The usage of phase differentiation also increased the internal validity, i.e. since the evaluation could isolate the effect on the UT phase where the new concept was implemented.

External validity. Since a case study was conducted, the results are only generalizable within the context of the study, i.e. they are dependent on the studied department having certain products, processes, and tools. However, the applied method should be generalizable to other environments as well.

5.3 Estimated Cost Savings

The case study evaluation in this paper has due to its quality focus not considered costs and benefits. However, since cost remains an important factor, this section estimates the impact the implemented test framework had on maintenance costs.

First of all, it is important to distinguish internal costs for the local organization and external costs, i.e. increased cost of sales from reported customer faults. These costs can be estimated as average cost per fault, which are available at the studied company. However, since these figures are confidential, only relative figures can be presented, i.e. the internal cost of a fault reported in maintenance is 30 times more expensive than when found in UT and a fault reported by customers is about 700 times more expensive than in UT. When using the average fault cost figures on the effort-adjusted difference in fault distributions between release 7 and release 5 of the two products, the cost savings in product maintenance correspond to 4 percent of the development effort spent on 'G R7' and 8 percent of the total effort spent on 'S R7'. When also including increased cost of sales from customer originated faults, the total cost savings correspond to 22 percent of the development effort spent on 'G R7' and 26 percent of the total effort spent on 'S R7'. Additionally if comparing cost savings to the investment costs estimated in our previous study [11], the investment cost corresponded to 39 percent of the saved internal costs and 8 percent of the total saved costs for R7 of the two products, which means a significant return on investment.

6 Conclusions

This paper describes results from implementing a component-level test framework together with Test-Driven Development (TDD). The evaluation comprises three subsequent projects of two products. The evaluation determined the impact the framework had on faults found after the products were put into operation. To determine the impact of the implemented framework, the study also suggested how to use a certain measurement approach for such evaluations, i.e. a measurement approach that classifies the faults after which phase they should have been caught in.

The evaluation determined that the number of faults decreased significantly after the framework was implemented, both regarding the total number of faults and the number of faults related to the unit test phase where the framework was introduced. That is, the ratio of faults found in operation that belonged to unit test decreased from between 60-70 percent in release five of the products to between 0-20 percent in release seven (depending on perspective). Further, when comparing the fault reductions to the effort spent on the development projects, the cost savings in maintenance comprised up to about 25 percent of the development cost for a project. Additionally, the study determined that faults that should have been found early but slip through that test level tend to slip all the way to operation, i.e. they are hard to catch in function/system tests if not found in for inspections or unit tests. Nevertheless, replicated studies in other contexts are required to determine the degree of generalizability of this trend.

Acknowledgments

This work was funded jointly by Ericsson AB and The Knowledge Foundation in Sweden under a research grant for the project "Blekinge - Engineering Software Qualities (BESQ)" (http://www.bth.se/besq).

References

[1] Bassin, K.A., Kratschmer, T., Santhanam, P.: Evaluating Software Objectively. IEEE Software 15(6), 66–74 (1998)
[2] Beck, K.: Test Driven Development - by example. Addison-Wesley, Boston, MA (2003)
[3] Beizer, B.: Software Testing Techniques, 2nd edn. Van Nostrand Reinhold Company, New York (1990)
[4] Bhat, T., Nagappan, N.: Evaluating the Efficacy of Test-Driven Development: Industrial Case Studies. In: Proceedings of the 5th International Symposium on Empirical Software Engineering, pp. 356–363. ACM Press, New York (2006)
[5] Bundell, G.A., Lee, G., Morris, J., Parker, K., Peng, L.: A software component verification tool. In: Proceedings of International Conference on Software Methods and Tools, pp. 137–146. IEEE Computer Soc, Los Alamitos
[6] Chillarege, R., Bhandari, I., Chaar, M., Halliday, D., Moebus, B., Ray, B., Wong, M.Y.: Orthogonal Defect Classification-A concept for In-Process Measurement. IEEE Transactions on Software Engineering 18, 943–956 (1992)
[7] Cockburn, A.: Agile Software Development. Addison-Wesley, Boston, MA (2002)
[8] Crispin, L.: Driving Software Quality: How Test-Driven Development Impacts Software Quality. IEEE Software 23(6), 70–71 (2006)
[9] Damm, L.-O., Lundberg, L.: Introducing Test Automation and Test-Driven Development: An Experience Report. In: Proceedings of the International Workshop on Test and Analysis of Component-Based Systems. Electronic Notes in Theoretical Computer Science, vol. 316, pp. 3–15. Elsevier, Amsterdam (2004)
[10] Damm, L.-O., Lundberg, L.: Identification of Test Process Improvements by Combining ODC Triggers and Faults-Slip-Through. In: Proceedings of the 4th International Symposium on Empirical Software Engineering, pp. 152–161. IEEE, Los Alamitos (2005)
[11] Damm, L.-O., Lundberg, L.: Results from Introducing Component-Level Test Automation and Test-Driven Development. Journal of Systems and Software 79, 1001–1014 (2006)
[12] Damm, L.-O., Lundberg, L., Wohlin, C.: Faults-Slip-Through - A Concept for Measuring the Efficiency of the Test Process. Wiley Journal of Software: Process Improvement and Practice 11, 47–59 (2006)
[13] Erdogmus, H., Morisio, M.: On the Effectiveness of the Test-First Approach to Programming. IEEE Transactions on Software Engineering 31(3), 226–237 (2005)
[14] Fenton, N., Pfleeger, S.L.: Software Metrics: A Rigorous Approach. PWS Publishing Company (1997)

[15] Gao, J., Tsao, J., Wu, Y.: Testing and Quality Assurance for Component-Based Software. Artech House Publishers (2003)

[16] George, B., Williams, L.: A structured experiment of test-driven development. Information and Software Technology 46, 337–342 (2004)

[17] Geras, A., Smith, M.R., Miller, J.: A Prototype Empirical Evaluation of Test Driven Development. In: Proceedings of the 10th IEEE International Software Metrics Symposium, pp. 405–416. IEEE Computer Society, Los Alamitos (2004)

[18] Harrold, J.: Testing: a roadmap. In: International Conference on Software Engineering, pp. 61–72. ACM, New York (2000)

[19] Hevner, A.R.: Phase Containment for Software Quality Improvement. Information and Software Technology 39, 867–877 (1997)

[20] Howles, T., Daniels, S.: Widespread Effects of Defects. Quality Progress 36(8), 58–62 (2003)

[21] Maximilien, E.M., Williams, L.: Assessing Test-Driven Development at IBM. In: Proceedings of the 25th International Conference on Software Engineering, pp. 564–569. IEEE Computer Soc. Press, Los Alamitos (2003)

[22] Robson, C.: Real World Research, 2nd edn. Blackwell Publishers, Oxford, UK (2002)

[23] Runeson, P., Andersson, C., Thelin, T., Andrews, A., Berling, T.: What Do We Know about Defect Detection Methods? IEEE Software 23(3), 82–90 (2006)

[24] Shull, F., Basili, V., Boehm, B., Brown, W., Costa, P., Lindwall, M., Port, D., Rus, I., Tesoriero, R., Zelkowitz, M.: What We Have Learned About Fighting Defects. In: Proceedings of the Eight IEEE Symposium on Software Metrics, pp. 249–258. IEEE, Los Alamitos (2002)

[25] Teiniker, E., Mitterdorfer, S., Johnson, L.M., Johnson, L.M., Kreiner, C., Kovacs, Z., Weiss, R.: A Test-Driven Component Development Framework Based On The Corba Component Model. In: Proceedings of the 27th Annual International Computer Software and Applications Conference, pp. 400–405. IEEE, Los Alamitos (2003)

The Impact of Test-Driven Development on Software Development Productivity — An Empirical Study

Lech Madeyski and Łukasz Szała

Institute of Applied Informatics, Wrocław University of Technology,
Wyb.Wyspiańskiego 27, 50370 Wrocław, Poland
Lech.Madeyski@pwr.wroc.pl, Lukasz.Szala@e-informatyka.pl

Abstract. Test-driven development (TDD) is entering the mainstream of software development. We examined the software development process for the purpose of evaluation of the TDD impact, with respect to software development productivity, in the context of a web based system development. The design of the study is based on Goal-Question-Metric approach, and may be easily replicated in different industrial contexts where the number of subjects involved in the study is limited. The study reveals that TDD may have positive impact on software development productivity. Moreover, TDD is characterized by the higher ratio of active development time (described as typing and producing code) in total development time than test-last development approach.

1 Introduction

Experimentation in software engineering is a relatively young field. Nevertheless, relevance of experimentation to software engineering practitioners is growing because empirical results can help practitioners make better decisions and improve their products and processes. Beck suggests treating each software development practice as an experiment in improving effectiveness, productivity etc. [1]. Productivity is usually defined as output divided by the effort required to produce that output [2]. An interesting survey of productivity measures is also presented by Fowler [3]. Test-driven development (TDD) practice [4], also called test-first programming (TFP) [1], is a software development practice that has recently gained a lot of attention from both software practitioners and researchers, and is becoming a primary means of developing software worldwide [5,6,7,8,9,10,11,12,13,14]. Moreover, one of the most important advantages of TDD is high coverage rate. In this paper, we present how we evaluated the impact of TDD practice on software development productivity and activity. The design of the study is based on Goal-Question-Metric (GQM) approach [15], and can be easily replicated in different industrial contexts, where the number of subjects that may be involved in an empirical study is often limited and the generalization of the results is not the key issue.

P. Abrahamsson et al. (Eds.): EuroSPI 2007, LNCS 4764, pp. 200–211, 2007.

2   Related Work

Several empirical studies have focused on TDD, as promising alternative to traditional, test-last development (TLD), also called test-last programming (TLP). Some of them concern productivity. Müller and Hagner [5] report that TDD does not accelerate the implementation, and the resulting programs are not more reliable, but TDD seems to support better program understanding. George and Williams [6,7] show that TDD developer pairs took 16% more time for development. However, the TDD developers produced higher quality code, which passed 18% more functional black box test cases. Other empirical results obtained by Williams et al. [8,9] are more optimistic, as TDD practice had minimal impact on developer productivity, while positive one on defect density. Geras et al. [10] report that TDD had little or no impact on developer productivity. However, developers tended to run tests more frequently when using TDD. Erdogmus et al. [16] conclude that students using test-first approach on average wrote more tests than students using test-last approach and, in turn, students who wrote more tests tended to be more productive. Madeyski [11] conducted a large experiment in academic environment with 188 students and reports that solo programmers, as well as pairs using TDD, passed significantly fewer acceptance tests than solo programmers and pairs using test-last approach, ($p = .028$ and $p = .013$ respectively). Bhat and Nagappan [12] conducted two case studies in Microsoft and report that TDD slowed down the development process 15%-35%, and decreased defects/KLOC 2.6-4.2 times.. Canfora et al. [13] report that TDD significantly slowed down the development process. Müller [14] conducted a unique empirical study and concludes that the TDD practice leads to better-testable programs.

Summarizing, existing studies on TDD are contradictory. The differences in the context in which the studies were conducted may be one explanation for such results. Thus, case study conducted and valid in a project's specific context is a possible solution that can be applied in industrial projects.

3   Empirical Study

It is important to present the context of the project. Java and AspectJ programming languages, and hence aspect-oriented programming (AOP) [17], were used to implement the web-based system. The presentation tier was provided by Java Server Pages and Servlets. The persistence layer was used to store and retrieve data from XML files. An experienced programmer, with 8 years of programming experience and recent industrial experience, classified as E4 according to Höst et al. [18] classification scheme (i.e. recent industrial experience, between 3 months and 2 years), was asked to develop a web-based system for academic institution.

The whole development project consisted of 30 user stories. Additionally, three phases (with random number of users stories in each phase) could be distinguished. The first phase (10 user stories) was developed with traditional, TLD approach, the second (14 user stories) with TDD and the last 6 user stories again with TLD approach, see Figure 1.

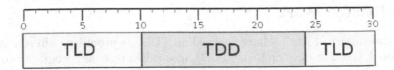

Fig. 1. User stories divided into development phases

3.1 User Requirements

The project was led with the eXtreme Programming (XP) methodology, as TDD is a key practice of XP. Therefore, it seems reasonable to evaluate TDD practice in the context of XP. Although some practices (such as pair programming) were neglected, user stories were used for introducing requirements concerning the developed system. The whole set of 30 user stories was prepared to outline the system, which is a web-based paper submission and review system. It defines different user roles such as *Author, Reviewer, Chair* and *Content Manager*, and specifies multi-level authentication functionality. The system involves the management of papers and their reviews on each step in their life cycle. Additionally the application provides access to accepted and published papers to all registered and unregistered users allowing users to select lists of articles based on earlier defined set of criteria (e.g. published, accepted works). The system supports a simple repository of articles with uploading of text files and versioning.

3.2 Procedure

The Theme/Doc approach [19] provides support for identifying crosscutting behaviour and was used to decompose the system into aspects and classes. Themes are encapsulations of concerns and therefore are more general than classes and aspects. They may represent a core concept of a domain or behaviour triggered by other themes. The procedure used during the TLD phase is presented in Figure 2, and the analogous one for the TDD phase in Figure 3. In TLD phase the participant chooses a user story and then develops its themes (only these parts which are valid for a specified user story). After finishing each theme, a set of unit tests is written. When the whole user story is complete, the participant may perform a system refactoring. The TDD phase differs in first steps. After choosing a user story, the participant chooses a theme and writes tests as well as production code to the specified theme in small test first, then code cycles. The activity is repeated (for other themes related to the selected user story) until the user story is completed. From this point the procedure is the same as in traditional approach.

3.3 Validity Evaluation

There are always threats to the validity of an empirical study. In evaluating the validity of the study, we follow the schema presented in [20].

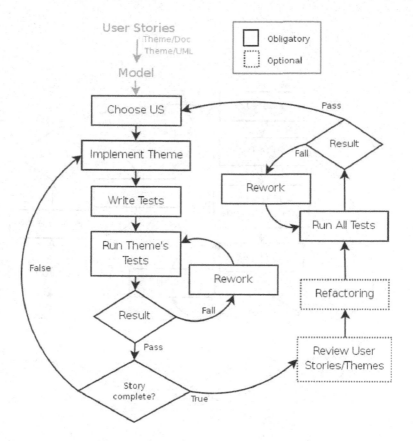

Fig. 2. Development procedure in the TLD phase

As a *statistical conclusion* validity threat, we see the lack of inferential statistics in the analysis of the results. However, the points at which TDD is introduced and withdrawn are randomly determined to facilitate analysis. As with most empirical studies in software engineering, an important threat is process conformance, represented by the level of conformance of the subject (i.e. developer) to the prescribed approach. Process conformance is a threat to statistical conclusion validity, through the variance in the way the processes are actually carried out [21]. It is also a threat to construct validity, through possible discrepancies between the processes as prescribed, and the processes as carried out [21]. Process conformance threat was handled by monitoring possible deviations, with the help of ActivitySensor plugin integrated with Eclipse IDE (Integrated Development Environment). ActivitySensor controlled how development approaches (i.e. TDD or TLD) were carried out (e.g. whether tests were written before related pieces of a production code). Moreover, the subject was informed of the importance of following assigned development approach in each phase.

The mono-operation bias is a *construct* validity threat, as the study was conducted on a single requirements set. Using a single type of measures is a

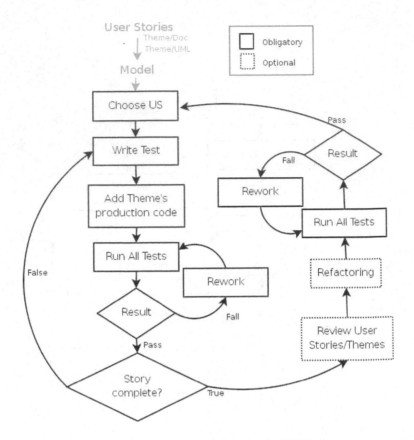

Fig. 3. Development procedure in the TDD phase

mono-method bias threat. To reduce this threat, different measures (e.g. number of acceptance tests, user stories, lines of code per unit of effort) were used in the study, as well as the post-test questionnaire was added to enable qualitative validation of the results. It appeared that the subject was very much in favour of TDD approach, which is in line with the overall results. Interaction of different treatments is limited, due to the fact that the subject was involved in one study only. Other threats to construct validity are social threats (e.g. hypothesis guessing and experimenter's expectances). As neither the subject, nor the experimenters have any interest in favour of one approach or another, we do not expect it to be a large threat.

Internal validity of the experiment concerns the question whether the effect is caused by independent variables, or by other factors. A natural variation in human performance, as well as maturation, is a threat. Possible diffusion, or imitation of treatments were under control with the help of ActivitySensor Eclipse plugin.

The main threat to the *external* validity is related to the fact that subject population may not be representative to the population we want to generalize. However, the programmer's experience is typical of a young programmer, with solid software engineering academic background and recent industrial experience. Thus, it seems to be relatively close to the population of interest.

4   Measurements Definition

The empirical study was conducted using the GQM method, described in [15]. The measurement definition relates to the programmer's productivity (in terms of source code lines written, implemented user stories, and number of acceptance tests passed).

Goal: The analysis of *the software development process* for the purpose of *evaluation of the TDD approach impact*, with respect to *software development productivity and activity*, from the point of view of *the researchers*, in the context of *a web based, aspect-oriented system development*.

Questions:

 – **Question 1:** *How does TDD affect the programmer's productivity in terms of the source code lines written per unit of effort?*

   Metrics: NCLOC (Non Comment Lines Of Code) per unit of effort (programming time) is one of productivity measures. However, NCLOC per unit of effort tend to emphasize longer rather than efficient, or high-quality programs. Refactoring effort may even results in negative productivity measured by NCLOC. Therefore, better metrics of a programmer's productivity will be used.

 – **Question 2:** *How does TDD affect a programmer's productivity in terms of user stories provided per unit of effort?*

   Metrics: Because in XP methodology the user requirements are introduced as user stories, the implementation time of a single user story may be considered as a productivity indicator. Therefore, the number of user stories developed by a programmer per hour is measured.

 – **Question 3:** *How does TDD affect a programmer's productivity in terms of Number of Acceptance Tests Passed per unit of effort?*

   Metrics: Because user stories have diverse sizes, we decided to measure the programmer's productivity using acceptance tests, as NATP (Number of Acceptance Tests Passed) per hour better reflects the project's progress and programmer's productivity. There were 87 acceptance tests specified for the system.

 – **Question 4:** *How does TDD affect a programmer's activity in terms of passive time, compared with the total development time?*

   Metrics: The programmer's productivity may be expressed as a relation of active time T_A to the total time (sum of active and passive times $T_A + T_P$) spent on a single user story implementation. The active time may be described as typing and producing code, whilst the passive time is spent on reading the source code, looking for a bug etc. The ActivitySensor plugin [22] integrated with Eclipse IDE allows to automatically collect development time, as well as to divide total development time into active and passive times. A switch from active to passive time happens after 15 seconds of a programmer's inactivity (the threshold was proposed by the activity sensor authors). To separate passive time from breaks in programming the passive time counter is stopped (after 15 minutes of inactivity) until a programmer hits a key.

5 Results

The whole development process took 112 hours. The finished system was comprised of almost 4000 lines of source code (without comments, imports etc.). The system had 89 interfaces, classes, and aspects. There were 156 unit tests written to cover the functionality. Branch coverage was over 90%.

5.1 Productivity Metrics Analysis

Although the XP methodology puts pressure on source code quality (programming is not just typing!), the differences in software development productivity are essential. Table 1 contains a comparison of productivity metrics in TLD1, TDD and TLD2 phases. TLD1 and TLD2 phases shown in Figure 1 are treated jointly in the last column named TLD.

Table 1. Productivity comparison in all development phases

	TLD1	TDD	TLD2	TLD (TLD1 and TLD2 combined)
Implementation time/US [h]	6.42	2.32	2.50	4.97
Lines of code/US	159.70	107.21	133.17	149.75
Lines of code/h	24.76	46.18	53.27	30.14

It appeared that the implementation time of a single user story during the TLD phase took, on average, almost 5 hours, while during the TDD phase only 2.32 hours, see Table 1. User stories are common units of requirements, but their size and complexity level are not equal. The average size (expressed in lines of code) of a user story, developed with TLD approach, was almost 1.5 times bigger than a user story developed during the TDD phase, see Table 1. It may mean that the code written in TDD phase is more concise than its TLD equivalent.

The next comparison concerns the number of lines of code written per one hour. The results favour the TDD approach with average 46.18 lines above the TLD with 30.14 lines per hour, see Table 1 and Figure 4.

More deatailed observation of boxplots, in Figures 4 and 5, allows to reveal an interesting regularity. Although the TDD phase is characterised by higher productivity in juxtaposition with TLD phase (TLD1 and TLD2 treated jointly),

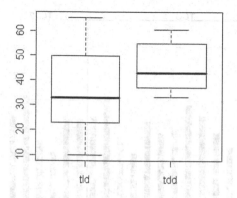

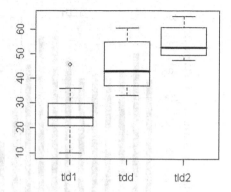

Fig. 4. Boxplot of average number of lines of code per hour in TLD, and TDD phases

Fig. 5. Boxplot of average number of lines of code per hour in TLD1, TDD, and TLD2 phases

when comparing all three phases, the productivity increases with the system's evolution. It may be explained by gaining skills and experience by the programmer, as well as making the programmer more familiar with the requirements, with each completed user story.

The productivity may be measured as a number of passed acceptance tests that cover added functionality, divided by number of hours spent on implementation. When looking at the development cycle divided into two phases (TDD vs. TLD), we measured the following values of passed acceptance tests per hour: 1.44 for TDD and 0.99 for TLD (TDD approach is characterised by a faster functionality delivery, see Figure 6). But when analysing the development cycle as 3 phases (TLD1, TDD and TLD2, see Figure 7), we found that the last two phases were similar while TLD1 phase was considerably worse.

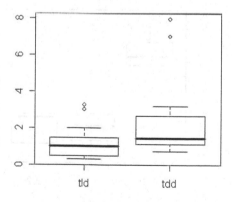

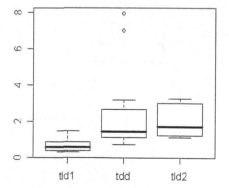

Fig. 6. Boxplot of the number of acceptance tests passed per hour in TLD, and TDD phases

Fig. 7. Boxplot of the number of acceptance tests passed per hour in TLD1, TDD, and TLD2 phases

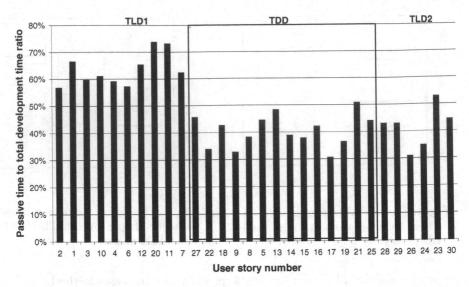

Fig. 8. The passive time to total development time proportion during the project

5.2 Analysis of Programming Activities

Figure 8 presents a proportion of passive time to total development time. We can observe that in first (TLD1) phase the passive time took the majority of total time (over 50%). This rule changed when the testing metohod was switched (the passive time only once exceeded 50% level).

The boxplots of active and passive times are presented in Figures 9 and 10. We can observe that the passive time is higher in TLD phase. However, the

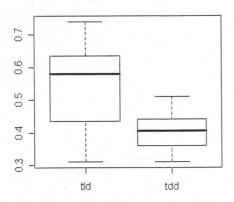

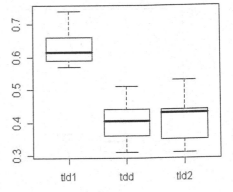

Fig. 9. Boxplot of the proportion of passive to overall development time in TLD, and TDD phases

Fig. 10. Boxplot of the proportion of passive to overall development time in TLD1, TDD, and TLD2 phases

difference is not so obvious when we analyse each phase separately, as results of TDD and TLD2 phases are similar.

6   Conclusions

If we analyse the development process divided into two phases (TLD and TDD), the programmer's productivity in TDD phase is definitely higher. A possible explanation is that TDD approach limits the feedback cycle length to minutes. Thus, the extent of potential bug is usually limited (a programmer knows exactly where should look for an improper system behaviour). Another plausible explanation, why TDD may increase software development productivity, is that improving quality by fixing defects at the earliest possible time (by means of continuous and rigorous testing and refactoring) costs up front but it pays off in the long run.

However, when the process is divided into three phases (TLD1, TDD, TLD2) a different pattern appears. In the case of source code lines written per unit of effort (Question 1) the productivity increases with the project development progress. The proportion of passive to overall development time (Question 4) falls in TDD phase, but in the last two phases (TDD and TLD2) is similar. In the case of user stories per unit of effort (Question 2), as well as acceptance tests per unit of effort (Question 3) the programmer's productivity increases in TDD phase, whilst in the last two phases (TDD and TLD2) is similar as well. A plausible explanation, why productivity in TLD2 phase does not fall, may be that the programmer gains experience, as well as knowledge of the application domain, during the course of the project. Thus not only TDD, but also experience and knowledge of the application domain would drive productivity.

The study can benefit from several improvements before replication is attempted. The most significant one is to replicate the study finishing with TDD in the fourth phase. In order to conclude that TDD has in fact positive impact on productivity, it might be advisable to conduct an experiment securing a sample of large enough size to guarantee a high-power design.

Acknowledgements

The authors thank Adam Piechowiak for ActivitySensor Eclipse plugin development.

This work has been financially supported by the Ministry of Education and Science as a research grant 3 T11C 061 30 (years 2006-2007).

References

1. Beck, K., Andres, C.: Extreme Programming Explained: Embrace Change, 2nd edn. Addison-Wesley, Reading (2004)
2. Maxwell, K., Forselius, P.: Benchmarking Software-Development Productivity - Applied Research Results. IEEE Software 17(1), 80–88 (2000)

3. Fowler, M.: Cannot Measure Productivity (accessed March 2007),
   http://www.martinfowler.com/bliki/CannotMeasureProductivity.html
4. Beck, K.: Test Driven Development: By Example. Addison-Wesley, Reading (2002)
5. Müller, M.M., Hagner, O.: Experiment about test-first programming. IEE Proceedings - Software 149(5), 131–136 (2002)
6. George, B., Williams, L.A.: An Initial Investigation of Test Driven Development in Industry. In: SAC 2003, Proceedings of the 2003 ACM Symposium on Applied Computing. pp. 1135–1139. ACM, New York (2003)
7. George, B., Williams, L.A.: A structured experiment of test-driven development. Information and Software Technology 46(5), 337–342 (2004)
8. Williams, L., Maximilien, E.M., Vouk, M.: Test-Driven Development as a Defect-Reduction Practice. In: ISSRE '03. Proceedings of the 14th International Symposium on Software Reliability Engineering, Washington, DC, USA, pp. 34–48. IEEE Computer Society Press, Los Alamitos (2003)
9. Maximilien, E.M., Williams, L.A.: Assessing Test-Driven Development at IBM. In: ICSE '03. Proceedings of the 25th International Conference on Software Engineering, pp. 564–569. IEEE Computer Society Press, Los Alamitos (2003)
10. Geras, A., Smith, M.R., Miller, J.: A prototype empirical evaluation of test driven development. In: METRICS '04. Proceedings of the 10th International Symposium on Software Metrics, pp. 405–416. IEEE Computer Society Press, Los Alamitos (2004)
11. Madeyski, L.: Preliminary Analysis of the Effects of Pair Programming and Test-Driven Development on the External Code Quality. In: Zieliński, K., Szmuc, T. (eds.) Software Engineering: Evolution and Emerging Technologies. Frontiers in Artificial Intelligence and Applications, vol. 130, pp. 113–123. IOS Press, Amsterdam (2005), http://madeyski.e-informatyka.pl/download/Madeyski05b.pdf
12. Bhat, T., Nagappan, N.: Evaluating the efficacy of test-driven development: industrial case studies. In: ISESE '06. Proceedings of the 2006 ACM/IEEE International Symposium on Empirical Software Engineering, pp. 356–363. ACM Press, New York (2006)
13. Canfora, G., Cimitile, A., Garcia, F., Piattini, M., Visaggio, C.A.: Evaluating advantages of test driven development: a controlled experiment with professionals. In: ISESE '06. Proceedings of the 2006 ACM/IEEE International Symposium on Empirical Software Engineering, pp. 364–371. ACM Press, New York (2006)
14. Müller, M.M.: The Effect of Test-Driven Development on Program Code. In: Abrahamsson, P., Marchesi, M., Succi, G. (eds.) XP 2006. LNCS, vol. 4044, pp. 94–103. Springer, Heidelberg (2006)
15. Basili, V.R., Caldiera, G., Rombach, H.D.: The Goal Question Metric Approach. In: Encyclopedia of Software Engineering, pp. 528–532 (1994)
16. Erdogmus, H., Morisio, M., Torchiano, M.: On the Effectiveness of the Test-First Approach to Programming. IEEE Transactions on Software Engineering 31(3), 226–237 (2005)
17. Kiczales, G., Lamping, J., Mendhekar, A., Maeda, C., Lopes, C.V., Loingtier, J.M., Irwin, J.: Aspect-Oriented Programming. In: Aksit, M., Matsuoka, S. (eds.) ECOOP 1997. LNCS, vol. 1241, pp. 220–242. Springer, Heidelberg (1997)
18. Höst, M., Wohlin, C., Thelin, T.: Experimental Context Classification: Incentives and Experience of Subjects. In: ICSE '05. Proceedings of the 27th International Conference on Software Engineering, pp. 470–478. ACM Press, New York (2005)
19. Clarke, S., Baniassad, E.: Aspect-Oriented Analysis and Design: The Theme Approach. Addison-Wesley, Reading (2005)

20. Wohlin, C., Runeson, P., Höst, M., Ohlsson, M.C., Regnell, B., Wesslén, A.: Experimentation in Software Engineering: An Introduction. Kluwer Academic Publishers, Norwell, MA, USA (2000)
21. Sørumgård, L.S.: Verification of Process Conformance in Empirical Studies of Software Development. PhD thesis, The Norwegian University of Science and Technology (1997)
22. ActivitySensor project (accessed March 2007),
    http://www.e-informatyka.pl/sens/Wiki.jsp?page=Projects.ActivitySensor■

Investigating the Software Fault Profile of Industrial Projects to Determine Process Improvement Areas: An Empirical Study

Jon Arvid Børretzen and Jostein Dyre-Hansen

Department of Computer and Information Science,
Norwegian University of Science and Technology (NTNU),
NO-7491 Trondheim, Norway
{borretze,dyrehans}@idi.ntnu.no

Abstract. Improving software processes relies on the ability to analyze previous projects and derive which parts of the process that should be focused on for improvement. All software projects encounter software faults during development and have to put much effort into locating and fixing these. A lot of information is produced when handling faults, through fault reports. This paper reports a study of fault reports from industrial projects, where we seek a better understanding of faults that have been reported during development and how this may affect the quality of the system. We investigated the fault profiles of five business-critical industrial projects by data mining to explore if there were significant trends in the way faults appear in these systems. We wanted to see if any types of faults dominate, and whether some types of faults were reported as being more severe than others. Our findings show that one specific fault type is generally dominant across reports from all projects, and that some fault types are rated as more severe than others. From this we could propose that the organization studied should increase effort in the design phase in order to improve software quality.

1 Introduction

Improving software quality is a goal most software development organizations aim for. This is not a trivial task, and different stakeholders will have different views on what software quality is. In addition, the character of the actual software will influence what is considered the most important quality attributes of that software. For many organizations, analyzing routinely collected data could be used to improve their process and product quality. Fault report data is one possible source of such data, and research shows that fault analysis can be a good approach to software process improvement [1].

The Business-Critical Software (BUCS) project [2] is seeking to develop a set of techniques to improve support for analysis, development, operation, and maintenance of business-critical systems. Aside from safety-critical systems, like air-traffic control and health care systems, there are other systems that we also expect will run correctly because of the possibly severe effects of failure, even if the consequences are mainly

P. Abrahamsson et al. (Eds.): EuroSPI 2007, LNCS 4764, pp. 212–223, 2007.

of an economic nature. This is what we call business-critical systems and software. In these systems, software quality is highly important, and the main target for developers will be to make systems that operate correctly [2]. One important issue in developing these kinds of systems is to remove any possible causes for failure, which may lead to wrong operation of the system. In a previous study [3], we investigated fault reports from four business-critical industrial software projects. Building on the results of that study, we look at fault reports from five further projects. The study presented here investigated fault reports from five industrial software projects. It investigates the fault profiles in two main dimensions; Fault type and fault severity.

The rest of this paper is organized as follows. Section 2 gives our motivation and related work. Section 3 describes the research design and research questions. Section 4 presents the results found, and Section 5 presents analysis and discussion of the results. The conclusion and further work is presented in Section 6.

2   Motivation and Related Work

The motivation for the work described in this paper is to further the knowledge gained from a previous study on fault reports from industrial projects. We also wanted to present empirical data on the results of fault classification and analysis, and show how this can be of use in a software process improvement setting.

When considering quality improvement in terms of fault analysis, there are several related topics to consider. Several issues about fault reporting are discussed in [4] by Mohagheghi et al. General terminology in fault reporting is one problem mentioned, validity of use of fault reports as a means for evaluating software quality is another. One of its conclusions is that "*There should be a trade-off between the cost of repairing a fault and its presumed customer value. The number of faults and their severity for users may also be used as a quality indicator for purchased or reused software.*"

Software quality is a notion that encompasses a great number of attributes. The ISO 9126 standard defines many of these attributes as sub-attributes of the term "quality of use" [5]. When speaking about business-critical systems, the critical quality attribute is often experienced as the dependability of the system. In [6], Laprie states that "*a computer system's dependability is the quality of the delivered service such that reliance can justifiably be placed on this service.*" According to Littlewood and Strigini [7], dependability is a software quality attribute that encompasses several other attributes, the most important are reliability, availability, safety and security. The term dependability can also be regarded subjectively as the "amount of trust one has in the system".

Much effort is being put into reducing the probability of software failures, but this has not removed the need for post-release fault-fixing. Faults in the software are detrimental to the software's quality, to a greater or lesser extent dependent on the nature and severity of the fault. Therefore, one way to improve the quality of developed software is to reduce the number of faults introduced into the system during development. *Faults* are potential flaws in a software system, that later may be activated to produce an error. An *error* is the execution of a "passive fault", leading to a *failure*. A *failure* results in observable and erroneous external behaviour, system state or data state. The remedies known for errors and failures are to limit the consequences of an active error or failure, in order to resume service. This may be in the form of duplication, repair, containment etc. These kinds of remedies do work, but as Leveson states in [8], studies have shown that this kind of downstream (late) protection is more expensive than preventing the faults from being introduced into the code.

Faults that have been introduced into the system during implementation can be discovered either by inspection before the system is run, by testing during development or when the application is run on site. The discovered faults are then reported in a fault reporting system, to be fixed later. Faults are also commonly known as *defects* or *bugs*, while another, similar but more extensive concept is *anomalies*, which is used in the IEEE 1044 standard [9].

Orthogonal Defect Classification – ODC – is one way of studying defects in software systems, and is mainly suited to design and coding defects. [10, 11, 12, 13, 14] are some papers on ODC and using ODC in empirical studies. ODC is a scheme to capture the semantics of each software fault quickly.

It has been discussed in several papers if faults can be tied to the reliability in a more or less cause-effect relationship. Some papers like [12, 14, 15] indicate that this kind of connection is valid, while others like [16] are more critical to this approach.

Even if many of the studies point towards a connection being present between faults and reliability, they also emphasize that it is not easy to tie faults to reliability directly. Thus, it is not given that a system with a low number of faults necessarily has a higher reliability than a system with a high number of faults. Still, reducing the number of faults in a system will make the system less prone to failure, so if you can remove the faults you find without adding new ones, there is a good case for the reliability of the system being increased. This is called "reliability-growth models", and is discussed by Hamlet in [16] and by Paul et al. in [15].

Avizienis et al. state [17] that the fault prevention and fault tolerance aim to provide the ability to deliver a service that can be trusted, while fault removal and fault forecasting aim to reach confidence in that ability by justifying that the functional and the dependability and security specifications are adequate and that the system is likely to meet them. Hence, by working towards techniques that can prevent faults and reduce the number and severity of faults in a system, the quality of the system can be improved in the area of dependability.

An example of results in a related study is the work done in Vinter and Lauesen [18]. This paper used a different fault taxonomy as proposed by Bezier [19], and reports that in their studied project close to a quarter of the faults found were of the type "Requirements and Features".

3 Research Design

This paper builds on a previous study [3] where we investigated the fault profiles of industrial projects, and this paper expands on those findings, using a similar research design. We want to explore the fault profiles of the studied projects with respect to fault types and fault severity. In order to study the faults, we categorized them into fault types as described in Section 3.2.

3.1 Research Questions

Initially we want to find which types of faults which are most frequent, and also the distribution of faults into different fault types:

RQ1: *Which types of faults are most common for the studied projects?*
When we know which types of faults dominate and where these faults appear in the systems, we can choose to concentrate on the most serious ones in order to identify the most important issues to target in improvement work (note that the severity of the faults are judged by the developers who report the faults):

RQ2: *Which fault types are rated as the most severe faults?*
We also want to compare the results from this study with the results we found in the previous study on this topic [3]:

RQ3: *How do the results of this study compare with our previous fault report study?*

3.2 Fault Categorization

There are several taxonomies for fault types, two examples are the ones used in the IEEE 1044 standard [9] and in a variant of the Orthogonal Defect Classification (ODC) scheme by El Emam and Wieczorek [12]. The fault reports we received were already categorized in some manner by the developers and testers, but using a very broad categorization scheme, which mainly placed the fault into categories of "fault caused by others", "change request", "test environment fault", "analysis/design fault", "test fault" and "coding fault". The fault types used in *this study* is shown in Table 1. This is very similar to the ODC scheme used in [12], but with the addition of a GUI fault type. The reason this classification scheme was used, is that it is quite simple to use but still discerns the fault types well. Further descriptions of the fault types used can be found in Chillarege et al. [13].

Table 1. Fault types used in this study

Fault types	
Algorithm	Function
Assignment	GUI
Checking	Interface
Data	Relationship
Documentation	Timing/serialization
Environment	*Unknown*

The categorization of faults in this investigation has been performed by the authors of this paper, based on the fault reports' textual description and partial categorization.

In addition, grading the faults' consequences upon the system and system environment enables fault severities to be defined. All severity grading was done by the developers and testers performing the fault reporting in the projects. In the projects under study, the faults have been graded on a severity scale from 1 to 5, where 1 is "critical" and 5 is "change request". The different severity classifications are shown in Table 2.

Table 2. Fault severity classification

Fault severity classification	
1	Critical
2	Can not be circumvented
3	Can be circumvented
4	Cosmetic
5	Change request

3.3 The Data Sample

The data collected for this study comes from five different projects, all from the same company, but from variously located development groups. The software systems developed in these projects are all on-line systems of a business-critical nature, and they have all been put into full or partial production. Altogether, we classified and analyzed 981 fault reports from the five projects. Table 3 contains information about the participating projects. The fault reports consisted of fault summary, severity rating, a coarse fault categorization, description of fault and comments made by testers and developers after the fault had been reported, while fixing the fault.

Table 3. Information about the participating projects

Project	P1	P2	P3	P4	P5
Project description	Registering data	Administration tool	Merging of applications	Administration tool	Transaction tool
Technical platform	J2EE	J2EE	Unix, Oracle	J2EE, Unix, Oracle	N/A
Development language	Java	Java	Java	Java	Java
Development effort (hours)	N/A	7900	14000	6000	2100
Number of fault reports	490	212	42	34	123

4 Results

4.1 RQ1 – Which Types of Faults Are Most Frequent?

To answer RQ1, we look at the distribution of the fault type categories for the different projects. Table 4 shows the distribution of faults types across all projects studied, Table 5 shows distribution of faults for each project. A plot of Table 5 is shown in Figure 1.

We see that "function" and "GUI" faults are the most common fault types, with Assignment also being quite frequent. Some faults like "documentation", "relationship", "timing/serialization" and "interface" faults are not frequent.

If we focus only on the faults that are rated with "critical" severity (7.6% of all faults), the distribution is as shown in Figure 2. "Function" faults do not just dominate

Table 4. Fault type distribution across all projects

Fault type	# of faults	%
Function	191	27,0 %
GUI	138	19,5 %
Unknown	87	12,3 %
Assignment	75	10,6 %
Checking	58	8,2 %
Data	46	6,5 %
Algorithm	37	5,2 %
Environment	36	5,1 %
Interface	11	1,6 %
Timing/Serialization	11	1,6 %
Relationship	9	1,3 %
Documentation	8	1,1 %

Table 5. Fault type distribution for each project

Fault type	P1	P2	P3	P4	P5
Algorithm	1,1 %	12,0 %	4,9 %	6,7 %	8,6 %
Assignment	9,5 %	7,4 %	14,6 %	26,7 %	14,0 %
Checking	6,3 %	15,4 %	2,4 %	0,0 %	7,5 %
Data	1,9 %	15,4 %	2,4 %	3,3 %	10,8 %
Documentation	1,4 %	0,6 %	0,0 %	0,0 %	2,2 %
Environment	4,6 %	7,4 %	2,4 %	3,3 %	4,3 %
Function	25,3 %	24,0 %	53,7 %	36,7 %	24,7 %
GUI	29,9 %	5,7 %	14,6 %	6,7 %	10,8 %
Interface	0,3 %	1,1 %	0,0 %	10,0 %	5,4 %
Relationship	0,3 %	1,7 %	0,0 %	3,3 %	4,3 %
Timing/Serialization	1,4 %	2,3 %	2,4 %	0,0 %	1,1 %
Unknown	18,2 %	6,9 %	2,4 %	3,3 %	6,5 %

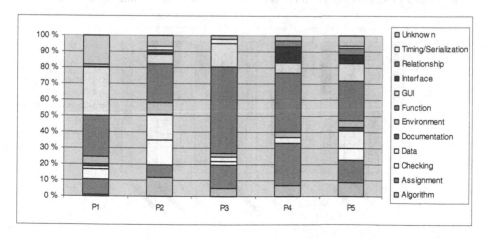

Fig. 1. Fault type distribution for each project

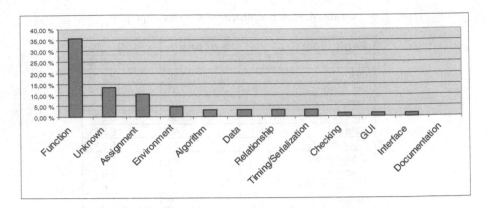

Fig. 2. Distribution of faults rated as critical

the total distribution, but also the distribution of "critical" faults. A very similar distribution is also the case for "can not be circumvented" severity rated faults.

When looking at the distribution of faults, especially for the high severity faults, we see that "function" faults dominate the picture. We also see that for all faults, "GUI" faults have a large share (19.5% in total) of the reports, while for the critical severity faults the share of "GUI" faults are strongly reduced to 1.5%.

4.2 RQ2 – What Types of Faults Are Rated as Most Severe?

As for the severity of fault types, Figure 3 illustrates how the distribution of severities was for each fault type. The "relationship" fault type has the highest share of "critical" faults, and also the highest share when looking at both "critical" and "can not be circumvented" severity faults. The most numerous fault type "function", does not stand out as a particularly severe fault type compared with the others. The fault types that show themselves to be rated as least severe, are "GUI" and "data" faults.

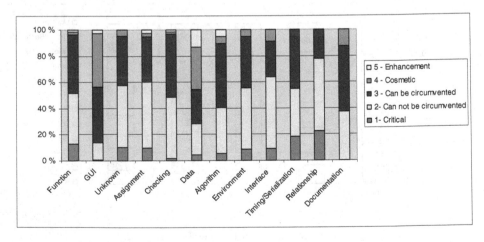

Fig. 3. Distribution of severity with respect to fault types for all projects

4.3   RQ3 – How Do the Results Compare with the Previous Study?

Previously, we conducted a similar study of fault reports from industrial projects, which is described in [3]. In the previous study, "function" faults were the dominant fault type, making out 33.3% to 61.3% of the reported faults in the four investigated projects. The percentage of "function" faults is lower for the five projects studied for this paper, but is still the dominant fault type making out 24.0% to 53.7% of the reported faults in P1 to P5 as shown in Table 5.

When looking at the highest severity rated faults reported, this study also shows that "function" faults are the most numerous of the "critical" severity rated faults as shown in Figure 2 with 35.8%. This is in line with the previous study where "function" faults were also dominant among the most severe faults reported, with 45.3%.

5   Analysis and Discussion

5.1   Implications of the Results

The results found in this study coincide with the results of the previous fault study we performed with different development organizations. In both studies the "function" faults have been the most numerous, both in general and among the faults rated as most severe. As "function" faults are mainly associated with the design process phase, as stated by Chillarege et al. in [13] and also by Zheng et al. in [20] as shown in Table 6, this indicates that a large number of faults had their origin in early phases of development. This is a sign that the design and specification process is not working as well as it should, making it the source of faults that are demanding and expensive to fix, as "function" faults will generally involve larger fixing efforts than pure code errors like "checking" and "assignment" types of faults. This means that we can recommend the developers in the projects that have been studied to increase the effort used during design in order to reduce the total number of effort demanding faults in their products. This finding is also similar to the one from the study of Vinter and Lauesen [18], where "Requirements and Features" faults were the dominating fault type.

When looking at each fault type in Figure 3, we see which fault types that tend to produce the most severe faults. One observation here is that although "function" faults dominate the picture for critical severity faults in Figure 2, it is the "relationship" and "timing/serialization" fault types that consist of the most critical severity rated faults.

Table 6. ODC fault types and development process phase associations [20]

Process Association	Fault types
Design	Function
Low Level Design	Interface, Checking, Timing/Serialization, Algorithm
Code	Checking, Assignment
Library Tools	Relationship
Publications	Documentation

It can therefore be argued that the fault types "relationship" and "timing/serialization" fault types are important to prevent, as it is likely that these types of faults have greater consequences than those of for instance "GUI" and "data" type faults. "Function" faults show themselves to be important to focus on preventing due to the sheer number of them, both in general and for the "critical" severity rated faults. Although "function" faults do not stand out as a fault type where most faults are rated as "critical", it is still the biggest contributor to "critical" severity rated faults.

When informing the organization involved of the results of this study, the feedback was anecdotal confirmation of our findings, as they informed us that they were indeed having issues with design and specification, even though their own fault statistics showed most faults to be coding faults. We would like to study this issue further in our future work on the subject.

In many cases, fault reporting is performed with one goal in mind, to fix faults that are uncovered through inspection and testing. Once the fault has been corrected, the fault report information is not used again. The available information can be employed in a useful fashion as long as future development projects are similar to, or based on previous projects. By reusing the information that has been accumulated during fault discovery through testing and during production, we are able to learn about possible faults for new similar projects and further development of current projects.

Measuring quality and effects on quality in a software system is not a trivial matter. As presented in Section 2, the opinion on how and if this can be done is divided. One of the means Avizienis et al. suggests for attaining better dependability in a system is *fault removal in order to reduce the number and severity of faults* [17]. By identifying common fault types, developers can reduce a larger number of faults by focusing their efforts on preventing these types of faults. Also, identifying the most severe fault types makes developers able to focus on preventing those faults that have the biggest detrimental impact on the system.

5.2 Further Issues Concerning Fault Reporting in This Organization

In addition to our quantitative study results, we were able to identify some points of possible improvement in the studied organization's fault reporting. Two attributes that we found lacking, which should be possible to include in fault reporting are *Fault Location* and *Fault Fixing Effort*. The location of a fault should be readily known once a fault report has been dealt with, as fault fixing must have a target module or software part. This information would be very helpful if the organization wants to investigate which software modules produce the most serious faults, and they can then make a reasoned argument if these modules are of a particularly critical type (like infrastructure or server components), or if some modules are simply of a poorer quality than others. Including fault fixing effort into the fault reports is also an issue that could be of great benefit when working to improve fault prevention processes. By recording such information, we can see which fault types that produce the most expensive faults in terms of effort when fixing them. These are issues that will be presented to the organization under study. Their current process of testing and registering faults in a centralized way hinders the testers and developers from including this valuable information from the fault reports. The testers who initially produce the fault reports do not necessarily know which software modules the fault is located in, and developers fixing the fault do not communicate the location it was found in after it has been found and fixed.

5.3 Threats to Validity

When performing an empirical study on industrial projects, it is not possible to control the environment or data collected as we would do in an experiment. The following is a short presentation of what we see as the main validity threats.

Internal validity. An issue here might be factors affecting the distribution of fault types. When the fault data was collected the intention of use was solely for fault fixing, it was not intended to be studied in this way. The coarse classification given by the developers could have been biased. Such bias or other inconsistencies were hopefully reduced by us classifying the fault reports with new fault types.

External validity. The small number of projects under investigation is a threat to external validity. However, the results of this study support the findings of a previous similar study of fault reports from other software development organizations. The projects under study may also not necessarily be the most typical, but this is hard to verify in any way.

Conclusion validity. One possible threat here is the reliability of measures, as the categorization of faults into fault types is a subjective task. To prevent categorizing faults we were unsure of into the wrong category, we used a type "unknown" to filter out the faults we were not able to confidently categorize.

6 Conclusion and Future Work

In this paper we have described the results of a study of fault reports from five software projects from a company developing business-critical software. The fault reports have been categorized and analyzed according to our research questions. From the research questions we have found that "function" faults, closely followed by "GUI" faults are the fault types that occur most frequently in the projects. To reduce the number of faults introduced in the systems, the organization should focus on improving the processes which are most likely to contribute to these types of faults, namely the specification and design phases of development. Faults of the fault types "documentation", "relationship", "timing/serialization" and "interface" are the least frequent occurring fault types.

The fault types that are most often rated as most severe are "relationship" and "timing/serialization" faults, while the fault types "GUI" and "documentation" are considered the least severe. Although "function" faults are not rated as the most severe type of fault, this fault type still dominates when looking at the distribution of highly severe faults only.

In additions to these results, we observed that the organization's fault reporting process could be improved by adding some information to the fault reports. This would facilitate more effective targeting of fault types and locations in order to better focus future efforts for improvement.

In terms of future work, we want to continue studying the projects explored in this paper, using qualitative methods to further explain our quantitative results. Feedback from the developers' organization would aid us understand the source of these results, and help us suggest concrete measures for process improvement in the organization.

Acknowledgements

The authors would like to thank Reidar Conradi for careful reviewing and valuable input. We also thank the organization involved for their participation and cooperation during the study.

References

1. Grady, R.: Practical Software Metrics for Project Management and Process Improvement. Prentice Hall, Englewood Cliffs (1992)
2. Børretzen, J.A., Stålhane, T., Lauritsen, T., Myhrer, P.T.: Safety activities during early software project phases. In: Proceedings, Norwegian Informatics Conference (2004)
3. Børretzen, J.A., Conradi, R.: Results and Experiences From an Empirical Study of Fault Reports in Industrial Projects. In: Münch, J., Vierimaa, M. (eds.) PROFES 2006. LNCS, vol. 4034, pp. 389–394. Springer, Heidelberg (2006)
4. Mohagheghi, P., Conradi, R., Børretzen, J.A.: Revisiting the Problem of Using Problem Reports for Quality Assessment. In: ICSE'06. Proc. the 4th Workshop on Software Quality, Shanghai, May 21, 2006, pp. 45–50 (2006)
5. ISO: ISO/IEC 9126 - Information technology - Software evaluation – Quality characteristics and guide-lines for their use. ISO (December 1991)
6. Laprie, J.-C.: Dependable computing and fault tolerance: Concepts and terminology. In: Twenty-Fifth International Symposium on Fault-Tolerant Computing. Highlights from Twenty-Five Years (June 27-30, 1995)
7. Littlewood, B., Strigini, L.: Software reliability and dependability: a roadmap. In: Proceedings of the Conference on The Future of Software Engineering, Limerick, Ireland, pp. 175–188 (2000)
8. Leveson, N.: Safeware: System safety and computers. Addison-Wesley, Boston (1995)
9. IEEE: IEEE Standard Classification for Software Anomalies. IEEE Std 1044-1993 (December 2, 1993)
10. Bassin, K.A., Kratschmer, T., Santhanam, P.: Evaluating software development objectively. IEEE Software 15(6), 66–74 (1998)
11. Bassin, K., Santhanam, P.: Managing the maintenance of ported, outsourced, and legacy software via orthogonal defect classification. In: Proceedings. IEEE International Conference on Software Maintenance (November 7-9, 2001)
12. El Emam, K., Wieczorek, I.: The repeatability of code defect classifications. In: Proceedings. The Ninth International Symposium on Software Reliability Engineering, pp. 322–333 (November 4-7, 1998)
13. Chillarege, R., Bhandari, I.S., Chaar, J.K., Halliday, M.J., Moebus, D.S., Ray, B.K., Wong, M.-Y.: Orthogonal defect classification-a concept for in-process measurements. IEEE Transactions on Software Engineering 18(11), 943–956 (1992)
14. Lutz, R.R., Mikulski, I.C.: Empirical analysis of safety-critical anomalies during operations. IEEE Transactions on Software Engineering 30(3), 172–180 (2004)

15. Paul, R.A., Bastani, F., Ling Yen, I., Challagulla, V.U.B.: Defect-based reliability analysis for mission-critical software. In: COMPSAC 2000. The 24th Annual International Computer Software and Applications Conference, pp. 439–444 (October 25-27, 2000)
16. Hamlet, D.: What is software reliability? In: Reggio, G., Astesiano, E., Tarlecki, A. (eds.) Recent Trends in Data Type Specification. LNCS, vol. 906, pp. 169–170. Springer, Heidelberg (1995)
17. Avizienis, A., Laprie, J.-C., Randell, B., Landwehr, C.: Basic Concepts and Taxonomy of Dependable and Secure Computing. IEEE Transactions on Dependable and Secure Computing 1(1) (January-March 2004)
18. Vinter, O., Lauesen, S.: Analyzing Requirements Bugs. Software Testing & Quality Engineering Magazine 2-6 (November/December 2000)
19. Beizer, B.: Software Testing Techniques, 2nd edn. Van Nostrand Reinhold, New York (1990)
20. Zheng, J., Williams, L., Nagappan, N., Snipes, W., Hudepohl, J.P., Vouk, M.A.: On the value of static analysis for fault detection in software. IEEE Transactions on Software Engineering 32(4), 240–253 (2006)

Author Index

Lecture Notes in Computer Science

Sublibrary 2: Programming and Software Engineering

For information about Vols. 1– 4079
please contact your bookseller or Springer

Vol. 4406: W. De Meuter (Ed.), Advances in Smalltalk. VII, 157 pages. 2007.

Vol. 4405: L. Padgham, F. Zambonelli (Eds.), Agent-Oriented Software Engineering VII. XII, 225 pages. 2007.

Vol. 4401: N. Guelfi, D. Buchs (Eds.), Rapid Integration of Software Engineering Techniques. IX, 177 pages. 2007.

Vol. 4385: K. Coninx, K. Luyten, K.A. Schneider (Eds.), Task Models and Diagrams for Users Interface Design. XI, 355 pages. 2007.

Vol. 4383: E. Bin, A. Ziv, S. Ur (Eds.), Hardware and Software, Verification and Testing. XII, 235 pages. 2007.

Vol. 4379: M. Südholt, C. Consel (Eds.), Object-Oriented Technology. VIII, 157 pages. 2007.

Vol. 4364: T. Kühne (Ed.), Models in Software Engineering. XI, 332 pages. 2007.

Vol. 4355: J. Julliand, O. Kouchnarenko (Eds.), B 2007: Formal Specification and Development in B. XIII, 293 pages. 2006.

Vol. 4354: M. Hanus (Ed.), Practical Aspects of Declarative Languages. X, 335 pages. 2006.

Vol. 4350: M. Clavel, F. Durán, S. Eker, P. Lincoln, N. Martí-Oliet, J. Meseguer, C. Talcott, All About Maude - A High-Performance Logical Framework. XXII, 797 pages. 2007.

Vol. 4348: S. Tucker Taft, R.A. Duff, R.L. Brukardt, E. Plödereder, P. Leroy, Ada 2005 Reference Manual. XXII, 765 pages. 2006.

Vol. 4346: L. Brim, B. Haverkort, M. Leucker, J. van de Pol (Eds.), Formal Methods: Applications and Technology. X, 363 pages. 2007.

Vol. 4344: V. Gruhn, F. Oquendo (Eds.), Software Architecture. X, 245 pages. 2006.

Vol. 4340: R. Prodan, T. Fahringer, Grid Computing. XXIII, 317 pages. 2007.

Vol. 4336: V.R. Basili, D. Rombach, K. Schneider, B. Kitchenham, D. Pfahl, R.W. Selby (Eds.), Empirical Software Engineering Issues. XVII, 193 pages. 2007.

Vol. 4326: S. Göbel, R. Malkewitz, I. Iurgel (Eds.), Technologies for Interactive Digital Storytelling and Entertainment. X, 384 pages. 2006.

Vol. 4323: G. Doherty, A. Blandford (Eds.), Interactive Systems. XI, 269 pages. 2007.

Vol. 4322: F. Kordon, J. Sztipanovits (Eds.), Reliable Systems on Unreliable Networked Platforms. XIV, 317 pages. 2007.

Vol. 4309: P. Inverardi, M. Jazayeri (Eds.), Software Engineering Education in the Modern Age. VIII, 207 pages. 2006.

Vol. 4294: A. Dan, W. Lamersdorf (Eds.), Service-Oriented Computing – ICSOC 2006. XIX, 653 pages. 2006.

Vol. 4290: M. van Steen, M. Henning (Eds.), Middleware 2006. XIII, 425 pages. 2006.

Vol. 4279: N. Kobayashi (Ed.), Programming Languages and Systems. XI, 423 pages. 2006.

Vol. 4262: K. Havelund, M. Núñez, G. Roşu, B. Wolff (Eds.), Formal Approaches to Software Testing and Runtime Verification. VIII, 255 pages. 2006.

Vol. 4260: Z. Liu, J. He (Eds.), Formal Methods and Software Engineering. XII, 778 pages. 2006.

Vol. 4257: I. Richardson, P. Runeson, R. Messnarz (Eds.), Software Process Improvement. XI, 219 pages. 2006.

Vol. 4242: A. Rashid, M. Aksit (Eds.), Transactions on Aspect-Oriented Software Development II. IX, 289 pages. 2006.

Vol. 4229: E. Najm, J.-F. Pradat-Peyre, V.V. Donzeau-Gouge (Eds.), Formal Techniques for Networked and Distributed Systems - FORTE 2006. X, 486 pages. 2006.

Vol. 4227: W. Nejdl, K. Tochtermann (Eds.), Innovative Approaches for Learning and Knowledge Sharing. XVII, 721 pages. 2006.

Vol. 4218: S. Graf, W. Zhang (Eds.), Automated Technology for Verification and Analysis. XIV, 540 pages. 2006.

Vol. 4214: C. Hofmeister, I. Crnković, R. Reussner (Eds.), Quality of Software Architectures. X, 215 pages. 2006.

Vol. 4204: F. Benhamou (Ed.), Principles and Practice of Constraint Programming - CP 2006. XVIII, 774 pages. 2006.

Vol. 4199: O. Nierstrasz, J. Whittle, D. Harel, G. Reggio (Eds.), Model Driven Engineering Languages and Systems. XVI, 798 pages. 2006.

Vol. 4192: B. Mohr, J.L. Träff, J. Worringen, J.J. Dongarra (Eds.), Recent Advances in Parallel Virtual Machine and Message Passing Interface. XVI, 414 pages. 2006.

Vol. 4184: M. Bravetti, M. Núñez, G. Zavattaro (Eds.), Web Services and Formal Methods. X, 289 pages. 2006.

Vol. 4166: J. Górski (Ed.), Computer Safety, Reliability, and Security. XIV, 440 pages. 2006.

Vol. 4158: L.T. Yang, H. Jin, J. Ma, T. Ungerer (Eds.), Autonomic and Trusted Computing. XIV, 613 pages. 2006.

Vol. 4157: M. Butler, C.B. Jones, A. Romanovsky, E. Troubitsyna (Eds.), Rigorous Development of Complex Fault-Tolerant Systems. X, 403 pages. 2006.

Vol. 4143: R. Lämmel, J. Saraiva, J. Visser (Eds.), Generative and Transformational Techniques in Software Engineering. X, 471 pages. 2006.

Vol. 4134: K. Yi (Ed.), Static Analysis. XIII, 443 pages. 2006.

Vol. 4119: C. Dony, J.L. Knudsen, A. Romanovsky, A.R. Tripathi (Eds.), Advanced Topics in Exception Handling Techniques. X, 302 pages. 2006.

Vol. 4111: F.S. de Boer, M.M. Bonsangue, S. Graf, W.-P. de Roever (Eds.), Formal Methods for Components and Objects. VIII, 447 pages. 2006.

Vol. 4089: W. Löwe, M. Südholt (Eds.), Software Composition. X, 339 pages. 2006.

Vol. 4085: J. Misra, T. Nipkow, E. Sekerinski (Eds.), FM 2006: Formal Methods. XV, 620 pages. 2006.